MINISTRY AMONG
GOD'S QUEER FOLK

The Center for Lesbian and Gay Studies in Religion and Ministry

Pacific School of Religion
1798 Scenic Avenue
Berkeley, California 94709
Phone: (800) 999-0528
Fax: (510) 849-8212
www.clgs.org

MINISTRY AMONG GOD'S QUEER FOLK

LGBT PASTORAL CARE

David Kundtz
and
Bernard Schlager

THE
PILGRIM
PRESS
Cleveland

For Robert (finally!) with love and gratitude (David)

For Gary, Barbara, Bill, and Johanna: Welcoming Ministers All (Bernie)

The Pilgrim Press
700 Prospect Avenue
Cleveland, Ohio 44115–1100
thepilgrimpress.com

© 2007 by David Kundtz and Bernard Schlager

❀ Printed in the United States of America on acid-free paper that contains post-consumer fiber.

17 16   5 4

Library of Congress Cataloging-in-Publication Data
Kundtz, David
  Ministry among God's queer folk : LGBT pastoral care / David J. Kundtz, Bernard S. Schlager.
    p. cm.
  Includes index.
  ISBN-13: 978-0-8298-1706-5 (alk. paper)
  1. Church work with gays. 2. Gays – Pastoral counseling of.
3. Homosexuality – Religious aspects – Christianity. I. Schlager, Bernard S., 1960- II. Title.
  BV4437.5.K86 2007
  359.086'64 – dc22
                                                      2007020588

Contents

Caring is the greatest thing,
caring matters most.
— F. Von Hügel

Preface to the Series

Gayatri Spivak, an important contemporary postcolonial theorist, entitled her famous 1988 essay, "Can the Subaltern Speak?"[1] in order to ask whether the Indian people who lived under the colonial power of the West could ever truly speak in their own voices. In the end, she decides they could not because their representation in society was always crafted not by themselves, but by the dominant voices of the colonizers' discourse, in which the colonized masses existed primarily as abstractions to be pointed to, not as real people with their own lives and views. They were the objects of social discourse, never its subjects. While the differences between the formerly colonized people of India and those who today identify as part of the lesbian, gay, transgender, bisexual, or queer communities are vast, the situation of being the objectified, silenced "Other" within the discourses of the dominant culture is remarkably similar.

Over the past century particularly, as debates over the moral and civil status of sexual minority groups have raged in churches, halls of government, courts, professional associations, and city streets, the loudest and often the only voices heard were those of the dominant heterosexual majority. Whether those voices were raised in denigration or, more rarely, in support, bisexuals, lesbians, gay men, and transgender people themselves were often visible only as silent abstractions within the violent logic of homophobia and heterosexism. They were allowed little or no public voice; whatever knowledge they possessed about their own situations was deemed inadequate, naive, biased, or simply irrelevant to the debate about them. The elite experts of the dominant heterosexual group, the doctors, lawyers, politicians, clergy, and scholars, established themselves as the only reliable sources of knowledge about those "others" whom their "expert witness" often condemned to silence — or worse.

---

1. Gayatri Chakravorty Spivak, "Can the Subaltern Speak?" in Cary Nelson and Lawrence Grossberg, eds., *Marxism and the Interpretation of Culture* (London: Macmillan, 1988).

Fortunately, within the last fifteen years, much of this enforced public silence has been shaken off by the concerted action of sexual minority groups themselves and their growing number of supporters. Significant legal and political victories upholding the equal civil rights of LGBTQ people along with the courageous determination of increasing numbers of LGBTQ people to be "out" and visible in society together seem to be slowly turning the tide of public ignorance and fear. However, full social and cultural acceptance of LGBTQ people will not be achieved by legal and legislative remedies alone. Only when other important social institutions open their doors to enlightened discussion will some of the final obstacles to full equality really disappear. Religion remains one of the major arenas in which ignorance about and hostility toward sexual minorities still dominate many groups. In most of these cases, LGBTQ people remain abstractions or objects, often portrayed only through the fantasies of the dominant group itself, rather than real people who can speak authoritatively about their own lives. Many faith communities continue doggedly to listen only to the characterization of LGBTQ people proposed by their own heterosexual leaders, assured, it seems, that no religious or spiritual understanding could possibly be found within the gay, lesbian, transgender, bisexual, or queer communities themselves. Such an assumption could not be further from the truth.

The very struggle for dignity in a hostile world, especially a hostile religious world, has brought with it remarkable religious knowledge and astonishing spiritual strength to LGBTQ people of faith. LGBTQ people of faith can be found in every religion, congregation, and faith community in the world. Because of their lived experience both within and outside of established communities of faith, LGBTQ people know what it means to stand courageously for who they are and for what they believe. They also know how to create and nurture family in the midst of rejection; how to care for and love friends even through illness and death; how to hang onto faith, even in the presence of persistent evil; and how to support each other faithfully and grow spiritually in the face of hatred and derision. Moreover, they know the deeply liberating joy of the good news preached to those who are oppressed, and they know how full of grace an embodied sexuality can really be. All of these gifts and graces of the spirit and more, all of this knowledge and strength are desperately needed today, not only by other marginalized populations, but perhaps even more so by faith communities at large in the dominant culture.

This book series, sponsored jointly by the Center for Lesbian and Gay Studies in Religion and Ministry at Pacific School of Religion and by The Pilgrim Press, is designed precisely to make more widely available the stories, insights, new knowledge and religious gifts of many within the transgender, queer, lesbian, gay, and bisexual communities — not only to support those who might be walking similar paths, but also to awaken the wider religious world to the spiritual genius of people it has all too often denigrated and rejected. For Jews and Christians, after all, there is strong precedent for attending to such people; as Jesus, quoting Psalm 118, pointed out, "The stone that the builders rejected has become the cornerstone" (Mark 12:10). The time has come for faith communities to listen to and learn from new voices and new perspectives.

Pastoral care and pastoral ministry describe the multitude of ways that faith communities reach out in care, assurance, counseling, and assistance to those within their groups who are experiencing the crises and transitions that life inevitably brings: illness, death, grief, relationship problems, addictions, family disfunction, and the stresses of life changes like marriage, childbirth, retirement, disability, and so on. With some notable exceptions, LGBTQ people of faith have in the past often been shut out of many institutional forms of pastoral care by the ignorance or religious intolerance of their communities. Yet, like many other minority groups, the LGBTQ communities experience more than their share of life crises, from the impact of the global AIDS pandemic and high rates of breast cancer to everyday stressors ranging from casual insults to homophobic violence on the streets. In most cases, members of the LGBTQ family have had to learn to comfort and sustain each other, and through those experiences they have discovered a great deal about love, support, honesty, spiritual integrity, and the real meaning of care. In the present volume, David Kundtz and Bernard Schlager draw together insights from years of their own experiences and those of many others to provide a guide for anyone who wants to offer pastoral care and support to LGBTQ individuals and families. This excellent volume will be especially important to the growing number of religious communities and religious leaders who are today finally coming to embrace their pastoral responsibilities for all of their congregants, including those who are gay men, lesbians, bisexu-als, and transgender, because those well-meaning ministers often quickly discover that they lack the resources and knowledge to work effectively with LGBTQ people. This book provides an important remedy for this situation. Here, major issues and transitions in the lives and families of LGBTQ people are detailed and explained, ways of providing helpful and healthful interventions are suggested and illustrated, and many available resources from a variety of other sources are listed and evaluated. This volume provides an indispensable guide for pastoral ministry to LGBTQ people and their families, a guide that is long overdue and much needed.

MARY A. TOLBERT

Executive Director
Center for Lesbian and Gay Studies
    in Religion and Ministry
Pacific School of Religion

Preface

This handbook aims to cover the basic skills that religious caregivers and ministry students (of all sexual orientations) need in order to be effective, enlightened, and supportive pastoral-care providers to sexual minorities, to whom we refer as LGBTQ. This more or less standard acronym stands for lesbian, gay, bisexual, transgender, and queer persons.

Perhaps the most obvious challenge for those writing about pastoral ministry to LGBTQ persons is that the topic exists in a divided world: some will be attracted to our starting-point principles and convictions (listed below), while others will be repelled. Fundamentalists and traditionalists on one side, progressive and liberal thinkers on the other, look out at each other over what seems an unbridgeable abyss.

Prospective readers, for example, might skim the Introduction to find out if it's the "right" kind of book for them. Indeed, some will make that decision based solely on the publisher. This deeply rooted dualism does not preclude a large "undecided" or "moderate" group in the center struggling for truth, wisdom, and practical advice about LGBTQ pastoral caregiving.

At the outset we want to make clear that we write for all pastoral caregivers, ordained or lay, who, in the name of God, a religious tradition, or spiritual identity, deal with, help, or otherwise minister to LGBTQ people. We especially write for students in Christian seminaries and theological schools as they prepare for their ministries.

We also include queer people's families and friends who are important in the whole pastoral care process, whether they benefit directly as readers interested in the spiritual welfare of their family members or friends, or indirectly though the effective pastoral caring of others. Our goal of being inclusive is related to our final goal, which is the spiritual good of lesbian, gay, bisexual, transgender, and queer people. These are the people whom we hope will be the ultimate beneficiaries of this work, through the blessings of your ministry.

Our equally sincere hope is that the process of becoming a more effective minister to this besieged minority of God's people will help you to develop deeper skills of ministry in general and, in particular, bring abundant blessings to your self-understanding as a pastoral caregiver.

Our knowledge and experience are within the Christian tradition and it is out of that tradition and to that tradition that we write. We sincerely desire that our work may also be of use for those who minister within the Jewish faith and other non-Christian faith traditions.

The authors were motivated to write this book based on their own personal involvement in pastoral ministry with LGBTQ people of faith.

David became aware of the immense need for this book based on his lived experience as a gay man growing up in, and later serving, churches in which queer people were not openly acknowledged, much less served. In addition, his teaching of clergy and seminarians over the years has made him keenly aware of the ongoing pain and remarkable gifts of LGBTQ people who are unfairly and needlessly separated from their communities of faith.

Bernie enthusiastically agreed to join David in writing this book after many years of teaching laity, seminarians, and clergy from a wide variety of religious traditions. His work as coordinator of the San Francisco Bay Area Coalition of Welcoming Congregations has also helped him to understand more deeply some of the many challenges and rewards involved in building local communities of faith that are genuinely inclusive of queer people.

Acknowledgments

There are many people who have contributed to our work, and we are honored to extend to them our heartfelt gratitude.

To Ulrike Guthrie, our editor at Pilgrim Press, and to Timothy Staveteig, our publisher, we say "thank you."

David thanks Shirlee Bromley, Louis Caissie, Greg Dell, Tom Faucher, Wanda Floyd, Bob Goss, Richard Hardy, Joretta Marshall, Bonita Palmer, Jim Schexnayder, Archie Smith, and Tom West for early and helpful input in deciding the direction of his chapters; he also thanks Jeff Kunkel and Mary Elyn Bahlert for valuable commentary on his writing.

Bernie and David thank Horace Griffin, Mary Hunt, Karen Oliveto, and Justin Tanis for their careful, insightful, and generous reading and suggestions on the text. Each of them contributed significantly to the betterment of this book.

Finally, we thank Mary Ann Tolbert and the staff, board members, and many volunteers at the Center for Lesbian and Gay Studies in Religion and Ministry (CLGS) at Pacific School of Religion in Berkeley, California.

Our book has been improved by you all. Again, we thank you. In the end, of course, we take full responsibility for what we have written.

Introduction

Ministry among God's Queer Folk

Only since the later years of the twentieth century have some religious bodies begun to develop a theology of pastoral care for sexual minorities — lesbian, gay, bisexual, transgender, and queer (LGBTQ) people in general. The obvious reason is that people in these categories were considered sinners in need of judgment, condemnation, and punishment. Churches, synagogues, and other religious communities, no different from society at large, ignored our existence based on the theological and psychological suppositions that LGBTQ identity and behavior were both chosen and sinful. Indeed, religion is often the vanguard of anti-LGBTQ prejudice and discrimination.

Here we are, though, at the beginning of the twenty-first century: out of the closet, proud of our LGBTQ identity, and candidly vocal.

What a time to be in ministry with us!

While issues directly relating to LGBTQ people threaten to cause schism in some denominations, those same LGBTQ people are living their lives with the rest of humanity and often as members of the same denominations. All the while they are being discussed and analyzed, excluded and feared, vilified and damned but especially judged by the society and the communities in which they live.

We don't have the luxury (and often not the patience) of waiting until our churches and synagogues pass from the debate stage to the decision stage about the moral acceptability of our queer lives and loves, whatever that might turn out to be for each denomination or congregation. No one knows how religious bodies will resolve the issues. Well-founded fears abound — on all sides.

1

Within religious traditions there is a broad range of opinion in regard to LGBTQ people. A few Christian and Jewish denominations and movements include complete acceptance of LGBTQ people in their official doctrine and teaching; some have welcoming and affirming programs of congregational education and LGBTQ acceptance; others penalize or discipline member churches or synagogues for the welcome that they extend to queer people.

But LGBTQ people have to live their lives and make their decisions *in the present moment,* and they are doing so more and more publicly as "out" individuals who belong to dynamic queer communities. This is "a new thing," and they are doing it now. As we read in the book of Isaiah, "Behold, I will do a new thing; now it shall spring forth; shall you not know it?" (Isa. 43:18–19).

The current work is an effort to contribute to the recently emerged and ongoing development of a pastoral theology and praxis for sexual minorities. We have written this book as a guide for pastoral ministry to, with, and among LGBTQ people.

Principles and Convictions

Here is a brief but critically important listing of the theological and psychological convictions that ground this book. These convictions/principles are important because they are the ones from which we write and thus will help clarify our approach.

LGBTQ people as gifts of God. God is the giver of all life to all people. This life is given in myriad ways, all of them reflecting something of the nature of the Giver. Thus, God gives each of us our sexuality (one's sexual makeup), which includes our orientation (to whom one is sexually attracted) and our gender identity (the gender one knows oneself to be), as a part of our total gift of humanity. We see sexual orientation and gender identity as significant aspects of God's gift. We believe that "God affirms the embodiment of human sexuality in our relationships with one another and within the community of faith."[1] Along with this first principle is the

---

1. Joretta L. Marshall, *Counseling Lesbian Partners* (Louisville: Westminster John Knox Press, 1997), 13. Marshall here is summarizing the theological support for this statement by Carter Heyward and James Nelson.

assumption, based on the primacy of love, that all of us are loved by God and thus are lovable as we are.

The justice that flows from love is the basis for the equal treatment for all God's people. This justice-based-on-love (or justice-love) gives rise to the oft-quoted but often ignored church phrase that "All are welcome." We also believe that the practices of theology and contemporary psychology need to pay deep attention and respect to each other. Although ultimately truth is one, at any given moment one field of study will arrive at its door sooner than another. When they differ, we believe we need to pay even deeper attention to the lived experience of the persons involved.

Bible and tradition. Many of the world's religions are "Religions of the Book." A sacred text is their foundation. Some also hold Tradition with a capital "T" in a very high place of honor and power. While acknowledging these sources and fundaments of religion, the present work does not attempt to examine, exegete, or otherwise analyze them and their effects on LGBTQ people. We do this not because they are unimportant. On the contrary, they are so basic that our brief treatment could add nothing significant. More importantly, there are many who have already done this critical work and still others who are continuing to do it. We commend their work to you.[2]

Most importantly, churches will no doubt continue to disagree strongly over interpretations of texts and traditions that are understood to refer to homosexuality and LGBTQ people. No matter what one concludes that the Bible or other sacred texts say or do not say about LGBTQ people, *we are still here.* We are in your congregations, a part of your communities, with needs, sufferings, gifts, and blessings, the same as everyone else. Here and now.

Pastoral care. Pastoral theology is practical, functional, and applied. Its bases are systematic, moral, and spiritual theology; its inspiration, the sacred texts and often the traditions of the religious body. To maintain effectiveness, pastoral theology must also be organic, vibrant, developing,

---

2. For example, see Robin Scoggs, *The New Testament and Homosexuality* (Philadelphia: Fortress Press, 1983); Daniel Helminiak, *What the Bible Really Says about Homosexuality* (San Francisco: Alamo Square Distributors, 2000); and, more recently, Jack Rogers, *Jesus, the Bible, and Homosexuality: Explode the Myths, Heal the Church* (Louisville: Westminster John Knox Press, 2006); and Alice Ogden Bellis and Terry L. Hufford, *Science, Scripture, and Homosexuality* (Cleveland: Pilgrim Press, 2002), 76–77.

and a vehicle for dealing with an always changing people in an always changing world. It is the basis and source of pastoral care. Thus, pastoral care becomes the principal expression of pastoral theology and brings it to life; it is "doing theology" day to day.

Insofar as it is practical and relational, pastoral care in turn embraces the insights of the science of human psychology and weds the two sources, theology and psychology, in a unique and holistic service of care. Yet pastoral care's distinctiveness is precisely that it is shaped by faith, and that this shaping is not incidental but quite central to such care. This basis in faith gives birth to and permeates the whole pastoral care experience.

Please note that this work is expressly about pastoral *care,* not pastoral *counseling.* The two areas certainly overlap, and some writers use "pastoral care" and "pastoral counseling" almost interchangeably. For our purposes, pastoral care, which certainly includes many skills used in counseling, is within the reach of all sufficiently trained ministers — indeed, in a broader way, within the capacity of all believers. We consider pastoral counseling as a form of psychotherapy, and thus it falls within the reach only of those educated in the discipline. We are aware that some of the examples we use could possibly be interpreted as crossing the difficult-to-define boundary into counseling. Thus, we urge pastoral caregivers, who naturally will have differing experience, skills, and expertise, to keep within their competencies. (See chapter 1 on referral and rejection.)

We define "pastoral care" as the relationship of concern and service between the minister of religion and the people he or she serves within the context and with the motivation of religious faith.

Contextualizing pastoral care specifically for LGBTQ people is difficult. On the one hand, there is very little formal expression of it, and its most common characteristic has been negativity: denial of our presence, embarrassment at our existence, labeling us as evil sinners, and at worst, aggressive pursuit and routing us out.

On the other hand, effective pastoral care of LGBTQ people has been going on for a long time, often informally and quietly, in specific times and places and by wise and often courageous ministers of care. Some of these caregivers who worked within the context of denominations — Christian, Jewish, and others — would be called progressive; still others became effective pastoral caregivers for LGBTQ people simply by following their pastoral instincts, their understanding of their faith message, and their hearts.

To these courageous caregivers, past and present, we owe much. Their pioneering work, writing, reflections, and experiences are the bases on which we have built the current work. Much joy must come to them from knowing how deeply appreciated and life-giving their compassionate ministry has been and in many cases continues to be. Often the result of their caring brings them serious trouble from the powers that be in their denomination. These pioneers have been censured and punished and have endured mortally damaging blows to their careers and, in not a few instances, dismissal or forced resignation from their churches.[3]

Heterosexual/homosexual rating scales. We believe that sexuality is a fluid state that often confounds those who try to simplify it. Following from that, we assume that the Kinsey Heterosexual/Homosexual Rating Scale is fundamentally accurate and that the Klein Sexual Orientation Grid is also accurate in a more detailed way. These scales were developed by Dr. Alfred Kinsey and his associates in the early 1950s and by Dr. Fritz Klein in the 1970s. Both scales indicate a broad and flowing spectrum of sexual orientations.[4]

Instead of understanding sexual orientation as an exclusively either-or condition (either heterosexual or homosexual), Kinsey and Klein developed continuums: Kinsey's is based on the degree of sexual responsiveness people have to others of the same or of different gender. Klein's scale is based on sexual attraction, sexual fantasies, emotional attraction, social attraction, lifestyle, and self-identification.

We recommend that all pastoral caregivers acquire an understanding of both scales. It is an understanding that will give you a helpful background to your dealings with all people. (We have included an appendix with a more complete exposition of these scales.)

---

3. For example, Rev. Jimmy Creech was excluded from ministry in the United Methodist Church for his support of LGBT people; see *www.umaffirm.org/cornet/jcomaha.html* (accessed November 2006). Rev. John McNeill, S.J., was asked to leave his religious order for the same reason; see John McNeill, S.J., *Both Feet Firmly Planted in Midair: My Spiritual Journey* (Louisville: Westminster John Knox Press, 1998).

4. For the Kinsey Scale, see *www.kinseyinstitute.org/resources/ak-hhscale.html*; for the Klein Scale, see *www.biresource.org/pamphlets/scales.html* (sites accessed November 2006). See also Fred Klein, *The Bisexual Option: A Concept of One Hundred Percent Intimacy* (New York: Priam Books, 1978); also see our appendix.

A significant detail of both scales is that they do not accommodate transgender people. Deeper understanding of the trans community is a more recent development. Indeed, Klein, in regard to its noninclusion in his scale, said, "I don't know how to do it so I leave it to the next generation. . . ."[5]

Choice/variation. Further, we assume that most people do choose how they express their sexual orientation and/or gender identity; that is, they choose their behavior. For example: some bisexual people decide to live their lives one way to the exclusion of other ways. That, of course, is a choice, but people rarely choose to be bisexual.

Transgender people have to make many significant decisions, often over a long period of time, about how they want to live their lives. A lesbian may decide to choose a partner, and both may then decide to live as an openly committed couple. A gay man might decide never to come out and thus live his life in the closet. But *being* bisexual, transgender, lesbian, or gay is almost never a choice. Again, this is the same for all: human beings very rarely choose their sexual orientation or gender identity — possibly never.

As we've said, in this work we consider sexual orientation and gender identity as God-given gifts that are good and holy variations of human sexuality.

Unique. Another important conviction which we share is that LGBTQ people are as capable of spiritual authenticity and holiness as anyone else. However, our lived experiences often lead us down challenging paths and through spiritual territories that are often unique to queer people of faith and, therefore, unknown to others; thus, our voices, too, are unique. We add significant new dimensions to the spiritual journey.

Labels. Many do not like the restrictions imposed by sexual minority categories or labels such as "gay" and "bisexual," and strongly resist using them for themselves and others. Still others consider lesbian, gay, bi, and trans to be social constructs that are distinctly modern. We respect both these opinions, but we believe that for now, at this moment in our history, these categories are functional because so many people use them.

"Queer," a term that is considered offensive by some and empowering by others, is used to refer to sexual orientations, gender expressions, and

---

5. From the obituary of Dr. Fritz Klein in the *San Francisco Chronicle*, June 1, 2006, B7.

gender identities that do not conform to predominant heterosexist societal norms. We use it here with the intention of simplicity and inclusivity.

A positive note. LGBTQ people are the way we are because we are the way we are, the same as everyone is the way they are.

We do not assume that sexual orientation and gender identity are conscious decisions that one makes at a certain point in life — even though there may be the rare individual who does that — or that they were chosen as one of several available options. Our assumption here is that for the vast number of LGBTQ people, who they are, as gendered and sexual beings, is an unchangeable given,[6] as it is for heterosexual people.

The analysis of *why* any of us are the way we are will continue for generations, maybe forever. We do not know in any complete way how human beings develop their sexual preferences or gender identities.[7] This, of course, is true of all human beings and of all ways of being sexual. The assumption/belief/opinion that LGBTQ people should try to change their sexual orientation or gender identity to conform with what is seen as "acceptable" is itself one of the most serious problems they face.

We hear more and more every day from LGBTQ people who come from various North American societies, as well as other parts of the world, who feel no need to apologize about who they are. Rather, an increasing number use words like "gift" and "blessing" when referring to their orientation or gender identity.

Of course all good-willed people can claim St. Paul's liberating proclamation of grace, "But by the grace of God, I am what I am" (1 Cor. 15:10) and add "and his grace toward me was not in vain" (1 Cor. 15:10). Or can they? LGBTQ people of faith are in the awkward and painful position of having to make a particular point of including ourselves in the statement. While others are presumed to be full-fledged members of faith communities, we, very often, are intentionally excluded.

Thus, by circumstances out of our control, we are often coerced into a defensive stance; that's where prevalent forces in the popular culture would have us begin. We don't want to begin there — namely by defending

---

6. See Richard Isay, *Being Homosexual* (New York: Farrar, Straus & Giroux, 1989), 20–21; also Andrew J. Weaver et al., *Counseling on Sexual Issues: A Handbook for Pastors and Other Helping Professionals* (Cleveland: Pilgrim Press, 2006), 191–92.

7. John Money, *Gay, Straight, and In-Between: The Sexology of Erotic Orientation* (New York: Oxford University Press, 1988), chap. 1.

LGBTQ people as we are examined and judged; we want to begin on a positive note.

Affirming attitude. In this book we assume that you, the reader, share with us a positive and inclusive attitude toward LGBTQ people and our lives, that in all aspects of human life you treat LGBTQ people like you treat everyone else, hold them to the same standards, and give them the same breaks.

Certainly "people have a right to disagree on a matter as difficult and complex as human sexuality. Thousands of years of precedent should not be taken lightly but neither should the living presence of hundreds of thousands of people whose sexual orientation does not fit traditional boxes."[8]

We disagree with religious leaders and communities that deny that LGBTQ people can live holy, moral lives while at the same time giving expression to their sexuality. Our position, which is far from unique or even unusual, is that those leaders and communities are simply wrong.

This is not merely a defensive and a priori position that says we disagree with you, *thus* we believe you're wrong. We base our position on four foundations: (1) the Jewish and Christian value of welcoming the stranger and freeing the oppressed; (2) the support of the human lived experience and testimonies of LGBTQ people of faith; (3) the overwhelming support of the scientific and psychological disciplines; and (4) the fact that historically, in literally *all* religious traditions, strong moral stances are often not immutable; they have changed.[9] "We must remember that we may change our position over time and still remain faithful."[10]

We do not deny that there are many historical causes for the negative position of churches. We simply believe it is far beyond time to move into the fuller truth from which we have been blocked. We believe the churches are wrong not only in their homo-negativity, but more broadly, in their deep fear of all forms of human sexuality, which is expressed as

---

8. Rabbi Steven Greenberg, *Wrestling with God and Men: Homosexuality in the Jewish Tradition* (Madison: University of Wisconsin Press, 2004), 32.

9. Usury, slavery, religious freedom, and marriage, for example. See also ibid., 16, and *www.indegayforum.org/topics/show/27105.html* (site accessed November 2006).

10. See Joretta L. Marshall, "Caring When It Is Tough to Care," *www.religion-online.org/showarticle.asp?title=300* (site accessed November 2006).

an anti-sex stance in many ways. All people are suffering and many are dying because of these intransigent stances.

Further, we believe that if one is unable or unwilling to reflect upon and revise in the light of faith those negative theological, psychological, and social biases toward LGBTQ people that we have all absorbed from our queer-phobic society, then one should not undertake any ministry to them. On the other hand, if you are a parish minister, for example, who wants to serve well the LGBTQ members of your congregation, then it is incumbent upon you to learn *how* to become a caregiver who ministers positively and effectively to LGBTQ persons.

To make our position even more specific (for those familiar with the sources), we endorse the fifth position taken by Jung and Smith[11] on the five possible moral positions in regard to homosexuality: "Homosexual orientations are natural; just, loving, and faithful homosexual behavior is good." We also endorse James Nelson's fourth option on the same question, which is described as "full acceptance."[12]

Fitting In? Left Behind?

Some readers will clearly know that you, as pastoral caregiver, fit comfortably into this positive and affirming group. Others will know that you clearly do not fit.

But for those of you who, after considering the above assumptions, still have some doubts, still have questions about how your practice of pastoral care is consistent with your theological beliefs, we encourage you to give yourself the benefit of your doubt and plunge in. That doubt could well be a sign of your desire to be honest before God, with yourself, and in your ministry.

For those of you whom this brief exposition has clearly left out, for whom our basic convictions are too broad, too "liberal," or simply wrongheaded — and you are still reading this (good for you!) — we hope you don't stop here. We recommend that you check the list of resources for other treatments.

---

11. Patricia Beattie Jung and Ralph Smith, *Heterosexism: An Ethical Challenge* (Albany: State University Press of New York, 1993).

12. James B. Nelson, *Embodiment: An Approach to Sexuality and Christian Theology*, new ed. (Minneapolis: Augsburg Fortress, 1979).

Our main criticism of some of the few writers who deal directly with the topic of pastoral care for LGBTQ persons is their underlying tone of withholding approval, of condescension, of lurking judgment, or in some instances, of outright disapproval and condemnation of "homosexual activity." They can be classified in the seriously flawed and misguided category of "love-the-sinner-hate-the-sin." (See chapter 1 for further treatment.) These attitudes are, at best, damaging to effective ministry, and, at worst, seriously damaging to LGBTQ people themselves. The efforts of these writers, however, are in some ways groundbreaking, in most cases appear to be good-willed, and in a broad historical perspective can be appreciated.[13]

An ever-increasing number of writers in the field of pastoral care for LGBTQ people, however, are unquestioningly supportive, deeply insightful, and extremely helpful. We quote from and refer to many of them; we are indebted to all of them.

Plan of the Book and Authors

Chapter 1, "The Pastoral Care Relationship," is an exploration of the relationship between the pastoral caregiver and the care receiver. After defining the relationship and discussing questions such as the caring intimacy of pastoral care with LGBTQ people and homophobia, it examines the understanding and keeping of boundaries, transference/counter-transference, and other issues between caregiver and LGBTQ care receivers. The chapter ends with a treatment of the five goals of systemic pastoral care with examples relating to ministry with LGBTQ people.

Chapter 2, "The Functions of Pastoral Care," is built upon the six functions of pastoral care as presented by Clinebell and Graham and their application to the lives of LGBTQ people: healing, sustaining, guiding, reconciling, nurturing, and prophetic pastoral care. It examines pastoral care with people of color and ethnic minorities, and presents a broad "Checklist for Pastoral Caregivers to LGBTQ People."

---

13. See David K. Switzer, *Pastoral Care of Gays, Lesbians, and Their Families*, Creative Pastoral Care and Counseling Series (Minneapolis: Fortress Press, 1999); this work is recommended to those who have hesitations in regard to our assumptions. H. Newton Mahoney, ed., *Pastoral Care and Counseling in Sexual Diversity* (New York: Haworth Pastoral Press, 2001), offers a broad spectrum of approaches.

Chapter 3, "Pastoral Care in the Tough Times," presents an LGBTQ perspective. It deals with shame, anger, fear, and isolation. It examines discrimination and stress in LGBTQ lives. In it we explore the caregiver's role in ministering to LGBTQ people who are ill (physically — including HIV/AIDS — or emotionally) or who are physically handicapped. We also discuss drugs/addictions, sex, and violence, and then conclude the chapter with discussions of youth, old age, and "ex-gay" ministries.

Chapter 4 explores the fundamental and pivotal experience of "Coming Out," in the lives of LGBTQ people. After a consideration of some of the most common features of coming out of the closet, this chapter uses Coleman's five-stage model as a framework to understand how many queer people of faith accept and embrace their gender identity and/or sexual orientation. The motif of journey is used to interpret the ongoing and life-affirming project that coming out can be for LGBTQ persons.

Chapter 5, grounded in a study of nearly two dozen welcoming and affirming churches and synagogues, invites the reader to consider how congregations can become communities of care for LGBTQ people of faith. In addition, "Creating Communities of Care" offers concrete suggestions for congregations interested in creating genuine welcome, integrating queer people into synagogue and church life, and building alliances with LGBTQ persons and communities beyond the walls of their congregation.

Chapter 6, "Caring for Relationships," invites the reader to consider the many ways in which queer people structure their relationships. Positing "Five Characteristics of Queer Relationships," this chapter includes case studies to illustrate how LGBTQ relationships and families are both similar to and different from their straight counterparts. Rather than assume that only those relationships and families based on the model of modern-day heterosexual marriage are morally acceptable for queer people, this chapter explores the variety of models that are found in LGBTQ communities today.

The work concludes with a list of resources (works cited, consulted, or related to the field, including books, Web sites, tapes, and films), an appendix on the scales of sexuality, and an index.

We have divided the chapters between us. Kundtz wrote chapters 1, 2, and 3; Schlager wrote chapters 4, 5, and 6. Together we wrote the Introduction and the Epilogue. Also, we have altered the examples and case studies in ways that protect confidentiality while keeping their essential significance.

We, the authors, are keenly aware of the similarities in our respective backgrounds and current social locations: both of us are white, gay, middle-class, and highly educated males who grew up as Roman Catholics and served for a time as official representatives of that church. Thus, we have consulted widely in our writing of the text. Since leaving the ordained ministry (David) and religious life (Bernie), we have continued to work in the fields of family counseling and seminar presentations (David), seminary teaching, and LGBTQ religious advocacy (Bernie).

Terminology

We use the word "minister" to refer to a person (professional or volunteer, ordained or lay) who in any way represents a faith tradition in a pastoral setting; who is Protestant, Catholic, or Orthodox; and who is in training or already providing pastoral care.

We use the term "pastoral caregiver" to mean the ministering person in his/her role of caring pastorally.

In referring to the recipients of pastoral care we most often use the terms "care receiver" or "care seeker."

We use the word "congregation" frequently. With this word we refer to the gathering of faithful in a local community. When we speak of a specific denomination or movement we will name it.

On the facing page are some definitions of terms regularly used in this work.

A Brief Definition of Terms

- "LGBTQ" refers to lesbian, gay, bisexual, transgender, and queer persons.

- "Queer" is a broad term that can include all categories of people whose sexuality or expression of sexuality is non-normative. Sometimes expressed "genderqueer," which can refer to someone who identifies with traits of both male and female.

- "Lesbian" refers to female persons who are primarily or exclusively attracted to other female persons.

- "Gay" (or "gay man") refers to male persons who are primarily or exclusively attracted to other male persons. Sometimes "gay" is used in a broader way to mean both lesbian and gay or even all LGBTQ people.

- "Bisexual" refers to male or female persons who are attracted to *both* same-sex and other-sex persons, although not necessarily to the same degree. Sometimes shortened to "bi."

- "Transgender" is a broad term to include those who contravene the commonly accepted definitions of gender, all or part of the time. Often shortened to "trans."

- "Transsexual" is a term which is "subset" to transgender and refers to those who change or have a desire to change their bodies to appear different from birth-assigned gender.

- "To come out (of the closet)" means to declare in some public way and to some degree (widely or narrowly) one's sexual orientation and/or gender identity.

- "Sexual orientation" refers to a person's innate sense of emotional, romantic, and/or erotic attraction to others (as opposed to "sexual preference," which implies a conscious choice).

- "Sexual identity" refers to the gender one knows oneself to be.

Chapter 1

The Pastoral Care Relationship

Pastoral care is a relationship. Beginning with the idea of relationship gets to the heart of all we deal with in this work. Pastoral care is the establishing and nurturing of a caring relationship between or among people that is based on religious faith. Commonly the relationship is between a minister of religion and member(s) of a religious congregation. More broadly speaking it is also the caring relationship between or among members of a congregation, for we are all called to the ministry of pastoral caring.[1]

The specific pastoral care relationship that is the focus of the present work is between the ministering person of the church or synagogue and its LGBTQ member(s). Often the member is seeking some specific service or guidance: help with a major life transition, the baptism of a child, a bar or bat mitzvah or confirmation, preparation for marriage, a consultation about his or her own or a family member's sexual orientation, a visit to a sick relative, making arrangements for a funeral service, consulting about a personal challenge, or a crisis in the family. Often, too, the relationship is simply what goes on between a minister of religion and the members of the congregation while interacting informally within the context of the community, such as a casual chance encounter between a Sunday school teacher and her student at the grocery store, rather than during designated formal sessions.

The motivation and unique characteristic of pastoral care, especially in the caregiver, is religious faith combined with a primary concern for the well-being of the care receiver(s).

The coming together, in the context of religious faith, of caregivers and LGBTQ care seekers, both individuals and groups, creates the unique relationship of pastoral caring that is our concern here.

---

1. Joretta L. Marshall, "Caring When It Is Tough to Care," *www.religion-online.org/showarticle.asp?title=300* (accessed November 2006).

The care relationship is also established between the ministerial representatives of the religious organization and any system that influences the queer care receiver. For example, a minister who is pastorally involved in the process of a young lesbian coming to responsible terms with her possible life choices by that very involvement is also relating in some way to her family; her girlfriend or partner; possibly to her school, her work, and her neighborhood; and to all the broader societal and human-interaction systems of which she is a part.

What is distinctive about this book is that we focus solely on care receivers who are LGBTQ.

The Relationship Is All-Important

Every pastoral caregiver needs to have the professional qualifications and training that is necessary for pastoral ministry. With these skills and insights the caregiver is prepared to care effectively. Practically, however, in pastoral care, the relationship you build with your care receiver is the primary way these skills become fruitful and effective, especially at the beginning — the key moment in determining the nature and success of the relationship. Consider: A gay man in your congregation talks to you about the challenges he faces in coming out to his family. In that moment, what you have to offer him is yourself, in all your manifestations: your attention or lack of it, your smile or frown, your body language, your words, the common ground of your faith — in a word, your willingness, your openness to begin a relationship of care. But the power and potential of that willingness can, and has, changed people's lives.

In previous pastoral experiences, many LGBTQ people have met with outright rejection at worst, and at best, a denial of care, or fear and incompetence masquerading as a denial of care. Many have encountered these attitudes so regularly in their churches and synagogues that they might understandably test to see if the caregiver really cares. For example, they may ask questions, perhaps about your opinion on public LGBTQ persons, or find other ways of determining if you are going to be respectful of who they are and safe to trust with the intimate details of their lives.

Recognize the possible "test" for what it most likely is: a natural instinct to avoid hurt and disappointment, and not a rejection or antagonism against you, the caregiver.

If, during any point within the ongoing work with your LGBTQ care receiver, you are in doubt about how to proceed or what is called for, refocus on the relationship and do something that will strengthen or enhance it.

Pastoral relationships with LGBTQ people have three particular characteristics that merit attention. The balance of the chapter explores these areas from the point of view of what is specifically applicable to pastoral work with LGBTQ people: caring intimacy, clear boundaries, and awareness of systemic functioning.

Caring Intimacy

The first thing to note as you approach pastoral care with LGBTQ people is that you are establishing and building a *relationship* with a gay, lesbian, bisexual, transgender, or queer/questioning person or group. What is the model for that pastoral relationship? The common ground of faith leads us to the fact that religion itself involves a relationship, a caring intimacy between God and God's people. Thus, our goal is to imitate God's relationship with us. Granted, it is a goal beyond our reach, but nevertheless I believe it is an ideal for which we can strive.

In human terms, the divine goal is transformed into building an effective pastoral relationship that creates a caring intimacy. This ideal stems in part from the expectations of people who seek pastoral care.

In a lecture on the differences between homoerotic and homosexual relationships, Robert Johnson, a straight Jungian analyst and writer, tells of a personal experience in India.[2] Johnson, a young, white man in search of his spiritual path, found himself unexpectedly alone in Calcutta. The poverty of the city depressed him, and he felt desperate and needed help. At that moment he recalled an Indian tradition he had learned and decided to try it; he would ask for help in a very specific way. He went to a public park and chose a middle-aged man, traditionally dressed, and seemingly educated. He approached the man and asked, "Do you speak English?" "Yes," was the answer. Then he looked into the stranger's eyes and asked, "Will you be the incarnation of God for me?" The man returned his earnest look, paused, and said, "Yes."

---

2. Robert Johnson, *A Study in the Contrast of Homoerotic and Homosexual Relationships,* audiocassette tape (Los Angeles: C. G. Jung Institute).

"Will you be God for me?" To our Western ears that sounds so improbable a question in such an unlikely story. Johnson told of the experience as an example of how comfortable Indian people are, compared to Westerners, with intimacy between men; yet it also beautifully expresses the desire that underlies many of the expectations that queer people, like all people, bring to their pastoral caregivers all the time: a desire for God.

Johnson poured out his soul, his fears, and his feelings to this man. The man said very little. "I felt much better after that," reported Johnson. "It's just what I needed, someone to be with me and listen to what was going on for me. He did that." They never saw each other again.

When people are living through a time of stress, pain, or confusion, the relationship they find at the time — often the relationship with the pastoral caregiver — can enhance life or not, can be a moment of grace or not, can be an occasion of meeting God or not.

Avoid Fear and Arrogance

Caring intimacy with LGBTQ people implies at least two specific attitudes in the caregiver, at different ends of a spectrum: one is an absence of fear and the other is an avoidance of a patronizing attitude. No fear, no arrogance.

A single, Latino male, about thirty-five, a successful lawyer, made an appointment with a priest who was director of seminary students for the local diocese. The next day he arrived on time and the first thing he said, with almost no introductory formalities, was that he was gay and he wanted to be admitted to the seminary. After these statements, he folded his arms and waited for a response, as if to say, "Let's see what you do with this one!" In other words, "Let's see if you care about me."

It turned out he had no lasting interest in the ministry. He was testing the degree of care in that particular minister of the church and, fairly or not, the care of the whole church, and even of God.

Because he was "openly" gay, he assumed that he would have been rejected. He was angry at the hypocrisy he observed in the church. The caregiver, far from being fearful or patronizing, engaged him in a meaningful and respectful conversation about those very issues.

This caregiver solved no specific problems, but he was able to establish caring intimacy mainly because he showed no intimidation or fear of the care seeker's anger and directness. He expressed neither a patronizing attitude nor arrogance in assuming he had all the answers. Though the presenting issues were not resolved, this is an example of successful pastoral care because the person felt cared for, and was invited into a pastoral relationship that could continue and grow.

Don't be afraid of LGBTQ people. The type of fear you might recognize, especially if you are not LGBTQ yourself (see below), is a fearful lack of confidence in dealing with them. You may think you don't understand them. Remember: queer people are people first and foremost. If there are specific issues that you do not understand, it is acceptable to admit to not understanding and ask the care seeker for clarification. If you are not LGBTQ, of course there will be gaps in your understanding due to lack of personal experience. Don't try to fake sophistication or experience in the queer "world"; much better for the relationship is to admit what is unfamiliar or fearful to you and look for information and insight directly from the care seeker, from a competent consultant, or from your own reading.

Certainly all people are put off by a patronizing attitude, but queer people are perhaps especially sensitive to it simply because we so often meet with it, especially in churches and synagogues. Any attitude that implies a superiority based on not being LGBTQ is guaranteed to kill the care seeker's hope of receiving helpful pastoral care.

Do You Care...or Not?

It's important to ask yourself from the very beginning: Do I really care about this person? What exactly are my feelings toward this person? That self-knowledge is more important for the outcome of the pastoral care than any "solutions" you might provide or wise words you might offer.

In the great majority of pastoral care relationships, the caregiver is ready and anxious to care, and there is no doubt about the presence or degree of concern and positive feelings. Some situations, however, we don't like to acknowledge: what if you really don't care about this person and his/her problems for whatever reasons, justifiable or not, mature or not? Maybe the issue hits too close to home for you to maintain equanimity. Maybe you are going through a challenge in your own life similar to the one the care seeker brings to you. There are many reasons that you might not care the way you need to care.

As in any pastoral care situation, if you know you lack sufficient care for the person you're dealing with, or your negative feelings are too strong to overcome, there are two choices: postpone the encounter, or refer to another competent caregiver. Ideally, postponement and referral will be rare. However, I believe too many pastoral caregivers reject postponement and referral because it represents a presumed weakness or limitations. This lack of honesty is a setup for a confusing and ultimately unsuccessful pastoral relationship. Much better to postpone or refer, especially if you have doubts about your preparedness.

Referral and Rejection

What is specifically important in pastoral care with LGBTQ people is that postponement or referral might well appear as rejection. Rejection is often a common experience of LGBTQ people as they encounter those with some kind of moral or physical authority over them. Your act of postponement or referral will often feel like more of the same old thing. Indeed, these responses *are* a form of rejection. Be willing to acknowledge that and use caution in the process.

Eleanor is a sixty-three-year-old, straight, white (parents from England) married minister with many years of pastoral experience and a lovable disposition. She has led two congregations through the welcome-and-affirming process for LGBTQ people (see chapter 5).

This Sunday afternoon after services she found herself in her office with Chris, a pierced and punctured, dyed and denimed, spiked and unscrubbed seventeen-year-old whose T-shirt proclaimed "Gender-Queer and Proud." Chris announced to her, "I want to join the church."

Eleanor was tired after the morning services, and even though she philosophically fought it, she felt disdain for the person in front of her. She cared ideally and philosophically; practically and immediately she just could not get to real care.

If you were Eleanor, what would you have done? Pause for a moment and consider.

Eleanor first tried to establish some kind of connection with Chris. None of her efforts worked; Chris remained monosyllabic and virtually

Pastoral Perspectives
Postponement and Referral

To mitigate the care seeker's possible feelings of rejection associated with postponement or referral, consider the following pastoral perspectives:

- Talk about it. Consider the possibility of bringing up the subject of rejection with the care receiver, explaining that you realize that it might feel like you're passing him/her off or denying care, but in fact you believe this is best for the success of the pastoral care relationship. It tells care receivers that you want to be aware of their possible feelings.

- If you postpone a session or meeting, set the time and date for the postponed meeting before the care seeker leaves.

- If you postpone establishing a pastoral care relationship, *never* fail to follow up on the postponement as planned. This gives a clear sign that you have cared and continue to care.

- If it seems appropriate and welcomed, pray with the care seeker. Prayer together is an excellent way to communicate your genuine care (to both God and the care seeker).

- Take as much care and time in the referral as in the original intervention. Don't rush. Perhaps continue in the session a little longer than you ordinarily might by spending a few more moments; it can be a sign of care.

- Perhaps you can find another way to involve the person in the life of the community in a way unrelated to the original issue: as a member of a committee? asking for help on a project? enlisting them in your efforts to influence some system of which they are a part?

nonresponsive. Then this seasoned pastor summoned all her years of experience and suggested in careful terms that the church's youth minister would be able to help more than she. Chris agreed: "Yeah, I think you're right. That's cool."

This serves as another example of a successful pastoral encounter, even though the minister involved could not carry through on its fulfillment. The care seeker left feeling cared for and placed with someone within the community with whom a more productive relationship could be established.

An important characteristic of this referral is that the youth minister to whom Eleanor referred Chris was comfortable and knowledgeable about gender-queer and transgender youth. A basic element of good referral is to know the capacities, specialties, and competence of those to whom you refer. A mere passing off of someone to someone else is death to effective care.

Since many pastoral encounters occur in those in-between moments, it is helpful to compile and keep up to date a referral list containing the names, contact information, and competencies of other caregiving people. The list will include pastoral counselors, psychotherapists, psychiatrists, other pastoral care ministers, and colleagues who have a particular expertise. Maintaining such a list avoids delays and thus possibly losing the energy of the pastoral moment.

If you really do care, it will become evident, no matter if you engage, postpone, or refer the care receiver. If you really don't care, whatever your response, your lack of concern will be transparent.

Are You Open?

The second question, and almost as important as the first, is: Are you really open to what the LGBTQ care seeker asks of you? Or do you have the assumption that your duty is to apply certain given teachings no matter the details of the situation? Do you have a predisposition toward the resolution of "this kind of problem"? If you have an open disposition, whatever someone brings to your care will elicit in your response a receptive mind and an open heart.

In this context, keep in mind that in many instances LGBTQ people are not working from any realistic moral guidelines or templates that they might have received from their religious traditions. Of course, they are included along with everyone else in the general moral principles offered by churches, but when it comes to being a moral LGBTQ person, churches seldom offer much guidance.

Thus, queer people often forge ahead in the moral process on their own, discovering for themselves what is healthy, what is moral, what is life-giving, and what is not. This is especially the case when LGBTQ people are trying to work out their relationships with other people: friendships and relationships with family and with authority, with peers, and especially with possible romantic relationships.

Issues of living together, parenting, sexual expression, and participation in normal civil rights are some areas in which LGBTQ people make up some of the rules as they go along. The rules that exist often don't work for them; that is, they are not life-giving or moral, intelligent, or indeed practical.

So this is what openness is about: willingness first to listen to the lived experience of the LGBTQ people with whom you work, and then to help them apply moral principles of their faith tradition that serve their needs.

I'll not easily forget a lesson I learned some years ago when I was an active member in a local Parents, Families & Friends of Lesbians & Gays (PFLAG) group. One evening a young man came to the meeting. He was, to my eyes, surly and unsightly. I remember wishing he had not come; I was embarrassed by him and not open to him. But the woman who served as leader of the group extended the same sincere and loving welcome to this young man as she had previously extended to me and would have extended to the most distinguished visitor. Under the loving care of this leader, the young man thrived in the group and went on to become one of its leaders. Thus, I too was able to see what the caring leader had seen from the beginning: goodness, beauty, talent, and a generous spirit. But without that caring welcome (if the welcome he received were influenced by *my* sentiments), the results would not have been so good. It was a lesson for me in the transformative power of care that is truly open.

Think of these pastoral situations: A sixteen-year-old girl tells you she is "in love with my girlfriend and I want to just hold her and live the rest of my life with her, and, and...! Oh what should I do?" A seventy-year-old man whose wife has just died comes to you for guidance and asks, "I would like to live with my male lover. How will this affect my relationship with the church? What do you advise?" A transgender woman applies for the opening that your church has posted for the directorship of Christian education. Her qualifications are excellent. "I am a perfect fit for this work," she tells you. "It's exactly what I did in my former church for eight years." Are you open?

A simple application of existing and traditional rules to these cases might not be pastorally effective. Be open to the experience of the individual by helping the young girl ask the right questions, applying the right moral principles to her thinking and behavior without judging her and closing the door to an ongoing pastoral relationship; understanding the man's dilemma of being old and alone and not having the moral alternatives of his straight counterpart — publicly accepted dating and marriage; hiring or not hiring the transgender woman based on her skills and qualifications, not on your discomfort or fears.

Ultimately the goal is to help the person arrive at a satisfactory resolution of the issue, morally and practically. The most important means to that end is to sustain the pastoral relationship. Don't give up simply because there seems to be no way out; keep the relationship open and progressing. Truth and moral choices are often elusive and take time to achieve.

This approach does not belittle nor deny the importance of any church's teachings and practice. But systemic (or dogmatic) theology without the benefit of pastoral theology can act like a weapon of destruction rather than a grace of healing. We are all at different stages of ability to assimilate the implications of our experiences. Good pastoral care accepts us where we are without giving away the ageless wisdom of the faith tradition. By establishing a solid relationship with the LGBTQ care receiver, you open the way to countless possibilities and blessings, as you forego the immediate, but often ineffective, quick fix.

Even if your church denomination does not officially accept homosexual behavior, which is the official position of most denominations in most religions, engaging pastorally with someone who is acting in contradiction to church teachings is neither affirming nor condemning the behavior; it's relating to the person. This simple distinction continues to elude the resources and imaginative powers of many church leaders who assume that even acknowledging LGBTQ people, much less serving and welcoming them, assumes that these pastoral acts will be seen as "affirming their behaviors." This attitude on the part of churches also encourages double lives in its ministers and members: *whatever you do, whoever you are, just don't talk about it.*

The goal for every pastoral caregiver should thus be to establish a relationship with care seekers that is an effective vehicle for the skills, insights, and training that the caregiver brings to the moment, and to remain as open as possible to them and to their lived experiences. Here's a suggested pastoral practice: When you begin to engage with any LGBTQ person or group in a pastoral situation, think to yourself: *It's the relationship, it's the relationship! Be open!*

So the most good that can be achieved in pastoral care is attained simply by the establishment, nurturing, and quality of the pastoral relationship. There need not be any "issue" or "problem" or "project" to deal with, although there generally is one. Simply the relationship with a pastorally based, caring person has remarkable power to heal and bless.

Thus, if at times you are not sure about the precise nature of your relationship with someone in or outside of your synagogue or church, focus on and be grateful for the fact of the relationship rather than its nature. Don't underestimate the simple power of the relationship itself. Keep it going, keep it fed.

Heterosexism/Homophobia/Transphobia

As pastoral caregivers, we are aware of the prejudice that is commonly called homophobia. In practice, it means the fear of — or more broadly, any kind of negative attitude toward — LGBTQ people and/or homosexuality in general. Transphobia is the same set of attitudes toward transgender people. These phobias are part of a broader and, in the long run, a more pervasive prejudice, which is heterosexism: a belief that male-female sexuality is the only natural, normal, or moral sexual behavior.

Because of our current moment in history, it would not be surprising if a significant number of pastoral caregivers have some degree of heterosexism and its accompanying phobias. They are surprisingly agile prejudices that are shape-shifters — they often appear as something else — as well as longtime survivors in our culture. They can even sneak out of those of us who would consciously and philosophically disavow them vehemently.

Here is a snippet from a conversation in a church courtyard between Martha and Joe (a married couple) and Reverend James (their minister), speaking about a newcomer to the church, a woman whom they have just noticed who is accompanied by a teenage boy.

Martha: ... Well, she's a lesbian, so she wouldn't have any children.

Joe: Of course, so the boy with her must be her brother, or maybe the son of a friend, or. ...

Rev. James: Martha, you shouldn't call her a lesbian! That's not fair.

Martha: But I'm quite sure she is. Her sister told me as much, and I know there is no man in her life.

Rev. James: Yes, yes, but still ... why would she be *here?*

Although the above text is brief and out of a broader context, it is clear that Martha and Joe and their minister need help with heterosexism and homophobia — the minister possibly more so because he has an added responsibility in his role as pastor and pastoral caregiver to the people in the conversation, as well as possibly with the woman in question. They consider being lesbian as somehow negative.

Of this pastor we might ask: Is it "not fair" to name someone as lesbian — as if it were a prejudicial term, a type of name-calling? Even though for some it still falls into those negative categories, assuming that lesbianism is somehow negative only affirms the prejudice, the homophobia, the heterosexism. Of Martha and Joe we might ask: Is it really the case that lesbians don't have children? The (assumed) knowledge that "there is no man" in a woman's life tells you nothing other than that simple fact. While their attitude might be defended as simple ignorance, it would seem fair to expect most people to know better.

Heterosexism, homophobia, and transphobia are thorny prejudices and can show up in the most unexpected places, even in LGBTQ people. Internalized homophobia is the negative attitude that LGBTQ people have toward themselves and other queer people. Our whole society has internalized heterosexism to various degrees. The attitudes of these prejudices have been internalized from the prevalent attitudes of the churches and synagogues of the wider society, the values of which people have made their own. Ultimately they are shame-based. Internalized homophobia can also be seen when one group within the LGBTQ community holds negative attitudes toward another of its groups.

I have often heard gay people say, "I just don't understand transgender people." The astute pastoral caregiver will diplomatically identify and help the person to see that there is nothing to "understand" about trans people any more than there is to "understand" about gay or lesbian or straight people. It's not a question of "understanding" but of believing and accepting their lived experience — or not.

Clear Boundaries

"Boundaries" refers to the person's physical, mental, or spiritual sense of self, or the "space" in which the person exists and holds as intensely personal and under the person's own control. Boundaries can differ from person to person in regard to their nature and strength. Respect for a person's boundaries directs that the caregiver recognize and acknowledge a person's boundary limits as early as possible in the care relationship and not go beyond the parameters of the invitation.

Clear awareness of and deep respect for the boundaries of your LGBTQ care receivers is an important aspect of caring intimacy. At the same time, I believe incompetent handling of boundaries is the most common reason that pastoral caregivers get into trouble.

The goal of caring intimacy calls for constant balance: balance between respecting boundaries and challenging the person to extend boundaries where it is called for, and between intimacy that leads to healing and intimacy that is inappropriate and leads to violations.

Boundaries are of particular importance when dealing with LGBTQ people for at least two reasons: first, because they are an intensely scrutinized, oppressed, and sometimes vilified subgroup of the culture; and second, because they are a people whose boundaries are often violated through false assumptions and misinformation.

In our context of offering pastoral care, the boundaries with which we are particularly concerned are the physical/sexual and the emotional/spiritual.

Physical/Sexual Boundaries

Put simply, it is not permissible to have any kind of a physical/sexual relationship with anyone in your pastoral care. The reasons and implications
of this are known and available in general compendiums of pastoral care.
One of the principal foundations for this moral imperative is the inherent
characteristic of power inequality in the pastoral care relationship. One
must always understand this responsibility: the caregiver is assumed to
have a moral power over the care receiver.

However, if it is possible to single out one group — besides children —
for whom this prohibition is especially true, it is people who are identified
by the general populace by their sexual orientation or their sexual identity:
LGBTQ people. Our culture sees LGBTQ people primarily as sexual beings
and often applies grossly inaccurate stereotypes to them; in the eyes of the
broader culture their primary identity is a sexual one. Some queer people
are susceptible to this cultural assumption. Of course, it is no more true
of LGBTQ people than it is of anyone else.

By violating this boundary the pastoral caregiver would, minimally,
reinforce this too-narrow identity and affirm a skewed and inaccurate
self-understanding in the care receiver, as well as gravely violate the trust
they have been given.

Some people, LGBTQ and others, perhaps especially those with poor
or no adult guidance in their formative years, have learned to use their
sexuality as the primary way they influence people and exercise power, how
they relate to others, and how they make their way in the world. Expressed
in the extreme, this can possibly be a sign of abuse in childhood or current
sexual addiction.

Thus, there might be a tendency in this type of care seeker to come on
to the caregiver — that is, to approach the caregiver in a sexually charged
manner. In the vast majority of cases, it is important to see this not as a
moral failure of the care receiver, but a failure of the social milieu in which
the individual was nurtured; not the behavior of a moral degenerate, but
the expression of a desire for care and acceptance by someone who has
not learned the appropriate ways to express those feelings. In other words,
this overexpressed behavior is a normal stage of development in people
who have been repressed.

Pastoral Perspectives
Respecting Physical/Sexual Boundaries

- It is not permissible to have any kind of a physical/sexual relationship with anyone in your pastoral care.

- There is an inherent inequality of power in the pastoral care relationship, for which the caregiver has the ultimate moral responsibility.

- Getting too close physically is a gesture that might easily be misinterpreted.

- Avoid making the assumptions that LGBTQ people are easily sexual, asexual, hypersexual, or don't feel bound by normal sexual mores.

- Don't assume that LGBTQ people are sexless, never had sex, never had sex with the opposite sex, were never married, or have no children.

- Avoid any kind of presumptive touch (until you have established enough of a relationship that might allow this). This would include even a pat on the back, a hand on the arm, an arm around the shoulder, and other similar touches, and certainly anything more overtly sexual.

- Avoid putting the person in, or being with a person, in a cramped physical space.

- Avoid looking at the person in inappropriate ways; flirting/cruising glances are unacceptable.

- Do not tell inappropriate jokes or stories or personal experiences at any time, and especially not in the presence of the LGBTQ care receiver.

- Do not make a comment — negative or positive — on the care receiver's appearance or clothing, which could be misinterpreted.

- Avoid anything that would make them feel either singled out or demeaned in any way.

Your response as caregiver? Understand this sexualized behavior as a developmental phase, have patience in the process, and always keep the balance between accepting and caring for the person and not allowing the behavior that would destroy the relationship and hurt the person. This is not a challenge for the unclear or weak-willed. To nurture the pastoral relationship while at the same time keeping the boundaries appropriate calls for a mature caregiver.

Emotional/Spiritual Boundaries

The emotional and spiritual boundaries of LGBTQ people can be the most challenging for the pastoral worker to recognize and respect. These boundaries are made up of feelings, convictions, and sentiments that are intensely personal and thus sensitive to any kind of negative invasion. Examples of invasions across these boundaries are: asking a too-personal question in regard to your care receiver's sexual history, or asking it too soon; assuming an intimacy of information between the two of you that is more than the care receiver is comfortable with; not recognizing fragile boundaries in someone who, for example, has just gone through a serious loss; and assuming that a care receiver wants to pray aloud with you in regard to the issue at hand, or assuming that they don't — always ask.

As a result of our history as an outcast group in the larger society, LGBTQ people may have a tendency to be hyper-alert and sensitive to possible invasions of emotional/spiritual boundaries. When pastoral caregivers do get into trouble around boundary violations, it often starts with a problem in the emotional or spiritual area. Regrettably, pastors and pastoral caregivers are often not well prepared for this set-up in their training. The "spiritual" and the "emotional" (and thus easily connected to the sexual) exist in all people simply as different facets of the same gem. They reside in the same spheres of the mind, in the same chambers of the heart. Religious leaders are often expected to delve into the spiritual realm with a great deal of intimacy, without a clear understanding that they are also entering another sacred realm: the emotional/sexual. Spirit and emotion: when you engage one, the other often responds as well.[3] Both the caregiver

---

3. Mary Burke et al., *Religious and Spiritual Issues in Counseling: Applications across Diverse Populations* (New York: Brunner-Routledge, 2005), 102; see also "The Faith Trust

and care receiver are vulnerable at this point to moving into an interpersonal involvement that is a violation of the care receiver's boundaries. Forewarned is forearmed.

Spiritual Boundaries: "Love the sinner..."

One of the most significant boundary violations against LGBTQ people is based on the dictum, "Love the sinner, hate the sin." It primarily violates the spiritual boundary by injecting hate and sin upon the soul of a person who is no more identified as a sinner than anyone else and deserves no hate; it easily leads to emotional violations as well. This seemingly useful catchphrase has done an immense amount of damage because at first it appears to be a logical and fair way out of a difficult question for some religious people: "What are we to do with LGBTQ persons?"

The reasons for its lack of validity are clear: On a practical level, it is extremely difficult to make the separation between "sinner" and "sin." What one hates, one works against, even destroys. It is difficult to hate an abstraction, such as sin, but easy to hate a person perceived as sinful. Hate always comes to land on the "sinner."

Sin, at least from a psychological point of view, does not possess a separate existence outside of human activity. There is no such thing as sin, only human acts that are considered sinful. So, ultimately, because we have no other "place" to put our hate, we hate those whom we perceive as sinners. Trying to love the sinner and hate the sin is, for this reason alone, impossible. The mentality of loving the sinner but hating the sin perpetuates hate, never gets to love, and must be challenged wherever it appears.[4]

Keeping Confidentiality and Outing

Outing is making known someone's sexual orientation or identity, most often without their knowledge or consent.

Institute and the work of Rev. Dr. Marie M. Fortune," *www.faithtrustinstitute.org* (accessed November 2006).

4. For a more complete treatment of "love the sinner, hate the sin," see J. R. Jacobsen and A. Pellegrini, *Love the Sin: Sexual Regulation and the Limits of Religious Tolerance* (Boston: Beacon Press, 2003).

Anyone in the public eye, like pastoral caregivers, is aware of meeting people in public places with whom they have a professional relationship. In these social situations there is a certain degree of unease, based on the absence of an accustomed, and thus a safe, place. How the caregiver deals with these out-of-context situations is important to the integrity and success of the relationship. I believe the pastoral care relationship partakes of both the professional and personal.

When the lesbian parents of a girl in your religious education class see you at a neighborhood meeting, how you encounter them and introduce them to others is important to them — and noticed by others. When you see a gay member of your synagogue in the hardware store and say hello, and a friend asks you how you know each other, your answer is important and influential on your pastoral relationship. Something as casual as saying to your friend, "Say hi to Sally for me," when Sally is your friend's female partner, could possibly be tantamount to outing your friend to others present; at the same time not saying it may be interpreted as dismissing or ignoring the relationship. Context and pastoral wisdom will determine your decision.

At issue is whose prerogative it is to make public that one is out or the degree to which one is out (see chapter 4). As a pastoral caregiver, it is your responsibility to know the importance of the information you have about your care receivers; other people may know they're LGBTQ — or may not. To avoid unintentional outing, be aware of how you interact in public with them, what you say, and how you introduce them. This responsibility of course also applies when speaking about them in their absence. Make it a point to ask your queer care receivers toward the beginning of your relationship to what degree they are out and whether or not you have their permission to acknowledge it, to what degree, or to whom.

LGBTQ Transference and Counter-Transference

The field of psychoanalysis elucidates two relationship phenomena that are important for maintaining effective pastoral care boundaries: transference and counter-transference. Transference is the psychic process by which one transfers emotions, needs, or unresolved conflicts directed to one person and places them on another. Within the context of pastoral care, the feelings of the care receiver are often projected onto the caregiver. Frequently, but not always, the feelings in question were originally directed toward parents or some other authority figure, precisely the people who often misunderstand, reject, or mistreat LGBTQ people.

Effective caregivers realize that they will often be placed, almost always unconsciously, in a parental/authoritative role. Because of the moral power that this transference of feelings often gives the caregiver, this is a good moment to recall that our underlying model for the pastoral care relationship is our relationship with the loving God. Be aware of your power and resolve to use it justly — and carefully.

The feelings and needs involved in this process are often negative, and thus you might receive the person's anger and frustration. By understanding the phenomenon of transference you will see that these attitudes are not personal toward you. Thus, to react to them personally would be incorrect, a response that could hurt the pastoral care relationship as well as hurt the care receiver. You are called on to carry these emotions with care — that is, to allow them to be placed on you (within reason, of course) without any negative or defensive reaction.

The feelings and needs of care receivers might also be positive and involve emotional and sexual attraction to you; they could be bestowing on you the love they were never allowed to give to a father, for example, or to an older sibling, or to a desired but unavailable partner.

Nor is it your direct responsibility as a pastoral caregiver to "help LGBTQ persons work through their feelings," since this is the work of a trained pastoral counselor or therapist. Nevertheless, your patience and understanding in the face of some undeserved feelings will be a kind of working through of the feelings by your care receiver and certainly will enhance the effectiveness of your care.

In terms of emotional boundaries, one might say that in this case LGBTQ persons are violating *your* boundaries; whatever they are feeling for you is not really yours — you don't deserve it, good or bad. This is not a true violation, however — simply a reality of effective pastoral care.

Inherent to the pastoral care relationship, at least in most cases, is an imbalance of power. The caregiver generally has more power. There can be situations when this is not so clear: If the care receiver is a major donor, years older, and chair of the parish board, she might well have more, or at least a different kind of, power over the pastoral caregiver. When it is a question of a juridical action against the pastoral caregiver, however, one must assume the power will be construed to reside in the caregiver. You have the responsibility to be both knowledgeable and able to carry what the receiver might need to place on you.[5] Like the power of a parent, this power is built into the role you have assumed and thus is nontransferable.

Now put the shoe on the other foot. Countertransference is the emotional energy that you, the caregiver, place on the person who is the recipient of your care. Does the young gay man on the finance committee remind you of your neighborhood friend when you were a child? Or maybe of your estranged younger brother? Does the lesbian woman who heads your church council have the same mannerisms as those of your first-grade teacher? Or maybe she looks just like a woman you were in love with once? Does the care receiver who comes to discuss his bisexuality conjure up memories of your college psychology professor?

These countertransference feelings happen to us all the time and have an influence on how you deal with the people involved; it's simply human nature. At these times you need above all to be aware of your countertransference feelings, to be as conscious of them as possible. Because awareness brings insight and safety, you will then be less likely to act on your feelings than your knowledge, less likely to act from your heart rather than from your head.

Self-knowledge is an essential part of caregiving. We must know just where we stand personally, intimately, experientially, morally, and sexually with the issues that we deal with in others. The specific experience of dealing with LGBTQ persons can sometimes bring up for caregivers unresolved sexuality issues of their own. It is important that the caregivers first of all recognize what is happening within themselves, especially if these issues deal with orientation or identity, and then seek an immediate process of consultation with a trusted and competent advisor. This is not an uncommon occurrence and can become a moment of grace for the caregiver. Not to deal with issues of self-knowledge in this area can easily lead the caregiver into serious trouble with keeping appropriate boundaries. As Marshall gently states, "Clients and parishioners are most helped

---

5. For a good understanding of the power imbalance in pastoral care ministry, see Richard M. Gula, *Ethics in Pastoral Ministry* (New York: Paulist Press, 1996).

when caregivers are not caught in their own moral struggles at the same moment in which they are trying to assist . . . their . . . congregations."[6]

Outside a fiduciary relationship, teachers within the Christian church have used transference in a positive way, urging people, for example, to see others as Christ (Matt. 25:40, 45). In other words, one is urged to project on to others the same feelings and attitudes one feels toward Jesus. In a way, this concept refers to the beginning of the chapter where the caregiver was encouraged to know his or her feelings toward the care seeker.

The patronizing attitude mentioned above in the section on "Caring Intimacy" is also important to mention here in the context of the feelings that the caregiver and care receiver might have for each other. On the one hand, the caregiver's patronizing attitude might be that "I am the pastor, and I know best what is good for you." While as a trained pastoral caregiver you do have special information and knowledge, this attitude is the patriarchal and futile attitude of authority having all the knowledge and the rest of humanity coming to get it.

On the other hand, it is possible to hear, "I am the bisexual person here, and I know what it's like; you have no idea!" If that's what you hear, whether you "know what it's like" or not, a simple invitation might be in order: "Then please help me understand so that we both can know." Getting defensive will not help. In any case, don't allow yourself to be manipulated through guilt, suffering, or any other guise.

Acknowledging one's own limits is often very effective. "No, I don't know what it's like to be transgender, but I would like to know more and I hope you will help me understand." Always remember, when you're not sure of a response to an LGBTQ care receiver, consider: what can I say or do that will keep the relationship going and growing?

Content and Process

Of significant help in keeping appropriate boundaries with LGBTQ people is to analyze what's happening in the pastoral relationship from the point of view of the content and from the point of view of the process. The content

---

6. Joretta Marshall, *Counseling Lesbian Partners* (Louisville: Westminster John Knox Press, 1997), 4.

is what you're actually dealing with: a stressful situation at the person's work, a death in the family, a problem with an aging parent, working on a problem with a fellow committee member, and so on. Content is very important.

The process is different. It's what's happening on an interpersonal level between (or among) you and the person (people) you're dealing with, no matter what the content is. The process is the ongoing state of the relationship between you, the caregiver, and the care receiver(s). Process, not content, is often the first aspect of the pastoral care relationship to which your LGBTQ care receivers will react.

For the lesbian couple who has come to you to talk about baptizing their infant daughter, the details of the baptism (content) are important, but not as important as the tone and feeling of how you are all relating to each other (process). For the transgender man who is looking for a deeper spiritual life (content), how he feels about the session as he leaves (process) is what will largely determine if he returns. Understanding the difference between these two aspects of the relationship is fundamental. Without this understanding, the relationship has little chance of success; with it, little risk of failure.

Make an attempt to keep in mind both these points of view within the pastoral care relationship as you are experiencing it. This two-level approach will give you clarity in your interventions. Your thoughts might run something like this: Is what she just said (or her tone of voice, or her choice of words) primarily about the subject we're talking about? Or is it more about what's going on between her and me?

Gay and Straight, In and Out

Effective pastoral care takes into account the sexual identity and orientation of both the caregiver and the care receiver. Two combinations are possible: The first is that the pastoral caregiver is LGBTQ and the care receiver(s) is (are) also LGBTQ. This sets up a very different dynamic from the other possibility: a caregiver who is straight (not LGBTQ). The point in specifying these combinations is to emphasize the need to understand the dynamic setup between the parties; it will influence the success of the pastoral care. Taking into account the degree to which parties are out adds further possible combinations of energies.

Caregiver and care receiver are both LGBTQ. When the caregiver and care receiver are both queer, the ideal is for both to know who both are in as natural a way as possible. At times you may be dealing with someone who does not immediately come out — someone who does not reveal their sexual orientation or identity to you at first. In these cases keep in mind the following:

- Never presume to know a person's sexual orientation or identity; playing "dumb" is ineffective as well.

- If the situation calls for information about the person's sexuality and gender identity in order to be complete and successful, inquire as needed, as in any other situation.

- Always begin with belief and acceptance of what the care receiver tells you. If you have basis for doubts as to the accuracy or truth of the information that care receivers give you, proceed with care.

The pastoral caregiver being in the closet sets up a possible additional tension mostly centered around the question of "who knows what?" which can be a serious distraction from the ultimate purpose of the relationship: the good of the care receiver. Generally speaking, I recommend that the pastoral caregiver be as transparent in this regard as possible and thus have his or her sexual orientation or identity commonly known. In reality, this is often not the case, nor even possible or desirable in some circumstances. When the pastoral caregiver is in the closet, keep in mind the following:

- It is possible that the care receiver will have a hunch or suspect that the caregiver is LGBTQ. Thus, the tension that this "knowledge" might add to the relationship must be acknowledged, at least internally, by the caregiver, to ascertain what kind of influence it might have.

- Keep integrity and honesty as your primary focus when, as caregiver, your closet is kept closed.

- In the long term, consider possible ways in which you, the LGBTQ caregiver, could successfully come out within the context of your church identity and pastoral position. While this question has a myriad of ramifications, I believe it must be at least considered in a serious way for the sake of personal integration and the broader LGBTQ cause.

• Seek competent, affirming, and knowledgeable support for yourself on an ongoing basis, whatever your decision about coming out.

In fairness, and particularly at this moment in the history of religion, it is important to acknowledge the significant challenges that face LGBTQ pastoral caregivers, who in some religious organizations work within a structure that not only fails to recognize their sexual orientation but also officially disparages or denies its existence.

Pastoral care for queer pastoral caregivers is especially important and necessary since they are vulnerable both to the anger of the LGBTQ community *and* to the reprimand or rejection of the church they love. Personal integrity is a constant challenge. At the very least, LGBTQ caregivers working within these oppressive bounds should find one another — and those caregivers within less oppressive churches — for support, prayer, and friendship, and seek ways to lead their churches to grace. Because your work is so important and necessary, and the pressures on you are stronger than on many others, I would strongly encourage all queer pastoral caregivers to seek camaraderie-in-the-ministry in some way, perhaps by participation in a support group.

One hears more and more often of pastoral ministers coming out in public and in responsible ways. Invariably and necessarily, they have good support systems in place before they do so. (See two examples on page 39.)

My own process of coming out as a gay man began with a pastoral relationship with a young man in the parish where I was assistant pastor. He came to me specifically for help in dealing with being gay. My initial stumblings, fears, doubts, and self-searchings gradually gave way — first to supportive help for the care seeker, and ultimately to enthusiastic espousal, not only of him and his process but of LGBTQ causes and of my own process of coming out. My specific journey of coming out began when I realized I wanted to imitate the courage of that care receiver. What wonderful gifts our care receivers have for us!

Caregiver is straight, not LGBTQ. In this scenario the possibility for tension is also lessened when both parties know the other party's orientation and it is a non-issue.

When the non-LGBTQ pastoral caregiver does not know the sexual orientation of the care receiver at the beginning of the relationship, it

Pastoral Perspectives
*Real-Life Pastoral Caregivers Coming Out**

Rev. Jane Adams Spahr: Janie was ordained a Presbyterian minister in 1974 and began her out liberation work very soon after. She is one of the founders of Spectrum Center for Lesbian and Gay Ministries in San Rafael, California. Because of her sexual orientation, she was denied a call to a pastorate by the denomination's highest court in 1992. The next year another Presbyterian church invited Janie to become their evangelist to spread the good news by "personing the issue" and challenging exclusive church policies. Janie has traveled throughout the country, educating and informing Presbyterians and others working on behalf of greater inclusiveness for gay, lesbian, bisexual, and transgender people.

Rev. Fred Daley: Fred is the pastor of St. Francis de Sales Roman Catholic Church in Utica, New York. "It wasn't until two years after his ordination, when he was twenty-seven and serving in a parish, that Fr. Fred Daley acknowledged he might be gay," stated an article in the *National Catholic Reporter.* In 2004, Daley came out to a local newspaper reporter soon after he received an award for service from the United Way of Greater Utica. He was given a standing ovation by his parish when he delivered a homily telling of his struggle. The wider church, by its stance, is "encouraging the oppression and physical violence against gays and lesbians," says Daley. "I hope I'm an example that being gay is not the end of ministry."

---

*Janie Spahr, *Religious Archives Network,* www.lgbtran.org/Profile.asp?ID=1 (accessed November 2006); Fred Daly, *National Catholic Reporter,* issue of November 11, 2005, *www.ncath.org* (accessed November 2006).

most likely will be revealed if it is significant to the issue at hand. If not, there should be no need to clarify.

If, through observation and intuition, the caregiver, whether straight or queer, believes that the sexual orientation of the care receiver is not being acknowledged *and* is a problem or an issue for that care receiver, always create safety first and establish your unqualified support for the seeker. Then proceed with caution to seek more information. Always be prepared to be wrong. Always believe what care receivers tell you about their sexual orientation. Even if you have doubts, act as if you believe what they say. It establishes trust and confidence and frequently creates welcoming ground for openness and truth.

There are particular challenges when dealing with these "gay/straight, in/out" issues with transgender people. First, the general awareness of transgenderism — and gender identity in general — is a relatively recent reality, and many people, including many caregivers, are still in the process of acquiring sufficient experience and accurate information to feel some competence in dealing with the issue, let alone in being helpful — thus the importance of up-to-date information and awareness.

Second, the processes through which trans people progress in their gender transition generally have extended stages and several variations. This adds to the need for openness, frankness about limits, accepting where they are in their process, and willingness to learn on the part of the caregiver.

Though one's sexual orientation and one's gender identity always influence how one responds to anyone in life, the goal is that the sexuality of both caregiver and care receiver be a "nonproblem," and to have each one appropriately transparent to the other in as natural a way as possible.

If the pastoral care relationship is specifically about a sexual issue of the care receiver, it is even more important for the combinations and distinctions mentioned here to be understood and acknowledged.[7]

---

7. See, for example, Andrew Weaver et al., *Counseling on Sexual Issues: A Handbook for Pastors and Other Helping Professionals* (Cleveland: Pilgrim Press, 2006), and Marshall, *Counseling Lesbian Partners.*

The Pastoral Relationship
with Systems Affecting LGBTQ People

In the systemic care of LGBTQ people, pastoral caregivers concern themselves not only with a relationship with the individual LGBTQ people within their purview, but also extend that concern to a relationship with the interconnecting and broader systems and social power arrangements which shape their lives or have some influence on them. These systems include significant others, spouses/partners, family, workplace, social groups, neighborhood organizations, schools, churches, political groups, societal matrices, cultural assumptions and forces, and extend even to the eco-centric system of our planet Earth.

The psychosystemic approach to pastoral care and the categories of care I use in this section are based on the work of Larry Kent Graham.[8] The term "psychosystems" is a combination of "psyche," which "delineates the soul... which is formed in relation to God, self and the world in which one lives," and "systemic," which "indicates that the elements of reality are regarded in religious terms as the interlocking dynamic forces of the natural and social forces..."[9] Think of a psychosystems approach to pastoral caretaking as primarily based on the philosophical, ecological, and religious precept that we are all interconnected with each other and with the world; the actions of the one affect the many, and the actions of the many affect each one.

Psychosystemic pastoral care is especially relevant to the care of LGBTQ people. It acknowledges that pastoral care with the faith-based values of justice and charity, for example, which are given to a person might not stand up to the influence nor match the power of the many secular systems that advance different, even contradictory, values and constrictions on that same person. Systemic care also acknowledges that some "secular" systems of service are more clearly based on justice and charity than are some of their religious counterparts. Many LGBTQ refugees from churches find excellent pastoral care in social centers, PFLAG, and other welcoming groups.

---

8. Larry Kent Graham, *Care of Persons, Care of Worlds: A Psychosystems Approach to Pastoral Care and Counseling* (Nashville: Abingdon, 1992).

9. Larry Kent Graham, "Prophetic Pastoral Caretaking: A Psychosystemic Approach to Symptomatology," *Journal of Psychology and Christianity* 8, no. 1 (1989): 53.

Effective pastoral care means cultivating an awareness of and challenging the systems in which people live. It involves broadening and deepening the pastoral caregiver's vision and sphere of influence from the exclusivity of this one person or congregation to the expansive matrices of relationships that the world contains. Psychosystemic care "sees" the broad implications and struggles of the individual in his or her world as it is, whether secular, sacred, or somewhere in between. Frequently it begins with and stems from a local, close-to-home occasion of pastoral care.

Churches and their pastoral care representatives have an unprecedented opportunity at the beginning of the twenty-first century to exert their influence for the just and fair treatment of LGBTQ people. Especially because of the outspoken nature of the more vocal, organized, and reactionary religious groups who work in opposition to LGBTQ people, any expression of care and enlightened wisdom from a church- or synagogue-based voice will be heard, perhaps more clearly than expected, simply by being different from the often-anticipated response from religion.

Following Graham's framework, here are descriptions of the five goals of psychosystemic pastoral care. After the explanation of each goal, I present brief examples or suggestions for the application of that goal to the ministry of the pastoral caregiver to LGBTQ people. Not intended to be a complete listing of opportunities, these are merely samples or possibilities for the living out of psychosystemic pastoral ministry. They ask the question: if pastoral caregiving were to embody the values and goals of the psychosystems approach, what are some examples of what pastoral interventions might look like?

Note that a "psychosystems approach to ministry" does not imply an either/or choice but an attitude, an understanding, a vision that can enhance everyone's pastoral ministry, whether carried out in the church office, in the town square, or on the Internet. The psychosystemically aware pastoral minister will always remember: we're all in this together, and what we each do influences everyone else.

Note too that all five of the goals of the psychosystems approach to ministry involve movement — movement from a state of pain and injustice to a state of fairness and joy, from a place of suffering to a place of peace, from transgression to grace.

The five goals[10] of psychosystemic pastoral care are to encourage movement

+ from being organizations that hurt to becoming organizations that help

+ from the unfair balance of power to the fair balance of power

+ from destructive conflicts over values to mutual understanding of values

+ from creativity kept powerless to creativity that blossoms

+ from being stuck in "no" to getting to "yes"

Becoming Organizations That Help

This goal is to see and respond to society's structures, groups, and organizations that are flawed and thus do harm to people, and to engage with those broken structures in the real world where they operate. The following are brief examples that present opportunities for the psychosystemic pastoral caregiver to be aware of and respond to harmful structures that influence LGBTQ people.

Contemporary feminist concerns. I begin with the rights of women for two reasons: First, I believe that the interests of women are the interests of LGBTQ people, and both are the interests of all.[11] Rabbi Steven Greenberg says, "We cannot address the question of homophobia without also addressing the question of misogyny."[12] Second, the way the world, including many of its religious bodies, treats women as second-class people must be at the forefront of all pastoral concern. The pastoral caregiver will recognize and engage these flawed systems, from local social service agencies and employers to national and international organizations. Any

---

10. Graham, *Care of Persons, Care of Worlds.* For purposes of simplicity and clarity, I have changed some of Graham's wording of these categories while making every effort to retain his meaning.

11. My statements are based on the assumption that homophobia and sexism derive from the same antifeminist attitudes. See Suzanne Pharr, *Homophobia: A Weapon of Sexism* (Little Rock, AR: Chardon Press, 1988).

12. Steven Greenberg, *Wrestling with God and Men: Homosexuality in the Jewish Tradition* (Madison: University of Wisconsin Press, 2004), 14.

system that mistreats women is based on what Gallo and Peck call the "wrong relationships of domination, exploitation, and dehumanization."[13]

Opening the closet door. The psychosystemic caregiver will not only care about the congregant who is in the process of coming out, but will move from that single experience into the reality of the societal-based LGBTQ closet throughout the congregation, town, city, and broader world. Many organizations, for various reasons of apparent self-interest, strive to keep closet doors closed. Life in the closet creates in the closeted ones attitudes that run counter to any wholesome religious experience and mature living in general. The closed door of safety and stagnation must give way to the open door leading to the wholesome promise of inner freedom. The pastoral caregiver becomes the careful and caring advocate of opening LGBTQ closet doors, and a helper in the process, to members of schools, churches, the military, social groups, the government, and so on.

The LGBTQ person's family of origin. When a family rejects a gay son, lesbian daughter, transgender parent, or bisexual uncle simply because of their sexual orientation or gender identity, the flawed structures that created that family become immediately apparent. Centuries of influence by broad-based social structures of which the family is a part (the church, for example) and deeply influential channels of authority are brought to bear on that family to create their counterintuitive attitude of rejection. The caregiver here has an opportunity to examine these structures and influences with this family and possibly with the broader communities involved.

Establishing a Fair Balance of Power

Another way to state this goal: there's a powerful energy loose in human culture that affects the ways power is distributed. The pastoral goal is to wrestle with the energy and bring access to power into a mutually satisfying and fair balance, while respecting and using power justly. Here are four brief examples of areas in which pastoral care can help create movement to fairness for LGBTQ people.

---

13. Jane Peck and Jeanne Gallo, "JPIC: A Critique from a Feminist Perspective," *The Ecumenical Review* 41, no. 4 (October 1989): 574. Cited in Graham, *Care of Persons, Care of Worlds*, 204.

Women in society. Again, one of the primary and most obvious of the power imbalances in the world is between the overarching power of world patriarchy on the one hand and the power of women, and by association, the power of LGBTQ people on the other. Pastoral care workers will see that the values of patriarchy have been well embedded in the structures of religious organizations, and thus they are called to become prophetic voices for wholeness (holiness) within the context of their denominations.

LGBTQ ethnic groups. Black, Latino, Asian, First Nations, and other ethnic minorities have their proportionate percentage of LGBTQ members. People in these populations struggle under two oppressions, both based on the prejudices and denial of power to them by the dominant groups in society. Psychosystemic care holds the religious ideal of equality as a constant template against which to see human interactions. Does it exist in this situation? Why not? What needs to be done here and now? (See chapter 2 for more on pastoral care with ethnic minorities.)

The AIDS-related power imbalance. The HIV/AIDS epidemic created a power imbalance from the moment it hit the human community. From denial of access to care and drugs, to becoming ostracized from society for perceived causes, people with HIV/AIDS have been and continue to be kept from the sources of power. To which organizations can you add your voice and power in the fight for fair and just treatment of people with AIDS? The psychosystemic caregiver knows the truth of the saying proposed by World AIDS Day: "We all have AIDS...If One of Us Does."[14]

LGBTQ homeless and marginalized. Because the impaired social structure of the family is prejudiced against the LGBTQ member, a disproportionate number of street youth are LGBTQ, having been disowned or physically thrown out by their families. Many of these children end up on the streets. Make no mistake: this still happens on a regular basis. Urban-based pastoral workers especially should be available to cooperate with agencies that care for street kids, bringing a values-based dimension of pastoral care to the challenge.[15]

---

14. For background of the saying, "We All Have AIDS...If One of Us Does" see Kaiser Family Foundation Web site: *www.kff.org/hivaids* (accessed November 2006); see also Larry Kramer, *The Tragedy of Today's Gays* (New York: Tarcher, 2005).

15. An example of this kind of ministry is Covenant House, which provides shelter and other services to homeless and runaway youth: *www.covenanthouse.org* (accessed November 2006).

Mutual Understanding of Values

This goal of psychosystemic care acknowledges that the virtues of love, kindness, and care are thwarted at every level of society and never seem to win, at least not at first, not easily, and not generally for the benefit of the poor and powerless. Psychosystemic care recognizes the presence of conflict in human values on all levels and is ready to cast its lot and its influence with the values it brings from its faith tradition. Examples of embodying this goal:

Harmonizing conflicting values: LGBTQ marriage. Directly from the pages, Web sites, and airwaves of today's news outlets comes the issue of same-sex marriage. It's clear that church-based teachings and convictions have formed the opinions of the vast majority of people who oppose it (and perhaps as often, ironically, those who support it). Psychosystemic care, no matter the individual caregiver's current opinion (personal, political, or other), will be engaged in this struggle and always seek the values of justice and truth and eschew avoidance of the issue.

Legal protections for LGBTQ people. Well-intentioned religious people often oppose antidiscrimination laws or hate-crime laws that are based on sexual orientation and gender identity. Are there opportunities in your pastoral care to point out these discrepancies between faith and action? Are there opportunities to join your voice to those who work against this type of inequality?

LGBTQ self-acceptance in a nonaccepting world. Perhaps the most fundamental LGBTQ issue, self-acceptance and self-love, is at the heart of all pastoral care with the LGBTQ community. There are many forces out there that foster nonacceptance and are expressed too frequently by murder, gay-bashing, taunting, bullying, and name-calling. Questions for the caregiver include: What and who are the forces for such harm? How can churches and synagogues confront and transform them effectively, especially when they happen in your town or city?

Keeping LGBTQ people from God. It's no secret that a significant percentage of queer people are angry at churches and religion in general. This anger is primarily based, I believe, on personal experience and on the anti-gay stances upheld by many churches. Notwithstanding churches' defense that they are not anti-gay, LGBTQ folks stay away in droves. At the same time a significant percentage are actively engaged with their churches.[16] Rather than avoid the discomfort, psychosystems-based care-givers will deliberately place themselves at the intersection of these groups, helping to clarify conflicting and misapprehended values.

Discounting LGBTQ experience: the double standard. The double standard is a common way to thwart values. With LGBTQ people it is expressed in the proclivity of many churches not to accept the simple truth and validity of the lived experience of queer people, while at the same time accepting the truthfulness of non-LGBTQ people's lived experiences. Representatives of churches often seem to say that they know what LGBTQ people experience better than they do — for example, the assumption that the goal for LGBTQ people should necessarily be quiet assimilation. The pastoral caregiver finds in this contradiction a rich opportunity for the voice of prophetic truth.

Promoting a Creativity That Blossoms

This goal recognizes that social matrices often intersect in such a way that human creativity is discouraged, unrecognized, or kept underground. The challenge for the pastoral caregiver is how to support its liberation. For example:

Keeping LGBTQ social roles rigid. In many instances society says "no" to LGBTQ people: They can't get married or adopt children or join the armed forces as out individuals (in most places in the world). In some places and times they are not allowed to teach children. Some schools will not accept them as students; most churches will not ordain them. Many civil jurisdictions do not include them in nondiscrimination policies. Many employers reject them. All that creativity, service, and life are denied to the world; all those opportunities to serve and create are lost to the individuals. These are great occasions for the systems-based pastoral caregiver to work to free creative forces that are kept down.

Creating rules and norms for moral relationships. Because LGBTQ people are not encouraged by society in general to have intimate or romantic relationships, at least not "legitimate" ones, they have

---

16. See Leanne McCall Tigert, *Coming Out While Staying In: Struggles and Celebrations of Lesbians, Gays, and Bisexuals in the Church* (Cleveland: United Church Press, 1996).

to create their own rules, customs, and standards as they form these re-lationships. Insightful pastoral caregivers will see an opportunity to apply moral standards to these new moral realities. They will also learn from these experiences and apply these "new" ways of human relating to the creation of stronger intimate relations in general.[17]

LGBTQ grief. Grief is often a window to emotional awakening and creativity. Grief abounds as LGBTQ people, both young and old, develop and become more aware of what they are denied and how negatively they are held in the public esteem.[18] The queer community has experienced considerable cumulative grief from the losses of AIDS. A common com-panion of grief is often, understandably, shame; one feels responsible in some way for the loss. And shame is a common road to addictions. Pastoral caretakers will seek opportunities to help LGBTQ people, even groups of people, deal with grief and shame, to emerge from these dark feelings with new life and, inevitably, with renewed creativity.

Getting to "Yes!"

At every level of human life there are formidable obstacles that keep human beings from getting through to each other, to sabotage our commu-nication, to keep us from understanding each other's intended meaning, which is a primary human need. This is as true within the dyad of marriage as it is between countries at the United Nations. This goal of psycho-systems pastoral care is to help open the lines of human communications. For example:

LGBTQ intergenerational issues. The psychosystems caregiver will recognize that one of the challenges for LGBTQ people, as for people in general, is for the young to accept the old and vice versa. So much wisdom is lost in generation gaps. This especially applies for the LGBTQ minority insofar as they need all the creativity they can muster to achieve equality and justice. Add to this dimension the generations that have been

---

17. See Anthony Kosnik et al., *Sexual Morality: New Directions in Catholic Thought* (New York: Paulist Press, 1966), 92ff. The characteristics of moral sexual acts are described: self-liberating, other-enriching, faithful, socially responsible, life-serving, and joyous.

18. See my article "Why Do They Hate Us So Much" on the Web site of the Cen-ter for Lesbian and Gay Studies in Religion and Ministry (CLGS), *www.clgs.org/5/pdf/kundtz_why_hate.pdf* (accessed November 2006).

decimated by AIDS. Bringing together young and old LGBTQ people is the challenge.[19] What better place than church?

The world of religion and LGBTQ people. On a broader basis, initiating and influencing the dialogue between LGBTQ people and their interests on the one hand, and the broad expanse of church communities and religion on the other, is a noble and urgent goal.[20] This service brings the wisdom of each within the understanding of the other: its eventual goal is harmony brought about by mutual understanding and appreciation. This can only be accomplished by actively destroying impasses that separate, and by building bridges that unite LGBTQ people with their churches.

LGBTQ and non-LGBTQ communities. The goal is to cause unity by removing the gap that exists between LGBTQ people and non-LGBTQ people. Queer culture is, in many ways, different from straight culture. An inevitable step along the way is bringing them together and encouraging them to listen to each other. Good pastoral experience shows that when that happens, attitudes begin to change. The psychosystems-based pastoral caregiver looks for opportunities to introduce LGBTQ persons to non-LGBTQ persons. On every level, human contact is a consistently transformative agent: it's more difficult to hate or fear queer people in general when you like Vickie, a particular lesbian, and Colin, a particular bisexual.

The Power of the Straight Voice

Here, at the conclusion of the section on systemic pastoral care of LGBTQ people, I want to call attention to a specific and often unrecognized source of power for the betterment of queer people and the systems that influence them: the supportive public voices of "straight" allies.[21]

---

19. Intergeneration is a good example. This organization brings together LGBT people across the age spectrum and around the arts. For more information see Queer Cultural Center (QCC): *queerculturalcenter.org/index.htm* (accessed November 2006).

20. A practical example of an engaging systemic ministry that seeks to influence and heal transactional impasses between the world and religion is the Center for Lesbian and Gay Studies in Religion and Ministry (CLGS) at the Pacific School of Religion in Berkeley, CA. CLGS is the sponsor of the book series of which the present work is a part. See *www.clgs.org* (accessed November 2006).

21. PFLAG (Parents, Families & Friends of Lesbians & Gays) is perhaps the best known and most influential of these voices. See *www.pflag.org/* (accessed November 2006). Many

Often non-LGBTQ caregivers do not seem to be aware of their power to influence the thinking of other non-LGBTQ people in regard to the issues that face the queer community. The power comes from a simple fact: "You [non-LGBTQ people] are not us [LGBTQ people]." "We" "have an agenda" that according to many is an undesirable agenda at best, and often is labeled much worse. "You" (non-LGBTQ people) don't have that agenda, according to this kind of thinking.

If you are non-LGBTQ, your pro-LGBTQ comments tend to make many other non-LGBTQ people stop and think. These are people who might otherwise dismiss the remark of any queer person as a self-serving example of the "gay agenda."

If you are a non-LGBTQ ally and pastoral caregiver, you are indeed a gift to LGBTQ people. We need you! Please never stop thinking that our concerns indeed are your concerns and the concerns of all. Keep Pastor Niemöller's poem[22] clearly in mind, and never underestimate the power and influence of your supportive words.

More than any technique, intervention, or ability to solve problems, is the strength and quality of the human relationship created within the context of faith-based pastoral care with LGBTQ people that enables the care seeker to move from the place of pain and challenge to the place of joy and resolution — and ultimately to peace. Pastoral care that affirms and strengthens the relationship, pastoral care that aims to heal the broad-based and interconnected systems within which LGBTQ people live, and pastoral care that ensures that the relationship remains open for future rekindling — such pastoral care indeed partakes of the divine.

---

churches have organizations specifically for their LGBT members; some official, some not. See the list of resources.

22. The poem by Pastor Martin Niemöller (1892–1984), a survivor of a Nazi concentration camp, is well known in various versions. For one version, see *www.en.wikipedia.org/wiki/First_they_came*.

Chapter 2

The Functions of Pastoral Care

The functions of pastoral care bring the foundations of theology down to earth, down to the daily ins and outs of the ministry. The functions of pastoral care tell us what it actually does. They are the type of services it provides to people, the kind of work it accomplishes.

In presenting the functions of pastoral care for LGBTQ people, I adopt the schema of Howard Clinebell as he has modified it from the work of Clebsch and Jaekle. Clinebell offers five functions of pastoral care: healing, sustaining, guiding, reconciling, and nurturing. In addition, and based on the work of Larry Kent Graham, I add the function of prophetic pastoral caring.[1] I consider each of these functions from the unique point of view of providing pastoral care for LGBTQ people.

Healing

The function of healing, according to Clinebell, "aims to overcome some impairment by restoring the person to wholeness and by leading him to advance beyond his previous condition."[2] Overcoming impairment: The impairments that present themselves first in most LGBTQ people are the wounds that are inflicted by the world into which they are born.

Woundedness. In varying degrees of intensity, woundedness is one characteristic you can count on in many of the LGBTQ people with whom you relate, and thus you will encounter a clear need for healing. Of course,

---

1. Howard Clinebell, *Basic Types of Pastoral Care and Counseling* (Nashville: Abingdon Press, 1984), 42–43; and Larry Kent Graham, "Prophetic Pastoral Caretaking: A Psychosomatic Approach to Symptomatology," *Journal of Psychology and Christianity* 8, no. 1 (1989).

2. Clinebell, *Basic Types,* 42. Clinebell is quoting from Clebsch and Jaekle, *Pastoral Care in Historical Perspective,* new ed. (New York: Jason Aronson, 1994). Stewart Hiltner, Wayne Oates, and others have contributed to the development of these functions.

LGBTQ people have all the wounds that are inherent in the human family. They do, however, tend to have a few battle scars that are particularly characteristic. With some people, the scars are truly devastating; with others, there is less damage. I do not hesitate to use the word "always" in regard to the woundedness of LGBTQ people: there is indeed always some woundedness. It would seem close to impossible to have avoided it given the history that has produced the predominant attitudes toward queer people in the early-twenty-first-century world in which we live.

Church-inflicted wounds. Too frequently the wounds have been inflicted by the church or synagogue, directly or indirectly. If that is the case, it is essential that the pastoral caregiver always keep in mind that these care seekers are engaging with the very reality that wounded them. The process might well feel risky and make them feel vulnerable anew. You as caregiver represent both the power and the responsibility of the church. Both power and responsibility might well involve an acknowledgment of the wounds and perhaps an apology.

A comment as simple as "You know, I'm really sorry for how the religious community has hurt you," can be an effective way to begin a process to undo decades of pain and enter into a healing relationship.

It seems to me there is no better place, no better community than the church to make up for the pain that the church had a role in creating. Thus, the healing of LGBTQ people will involve making the specifically healing elements of church life as easily available as possible. For sacrament-based churches this clearly involves sacraments, all the sacraments. For all, it involves making access to worship and fellowship not only available, but easy and welcoming (see chapter 5).

Most church communities are blessed with people who have the gift of affirmation; they are the enthusiastic and sincere supporters of people and good causes. Imaginative pastoral care will find ways to unite your hesitant care receivers and these loving, affirming people.

Family-of-origin wounds. Most LGBTQ people leave their family of origin with some wounds, wounds that have been directly or indirectly inflicted.

Reason and experience tell us that all wounded people can be unpredictable and isolated, and understandably so. They have reasons not to trust; they have experience that tells them they will be hurt, and scars to remind them. Some LGBTQ people have been worn down by wounds inflicted deeply and early in life by those who should have loved them most, and they have either retreated into unfriendly isolation or become aggressive and defensive. With the eyes of pastoral care, we can see through the hard exterior into the bright souls hoping for healing.

I have already mentioned internalized homophobia as something to watch for in your LGBTQ care seekers. In the same vein are shame-based attitudes of self-denigration or low self-esteem. An aware pastoral care provider will notice these isolated individuals, no matter the cause, and act to heal by facilitating their incorporation into the broader community of faith. One frequently encounters this woundedness in both older and younger LGBTQ people who make assumptions that indicate they do not expect or think they deserve anything better than the back-of-the-bus and don't-ever-talk-about-it treatment that our culture has traditionally offered them.

One Sunday morning after the last service, I asked a fellow pastoral worker, "Did you notice that frail kid in the last row? He always seems to be alone." We all had noticed him. It turns out that he was a thirteen-year-old white boy from a large, poor, unchurched, local family that was literally being destroyed by an alcoholic and rage-aholic father. The youngster had come to our church because it was the closest one to his home and just sat in the back row every Sunday morning, arriving late and leaving early. One morning the director of religious education corralled him in her unique and loving way, and that was the beginning of a long, complex, but ultimately redemptive saga of a whole family and a small-town church. (That's another book!) Fortunately for him, he had a winning personality and an indomitable spirit, and in time, the whole parish sort of adopted him.

His father had identified him at ten years old as "a faggot kid" (the father's words). The details he revealed of his father's mean violence, his mother's helplessness, and his siblings' avoidance and fears startled all who heard them. He at first easily acknowledged (to anyone who would listen) that he was gay; later in life he came out as transgender and is now living, happily partnered, as a woman.

This kid's sitting alone in the back of a church was initially the sole impetus for whatever very limited healing the family eventually achieved. This particular kid expressed an exceptional personality by reaching out and by having a rich and expressive imagination. Most kids in that situation end up on the streets of the nearest large city and have very short lives.

The point for pastoral caregivers: Don't miss the subtle cries for help, especially in the old and young. Don't underestimate the depth of the wounds that a family is capable of bestowing.

Trading places. As a pastoral caregiver to wounded queer people, especially if you are not LGBTQ, learn to develop the virtue of understanding, and specifically of trying to put yourself in their place. In other words, "Walk a mile in their shoes." Such an attitude will go a long way in allowing your care to be effective.

For a moment, imagine living in a world in which what seems like your very being is questioned and found to be wanting — if not downright evil. Such a response would have a strong effect on anyone. The "closet" seems safe, quiet, and peaceful by comparison. The problem, of course, is that it is also dark, hidden, and can be lonely — and ultimately not a healthy choice. (See "Queer for a Day: An Exercise for Non-LGBT Caregivers" on page 89.)

The healing of wounds takes time and care. Recall the centrality of the relationship you have with care receivers. It is within the context of your relationship that much of the healing will take place, whether you are relating to your people in the context of worship, working together on a committee, or eating supper together at the church picnic.

Healing systems. Woundedness exists not only in individuals but in the organizations they create. The seasoned pastoral sense of Leonard, a sixty-eight-year-old, African American, retired pastor emeritus, led to some broad changes in the whole geographic region of his church.

Leonard's story begins with a casual conversation with a sixty-three-year-old member of the church, Helen, who told him tearfully that she did not know how she would get along now that "my friend Sarah is moving away." What Leonard noticed were the tears and the strong emotional response that Helen's statement brought out in her. He followed up, inquiring more deeply into her experience.

What he found out over a period of caring follow-up to that conversation was that Helen, who was African American, and Sarah, Irish American, had shared a life and a home for twenty-one years and were indeed life partners. Sarah needed to live at a medical care facility because of her health, and Helen was not eligible to go with her. Leonard became not only Helen's supporter in the church community but her advocate with the care facility, which eventually allowed the two women regular extended and private visits. Leonard also influenced the facility's administration to extend this policy of recognizing same-sex relationships to its other facilities in the region. Equality and justice for LGBTQ seniors became the focus of ministry for this straight, widowed, retired minister.

This wide-ranging series of healings, both individual and psycho-systemic, began with a moment of noticing — with Pastor Leonard's noticing in her seemingly casual announcement to him that Helen was deeply upset. He didn't miss it!

Sustaining

Sustaining is "helping a hurting person to endure and transcend"[3] circumstances that in all probability will not change.

The circumstances of the function of sustaining can range from a general need for encouragement in the face of angry and mean-spirited politicians to trying to deal with the very personal problems we share with everyone else. The function of sustaining recognizes that the world offers very few supports for LGBTQ people.

At the beginning of the twenty-first century, what do LGBTQ people have to endure and transcend?

Being queer. The place to begin is perhaps so obvious that it is easy to miss: we are LGBTQ people who live in a frequently unfriendly or belligerent world that is not going to change any time soon. Many LGBTQ people, certainly not all, need encouragement simply to be who they are in a proud, dignified, and self-accepting way. The yearly "Gay Pride" event celebrated in most cities is a celebration of all things LGBTQ. No matter one's political or cultural appraisal of these events, for many, such a celebration was the first time we felt affirmed, celebrated, and happy to be who we are. No small moment.

LGBTQ people have different experiences based on where they live — and whether or not they are out. Those in the urban centers of North

---

3. Ibid., 42.

America have the advantages of numbers, resources, and generally more enlightened attitudes in the population. They will often not have the same kinds of needs as those in rural and isolated regions. Typically, there is little acceptance and understanding of queer people in many rural areas, and often there are dangerous levels of ignorance and homophobia. Pastoral caregivers in these less populated areas are called to develop a special sensitivity of their LGBTQ people's needs, which might not be so readily expressed.[4]

The affirming and accepting pastoral caregiver will deepen and broaden this life-giving sense of self-worth in whatever ways possible, but probably most effectively by day-to-day interactions of care and joy with his or her LGBTQ congregants. These low-key, ordinary-seeming pastoral interventions can be "high-key" in effectiveness.

The power of affirmation is often remarkable. Ask members of Parents, Families & Friends of Lesbians & Gays (PFLAG)[5] what it was like for them to march in their first gay pride parade, and many will tell you it was "life-changing." Ask those LGBTQ people who cheer them along the parade route what it's like to see parents and friends marching and you'll hear, "I can't explain to you how much it means to me to see parents out there supporting us!"

Under siege. Presently LGBTQ people are practically under siege by the cultures of almost the entire world. Our very legitimacy is often questioned in a public and vociferous way, and we are constantly under public scrutiny. The fact that we are the subject of an emotionally charged news story practically every day of the year is enough to tell you we are a population that could use some help to "endure and transcend."

Arguably, the institutions that are debating the status of LGBTQ people the most loudly and argumentatively are churches and political parties. I hope you see this as an opportunity, not as a roadblock. Your sustaining

---

4. Three resources: William D. Fellows, *Farm Boys: Lives of Gay Men from the Rural Midwest*, new ed. (Madison: University of Wisconsin Press, 2001); *Farm Family: In Search of Gay Life in Rural America*, a documentary film by T. Joe Murray, *www.imdb.com/title/tt0409954/* (accessed November 2006); James Donald Smith and Ronald Mancoske, eds., *Rural Gays and Lesbians: Building on the Strengths of Communities* (New York: Haworth Press, 1997).

5. For more information on and listings of local contacts for PFLAG, see their Web site: *www.pflag.org* (accessed November 2006).

pastoral care in the form of support and encouragement can indeed bear immediate and abundant fruit.

Anyone under siege is likely to have strong feelings. I have referred before to the anger and frustration that many LGBTQ people hold toward some churches and synagogues in particular and religion in general. The sustaining pastoral caregiver will accept the anger and then find ways to help them sublimate these feelings into constructive and fulfilling channels of activity or interest. Frequently the most effective response is to enlist these strong-feeling people into the ranks of the reformers, the rebels, and others working for justice and equality.

LGBTQ relationships. Gay marriage is certainly one of the hot issues of our times. Everyone weighs in with a particular insight, a unique approach, or a critical comment on what's going on. However, above and beyond those variables remains the simple reality that queer people form relationships — whether or not they are sanctioned (see chapter 6). This is another example of our not being willing to wait for the world to decide who we are and what we can or cannot do. We live now. It would be both unreasonable and unhealthy to put one's life on hold until some religious or civil authority finally makes up its collective mind. Good pastoral care will help LGBTQ people sustain healthy, life-giving relationships now, like Carolyn did.

Carolyn, an Asian American, is the new, young, recently married assistant minister to the congregation. Martin, the Latino care seeker, is forty-five, in an almost-two-year relationship with Paul, white, forty-three, who has recently tested positive for the HIV virus. Martin is distraught and reports that his family and many friends are urging him to get out of the relationship. Carolyn mostly just listens carefully to Martin as he relates at some length the elements of his story, his feelings, and his worries. Caregiver Carolyn believes she hears, mostly between the lines, that Martin does not really want to leave Paul, that he loves him, and he believes it is mutual. Carolyn says as much to Martin.

Martin in turn responds with relief: "What I need is someone to encourage me and not to think I am crazy to stay. I love Paul deeply, and I am willing to go through the challenges that surely await us together."

It is worth noting that the reason Martin chose Carolyn as a pastoral caregiver — rather than the LGBTQ-affirming, older male pastor — was because of her quiet, contemplative nature. In turn, Carolyn recognized in her care seeker a religiously motivated desire for virtue and sacrifice and a good probability of success, goals to which she could give her encouragement and sustaining energy.

An important part of Carolyn's sustaining pastoral care would, of course, be follow-up and continuing involvement in the challenges that will certainly be part of this family's life.

Illness and suffering. Another clear application of the sustaining function is caring for people affected by sickness, especially AIDS, and any other ongoing suffering. This topic is discussed in chapter 3.

Guiding

Guiding is "assisting perplexed persons to make confident choices between alternative courses...affecting...the state of the soul."[6] Guidance is a wonderful gift, especially when received at just the right time. It involves several elements: educating your care seekers in the implications and ramifications of their possible choices; educating the young who are unexposed to many confusing choices; reminding the elderly of what might have faded from mind in forgetfulness; serving as the well-grounded guide, asking the right questions, and encouraging virtuous responses.

Competence with LGBTQ issues. Often ministers of religion give in, or fear being perceived as giving in, to the cultural stereotype which says, "If I know too much about gay issues or if I seem too well acquainted with gay people I am somehow 'tainted' or *one of them*," or some other such unreasonable conclusion. Part of pastoral competence for *all* caregivers is to understand the basic issues of being both LGBTQ and religious in contemporary society; this knowledge says nothing about anyone's sexuality.

Those who are confident give the best advice; guidance by committee or by consultation is often ineffective. Confidence is not arrogance. It is born of preparation, care, study, and experience.

Johnny is a quiet, polite, fourteen-year-old member of a large Reformed Jewish congregation. One evening after a youth group meeting he asks to see Rachel, the rabbi who serves as youth director. During their session he tells her he's gay. "I've known it for a long time now, and I just want

6. Clinebell, *Basic Types*, 42.

everyone to know," he says smiling and confident. "I've just told my parents. They're pretty bummed, but they'll get over it, 'cause they're really liberal and all that."

To this announcement, Rachel, fortyish, straight, married, mother of two, generally quick-witted and ready with a retort, responds with a stunned silence. She has been taken by surprise, and she does not know what to say.

"So anyway, thanks," says Johnny, leaving. "I gotta get going. See you soon and thanks again."

Rachel is left sitting there, feeling very unsettled.

Early the next morning Rachel gets a call from Johnny's father. "We want to see you as soon as possible," he says. "Can we come over right away?"

The first thing to say about this case is that Rachel, as an ordained rabbi and youth minister of a congregation, has the responsibility to know what do in this situation. The fact that she was surprised is a sign of how ill-prepared many pastoral caregivers are when it comes to being LGBTQ-aware, knowing facts, understanding implications, and simply feeling confident and competent to deal with LGBTQ issues and persons. (Another reality that this case demonstrates is that kids are coming out younger and younger. This topic is treated in chapter 3.)

Johnny and his parents need guidance. They need someone who knows the territory, the questions to ask, the dangers to watch for, how to relate to a fourteen-year-old gay boy, someone who has the skill to help with the parent-child relationship, advice for limit-setting and guidelines for companionship, someone who knows the referrals to make, and especially the referrals not to make. Too frequently people who come out young are forced by their parents' abandonment of them to take over their own parenting (always with poor results), or they receive only censures, rejections, and thus years of unnecessary pain.

After a rocky start, Rachel fulfilled her role as pastoral caregiver and guide for Johnny and his family. Indeed, she became a strong voice for LGBTQ issues. Non-LGBTQ religious leaders who express public advocacy for queer people explore a lonely and uncharted territory, which takes courage and dedication, and sometimes a tough skin.

What Rachel realized as she moved into the situation that confronted her is that she indeed had the skills needed: after all, she would have known what to say and do if the situation were of a heterosexual nature. What she had to overcome was her feeling of being in unknown territory where she felt incompetent. She began a crash course in self-education. Of course she could be helpful, insightful, and knowledgeable in this situation! Why couldn't she?

As a pastoral caregiver who gives guidance to LGBTQ people (as well as to all), you need to have a broad, general knowledge of human sexuality. Without it, you can actually add to the challenges of those seeking your care, rather than helping them. I mention this issue of awareness simply because it is frequently passed over in training. Do you know about bondage and discipline (B&D), sadism and masochism (S&M), polyamory, paraphilias, or fetishes? If someone says she's femme or butch, he's into leather or he's a bear, would the blank, uncomfortable look on your face immediately tell them to look elsewhere? If so, you need to learn. Since education in sexuality is not the purpose of this work, I recommend you to (1) the list of resources, (2) your favorite search engine, and (3) local resources, contacts, colleagues, and authorities who can educate you.

Public guidance. Another way to provide guidance for your LGBTQ people is by public statement. This is also a systemic application of guidance.

In the midst of a local gay marriage controversy, and clear anti-gay-marriage pronouncements from many church denominations, including his own, a pastor wrote an op-ed piece in the daily newspaper of a mid-size western city in support of gay marriage.[7] Succinctly and convincingly he stated his reasons and priorities. It was a risky and courageous act. But think not only of the LGBTQ people of the whole city who received guidance, encouragement, and pastoral care through this article, but think also of all the other readers who had their assumptions challenged.

The "sins" of omission. If you find that you do not have the information that you feel is necessary, don't be afraid to ask the care receiver for the information that you need. Also, don't hesitate to inquire more deeply into an issue if your pastoral instinct tells you to do so — always, of course, with care and skill. I believe that more poor pastoral caregiving is the result of *not* doing than of doing poorly. It's often what you did not ask and did not suggest that leaves your care seeker unfulfilled. LGBTQ

---

7. *Boise Idaho Statesman*, February 25, 2006, op-ed column by Rev. W. Thomas Faucher.

issues, although much more out and dealt with than just a decade ago, still cause embarrassment, shame, and shyness in both the caregiver and care seeker.

Proactive guidance or confrontation is something most of us don't like, whether we are the receivers or the givers. It can lead to anger and resentment. Your function as a source of guidance, however, sometimes demands it. Confrontation of LGBTQ people can be challenging, especially if the one confronting is a representative of the church. The caregiver might be hesitant to confront the care receiver for several reasons. Unfamiliarity with the territory and fear of being seen as unsympathetic with a minority are two excuses that come to mind. My advice: plunge in with care. Responsibility demands that we challenge LGBTQ people just as we would challenge any other people if they are seeking advice or acting irresponsibly and unwisely.

Moral guidance; exploring options. People will often approach the pastoral caregiver seeking moral guidance in regard to a practical situation in their lives:

A man in your church is ill with AIDS and wants to have a discussion about the future possibility of ending his life; he wants to "talk about it" with you.

A young, interracial lesbian couple is considering artificial insemination and asks about the moral implications of what they are planning.

A sixteen-year-old high school boy in your youth group tells you he is gay and he has been asked out on a date by a twenty-year-old college freshman. He is confused and seeks guidance from you.

A preoperative transgender woman comes to you and asks what is the teaching of the church on the morality of having gender-reassignment surgery.

A twenty-five-year-old woman asks you if it is a sin to be involved in a lesbian sexual relationship.

A sixty-five-year-old married woman consults you with the question, "Do you think that people can really be bisexual?"

These, of course, are just a few of the very real moral dilemmas and questions that face LGBTQ people all the time. I believe the best advice in all these situations is not to give an immediate answer, certainly not to make a pronouncement. True pastoral care and guidance call you to explore the options, examine the moral implications and their meanings, and clarify the moral principles involved with your care seeker. Joretta Marshall puts it succinctly: "The important thing in pastoral care with people facing moral crises is neither to pretend we can be morally neutral nor to pronounce moralisms; rather, it is to discern with people as they engage their life issues. We must not deny our moral stand nor should we insist that others stand where we do."[8]

Talking about it. Over the years I have taught classes to midlife clergypersons. I always ask how many have ever mentioned LGBTQ people in a sermon or homily during Sunday worship. Typically one (or none) had done so, and that was in a negative way. The point is to talk about LGBTQ people and their issues in some kind of positive light and in some kind of public way, the same way you mention straight persons — such as during the weekly sermon or homily or other occasion of teaching. Even mentioning LGBTQ people as one group in a grouping of several, or as an example, will teach your congregation to be more aware. By never mentioning LGBTQ people and issues, one makes a powerful negative statement and further renders them invisible.

In addition to talking about queer issues publicly, there's just plain talking about sex in general. It's no secret that sex is a difficult subject to talk about in our culture. It is considered off-limits in many circumstances and off-putting in many others, yet there remains a tremendous need to talk about it. Nothing takes the place of sharing information and feelings honestly, carefully, and kindly in a safe place. People inevitably grow in understanding, appreciation, and wisdom from such "holy conversations."[9] How can you further that goal?

Spiritual direction, a longtime staple in the Catholic spiritual repertoire, has found popularity in much broader spiritual circles in the last fifteen years. I understand spiritual direction to be a person of faith accompanying a co-religionist in a supportive and encouraging way on the journey of faith in order to clarify and understand its challenges and issues and move closer to God. I endorse the approach of James Empereur,

---

8. Joretta Marshall, "Caring When It Is Tough to Care," in *www.religion-online.org/showarticle.asp?title=300.*

9. See Karen Oliveto, Kelly Turney, and Traci West, *Talking about Homosexuality: A Congregational Resource* (Cleveland: Pilgrim Press, 2005). This is part of the Holy Conversations series.

S.J., who emphasizes the giftedness of being gay and its centrality in the process of spiritual direction with queer people.[10]

Offering spiritual direction to LGBTQ people in your congregation, people who have so frequently been kept at a distance from the rich and refreshing waters of the spiritual well, will bring welcome rewards.

Reconciling

If there is one function that stands out as urgent in dealing with the LGBTQ community, it is reconciliation. This is the function that "seeks to re-establish broken relationships"[11] among persons, and between persons and God. I will add: between persons and the church. The exodus of LGBTQ people from churches continues to be steady and widespread. The stereotypical process is for an individual to reach teenage or young adulthood, come out, and leave the church. Statistics on queer membership in churches are expectedly hard to come by, but experience and casual survey indicate that the number of older LGBTQ people leaving or not participating is also significant. Leanne Tigert's *Coming Out While Staying In*[12] is a good history and analysis of LGBTQ participation in church.

Alienation/reconciliation. Alienation currently is the dominant relationship mode tendered to LGBTQ people in the majority of churches, with few but notable exceptions.[13]

Consider when you approach queer people that they are, in all probability, alienated to some degree from this church in particular or from the church in general. Even if they are active members, I believe on some level that no one who is LGBTQ can escape the pervasive energy of alienation that currently divides so many denominations. The basis of that feeling of alienation is the depth of the rejection, the breadth of the avoidance,

---

10. James L. Empereur, S.J., *Spiritual Direction and the Gay Person* (New York: Continuum, 1998).

11. Clinebell, *Basic Types*, 42.

12. Leanne McCall Tigert, *Coming Out While Staying In: Struggles and Celebrations of Lesbians, Gays, and Bisexuals in the Church* (Cleveland: United Church Press, 1996).

13. There are churches that make welcoming and affirming LGBT people an official part of their teaching. Among them are the United Church of Christ, the Metropolitan Community Church, the Unitarian Universalists, and the Religious Society of Friends (Quakers).

the power of the revulsion, and the overall enormity of the negative energy that emanates from so many religious people toward their LGBTQ
neighbors. It can be overwhelming.

Most LGBTQ people over the age of eighteen, and probably many
under, have been struck by the force of the enmity that often comes at us.
We know, on some level, that we have become, unfairly, the scapegoats
of some dark and alien representation of "otherness" — that rather than
being seen as "gifted by otherness,"[14] we are damned because of it.

Religion/spirituality. Many LGBTQ people have joined with others
in contemporary society in the practice of separating spirituality from
religion. It's a step that excludes involvement in the church and the community it offers, while keeping clear and open the way to God and religious
values. It is a common reality in practice if not in name. On the one hand,
it deprives the person of being part of a rich and long tradition and a member of the supportive community of the church; on the other hand, given
the circumstances, it allows spirituality to flourish and grow and be part
of one's life.

This group of LGBTQ people would seem to be the most promising for
reconciliation. They already have the commitment to the spiritual life. Can
you, as pastoral caregiver, offer reconciliation in which that spiritual life
would be enhanced and affirmed for queer people by becoming members
of your religious community?

Sacramental reconciliation. Churches with a sacramental system —
Roman, Anglican, and Orthodox Catholics; Lutherans; and others —
have a wonderful opportunity for reconciliation in the sacrament of
the same name. But how available is this sacrament to your LGBTQ
people? It's a complicated issue but one also ripe for pastoral creativity.
Consider these pastoral perspectives as you contemplate LGBTQ people
participating in the sacrament of reconciliation:

• LGBTQ people who are not celibate are excluded in some churches
  from communion, a source of unity in the church, and from reconciliation.

---

14. See L. William Countryman and M. R. Ritley, *Gifted by Otherness: Gay and Lesbian Christians in the Church* (Harrisburg, PA: Morehouse Publishing, 2001), for a treatment of a positive understanding from a faith perspective of being LGBT.

- Why should people who are excluded from the sacraments of unity and reconciliation be expected to participate in the life of the church? As with the divorced (and remarried) in some denominations, LGBTQ people are, in practice if not in theory, treated as second-class members.

- From the point of view of LGBTQ people of faith, the exclusion is based on living out one's unchangeable identity, of being and acting who one was created to be by God. Exclusion and judgment hardly embody the ideals of sacramental theology.

These reflections and questions bring me to the last and perhaps most important consideration in regard to the pastoral function of reconciliation with LGBTQ people:

"In the meantime . . . " That which you actually do in situations when you don't know what to do, and when the consulting of laws, customs, and precedents does not help, is often referred to as the "pastoral solution." It always favors the person over the rules. A pastoral solution emphasizes God's loving-kindness, not cut-and-dried regulations and laws.

Sometimes reconciliation seems quite impossible between LGBTQ people and the church. The differences are too clear and too strongly held to give way to compromise and reconciliation. What's the solution when there seems to be none? When both parties are left in the pain of isolation, frustration, and probable defeat? The experience of Rabbi Steven Greenberg serves well as a response.

As he came out of the closet as a "gay Orthodox Jewish rabbi," these are some of the comments Rabbi Greenberg received from other representatives of his faith: "You're an absurdity . . . an oxymoron, a dangerous perversion of truth." "Change is possible and homosexual desire is a test. God has given us a spiritual challenge to struggle with same-sex desire and defeat it with abstinence." Your choice is to choose your faith or "be gay and leave the community."[15]

These are the kinds of comments many of us hear when we take our pain to our communities of faith, and they surely represent a reconciliation impasse. Or do they?

I cite the example of Steven Greenberg and his supporters because of their refusal to make an either/or choice but perpetually to move toward

---

15. Rabbi Steven Greenberg, *Wrestling with God and Men* (Madison: University of Wisconsin Press, 2004), 12.

what seems to be an impossible reconciliation of faith and same-sex love. After years of struggle, pain, and ongoing doubt and conflict, Rabbi Greenberg is a living example of reconciling the seemingly irreconcilable simply by not giving up, by not ending the process, by becoming comfortable with doubt. As Greenberg says, "There is great hope in a tradition that loves good questions even more than good answers, a tradition that teaches that God listens to the deliberation of the sages in order to know"[16] the Jewish law.

Rabbi Greenberg simply is. His existence is a powerful statement; his presence, a constant symbol of trust.

And there is no refuting that! Just how will it all work out? Well, paraphrasing the words of one of his supporters, "We'll just have to see what God wants us to do about this. Sooner or later we'll know; in the meantime we do what we can."[17]

Here is an example of "reconciliation-in-waiting," or "refusal to give up," or "perpetually ongoing reconciliation." Here's an example of a "pastoral solution." Nothing has been definitely resolved but — and this is the point for pastoral care of LGBTQ people — nothing has been ended, no one has been abandoned; the process is ongoing, forever, if necessary.

It's not perfect. There are still many who reject Steven Greenberg. It's an open-ended, ongoing, faith-based reality that he, his partner, and their supporters live daily.

Nurturing

Clinebell notes that nurturing has always "been a persistent motif in the history of the church"; he defines it as enabling "people to develop their God-given potentialities throughout the journey of life with all its valleys, peaks, and plateaus."[18] In some times and places it is referred to as sanctification, the process of becoming holy/whole.

---

16. Ibid., 23.
17. This is a paraphrase (my wording) of Daniel Boyarin, professor of Talmudic culture at the University of California, Berkeley, during his public response to a lecture by Rabbi Greenberg, sponsored by the Center for Lesbian and Gay Studies in Religion and Ministry (CLGS) at the Pacific School of Religion in Berkeley, on April 12, 2005.
18. Clinebell, *Basic Types*, 42.

I see the most important application of the function of nurturing to queer people in its systemic sense — that is, helping to create structures and systems that deal with LGBTQ people justly, fairly, and with acceptance and affirmation. In other words, seek opportunities to nurture systems. The previously mentioned case of Leonard, the retired pastor, influencing the retirement care system is a good example of this function. Here's another:

Nurturing exposition. Claire, Caucasian and German-born, is the pastor of a progressive suburban parish of an eastern city. She is lesbian and lives with her partner in the parish-owned parsonage. Allen, one of their close friends and a member of the church, is bisexual and out. Through her friendship with Allen, Claire has learned much about being bisexual. Over the period of a year and in various ways — preaching, mentioning it in conversation, writing about it in the church bulletin, reading up on current books on the subject — Claire has brought bisexuality into the consciousness of her church community. As a result, both she and her partner and their bisexual friend have noticed a heightened and more enlightened awareness of the subject.

Thus, through a nurturing exposure of the reality of being bisexual, the system — in this case, the church community — can become more understanding, more conversant, and thus more accepting of bisexuality.

Human and faith development. There is an important application of the nurturing function to LGBTQ people on a more individual level as well. It deals with the characteristic way that we tend to develop as human beings. Or don't. Developmental patterns, both in faith and society, are not clear-cut, of course; but while some non-LGBTQ people may have developmental gaps, many LGBTQ people do, and it tends to be the same one: we characteristically get stuck around the stage of securing our identity and moving on to intimacy.

LGBTQ people follow the familiar stages described by Erikson, Levinson, Fowler,[19] and others, often with one exception: when it comes time

---

19. See works by Erik Erikson, notably *Childhood and Society* (New York: W. W. Norton, reissue 1993); also Daniel Levinson, *The Seasons of a Man's Life* (New York: Ballantine Books, reissue 1986); James Fowler, *Stages of Faith: The Psychology of Human Development* (San Francisco: HarperSanFrancisco, 1995); and Sheila Greene, *The Psychological Development of Girls and Women: Rethinking Change in Time* (New York: Routledge, 2003).

to advance to the stage of maturity that resolves the conflicts around social development (the Eriksonian adolescent stage), many LGBTQ people
typically get stuck because there seems to be nowhere to go.

The reason for this developmental fixation is that the intimacy which
we naturally seek is not allowed by the systems that have the strongest
influence on us: family, church, and school. Normally this occurs in the
teenage years, and thus most are not sufficiently independent or self-reliant
to go against the systems. So we stop developing in that area and generally
find a substitute. Unfortunately, the substitutes are not always the stereotypical tomboyish swagger and car repair or Broadway tunes and fashion
trends. Too often they are less healthy and uplifting.

As a pastoral caregiver, please take this stoppage (at times it almost
seems like a moral paralysis) into consideration with your LGBTQ people.
Taking care not to be invasive, notice, for example, when a member of your
congregation seems to be overly absorbed in an isolating activity or sinks
too deeply into work/school to the exclusion of all else. Both behaviors
might attract pastoral care notice to the area of problematic development.

Parallel to stages of social development are stages of faith development.
Frequently there are parallel stoppages. In terms of Fowler's schema[20]
the LGBTQ person frequently gets stuck between stage 3, Synthetic-
Conventional faith, and stage 4, Individuative-Reflective faith. If there
is enough compartmentalization going on with the individual (that is,
they can keep the different aspects of their lives separate from each other;
in a sense lead a "double life"), it is possible to skip a stage and continue
through the progression of the faith stages. But in order to do this, the
person must clearly isolate these two areas of life: development in social
intimacy and development in faith. There are many adult religious people
who have done just that. Of course it is not the ideal; it can result in an
immature faith and retarded social skills.

It is important to note that women and people of color were generally
not included in the development of these theories of human development,
and thus their usefulness and general application is limited. (See Sheila
Greene's work mentioned in note 19.) I present the forgoing discussion
primarily so that pastoral caregivers can become aware of the developmental process, recognize when it possibly becomes problematic in a member

---

20. Fowler, *Stages of Faith*.

of the congregation, and thus become a supportive, nurturing presence in the process.

On a positive note, even if one misses a stage in development, one can generally go back and catch up, so to speak. It's not the same, but it can work. A forty-year-old going through some of the squirrelly processes of adolescence and learning intimacy is often not an easy challenge. The support of a nurturing pastoral caregiver and a supportive community, and of course a good sense of humor, are big helps.

Pastoral Perspectives
Pastoral Interventions for Nurturing in the Developmental Gap

- Cultivate the practice of noticing the lives of your people from a developmental point of view.

- Recognize in them the presence of delayed development, perhaps helping them recognize and accept it (and thus be able to do something about it).

- Refer them to a pastoral counselor or other therapist, when appropriate, to more efficiently and quickly resolve developmental issues.

- Patience and understanding are the needed virtues here.

- Continue to observe to see if the impasse simply passes or becomes a more serious problem.

Noticing. The function of nurturing calls forth an important trait of good pastoral caregiving: noticing. So many of our human pleas for help go unnoticed by those around us. The caregiver who notices these signs — the tone of voice, the drooping shoulders, what people don't say, the look in their eyes, the subject of conversation, the attitude of mind — is the caregiver who is in a position to nurture. Noticing means that you are aware of what is going on between the lines in your people's lives. It is frequently this space that holds the most important meanings.

Prophetic Pastoral Care

Here is where psychosystemic pastoral care (see chapter 1) and prophetic/ ecological awareness come together. As in the psychosystems part of chapter 1, here too I am indebted to the work of Graham and Clinebell.[21]

For the most part, the pastoral care tradition that we have inherited has been what Graham terms the "existentialist-anthropological model of care."[22] That is, it focuses on individuals, their problems, and their ultimate happiness within a context of self-realization. This type of pastoral care, which has achieved a tremendous amount of good, assumes a certain distance or disconnectedness between the person and the larger realities of the world and its cultures. Also, "In spite of many positive outcomes, the pastoral caretaking enterprise has become increasingly isolated from many of its communal and religious roots, and from the formative experience of the oppressed in our culture — especially women, non-whites, and gay persons."[23]

Prophetic pastoral care is thus more communal than individualistic and primarily based on the fact that we all live and move and have our being within a wide variety of systems that are continually influencing us, and upon the lived experiences and values of oppressed groups in our culture. The ultimate system that we must care for, of course, is the Earth, our home.

The joining of these bases with two characteristics from the ancient prophetic tradition of Israel give us the foundation for prophetic pastoral caring. From the prophets: "First ... they provide a critique of what is currently dominant. Second, they offer a direction toward health, salvation, shalom, justice and fulfillment."[24] In other words, the prophets were always talking about the hottest topics of the day and, despite many differences in style and circumstances, they called the people to work for the "welfare of the nations and of the created order."[25]

---

21. Graham, "Prophetic Pastoral Caretaking"; Howard Clinebell, *Ecotherapy: Healing Ourselves, Healing the Earth* (New York: Haworth Press, 1996).

22. Larry Kent Graham, *Care of Persons, Care of Worlds: A Psychosystems Approach to Pastoral Care and Counseling* (Nashville: Abingdon, 1992), 14.

23. Graham, "Prophetic Pastoral Caretaking," 50.

24. Ibid.

25. Ibid.

Bringing the elements together, we can say that prophetic pastoral care is

◆ Speaking out in justice and compassion, in one way or another...

◆ ...to the people and systems of our communities and of our world...

◆ ...for the healing of the people, especially the oppressed, and the right relationship of all on earth with each other and with God.

Prophetic pastoral care takes its roots from process theology, liberation theology, feminist theology, ecology[26] (and ecotherapy[27]), family systems theory (psychology), and certain aspects of personality theory.

This is not to say that prophetic pastoral care is anything new to contemporary eras. People like Albert Schweitzer, Martin Luther King Jr., Mahatma Gandhi, and others long before and after them have raised prophetic voices from within the religious world; and not only on the world stage have these voices cried out. Often we have to look no further than the church or synagogue around the corner to find strong prophets raising their voices in righteous anger toward the injustices of the world's blindly accepted systems. Often too, those prophetic voices emanate from unexpected places, like PFLAG — what a wonderful example for churches this worldwide organization gives for loving and affirming our children, not rejecting them — and GLSEN, which "strives to assure that each member of every school community is valued and respected regardless of sexual orientation or gender identity/expression."[28] For those with ears to hear, prophetic pastoral voices can be heard all the time and anywhere.

The need for specific application of prophetic care to LGBTQ people is clear, especially since the queer experience is central to its development. One can easily make a case for LGBTQ people needing all the help possible in trying to deal with the systems of the world. For example, the relationship of LGBTQ people to the military, to all levels of government, to educational institutions, and especially to all religious institutions, churches, and synagogues offers fertile ground for the contemporary prophet.

---

26. Ibid., 52.
27. See Clinebell, *Ecotherapy.*
28. See *www.pflag.org* and *www.glsen.org* (sites accessed November 2006).

Imagination. I end this section on the prophetic dimension of pastoral care with the issue of the human imagination, a sure sign of the effective prophet, and as a reminder that no one can come out of the closet as queer, embrace their own identity, or proclaim it to their world unless they are first able to imagine themselves doing and being all those things. The imagining must precede the realities.

Your prophetic pastoral care thus has a more specific application as well. Your interventions with LGBTQ people who are solidly closeted and suffering from it might be along the lines of "What would it be like if ... ?" "Can you imagine yourself ... ?" "How might that happen ... ?" or "What might prohibit its happening ... ?" Develop ways to encourage their imagining themselves out and free. So often one hears from queer people of all varieties and ages, "I can't even imagine being out to my father (mother, family, etc.). It's totally impossible. It's not even thinkable." These remarks indicate the power of the locks on some closet doors. Freedom from the closet must begin in the imagination of the person. If you cannot imagine it, you cannot achieve it.

Pastoral Care with People of Ethnic Minorities

The first idea to note here is that this entire work, in all of its chapters and parts, includes *all* LGBTQ people as both caregivers and recipients of pastoral care, whether members of a specific minority or not. It excludes no one. However, there seem to be enough particularities to being a member of a minority in our North American culture to warrant, in addition, some specific treatment.

The plan in this section is first to identify several key issues that I believe are common to LGBTQ members of minority groups, then to name some specific characteristics in the areas of religion and tradition, and lastly, to present general guidelines and a few insights for the pastoral caregiver. For more references, see "Ethnic Studies and Issues" in the list of resources; these originate, for the most part, with LGBTQ members of the specific minority. Unfortunately they are not numerous.

I use the word "minority" here to mean what I believe is the general meaning North American people give it: a part of a population, significantly smaller in numbers from the majority, identifying with a particular national or racial culture or identity (both of which can include a religious dimension), and often subjected to different treatment.

Key issues. I believe that the key challenging issues for LGBTQ members of minorities are the same ones as for the majority culture, but to differing degrees of strength and emphasis. I would identify key challenging social issues as religion, tradition, work, family, peer pressure, and personal issues, such as shame and fear. I believe these are always the ultimate sources of our pain — LGBTQ or not, minority or not — because they are the primary sources of meaning in human life. Although these same sources of pain can serve as sources of ecstasy as well, it's the pain I am concerned with here.

Each minority emphasizes one or the other of these key issues and perceives them to varying degrees as reasons to deny the validity of the experience of their LGBTQ members.

Religion and tradition. Ethnic church communities have generally been much more than simply religious organizations. In many instances the church also serves the educational and leadership needs of the community and is the place where people learn their traditions and values. Because LGBTQ people grow up in those churches, they often also take on their homophobic assumptions.

"I Don't Mean to Offend, but I Won't Pretend" is the title of a perceptive essay by D. Mark Wilson.[29] In it he presents and examines the challenges for African American gay men in a specific church community in keeping the balance between the love, respect, *and* full participation in their church family (the "I-don't-mean-to-offend" part), while at the same time acknowledging their pride in being gay and all that it implies in their lives (the "but-I-won't-pretend" part). His essay offers helpful insight for pastoral caregivers into the delicate balance that minority LGBTQ people are forced to maintain to ensure a life of equilibrium.

A value for the African American is the validation of the individual by others, especially by the family, broadly understood. They also tend to be, as an ethnic grouping, more holistic than dualistic, self-knowledge being revealed through symbol and interpersonal relationships that are

---

29. D. Mark Wilson, "I Don't Mean to Offend, but I Won't Pretend," in K. Brynolf Lyon and Archie Smith Jr., *Tending the Flock: Congregations and Family Ministry* (Louisville: Westminster John Knox Press, 1998).

harmonious. Oral traditions are an important source of wisdom, humor, and insight.[30]

The church is central also to the Latino experience. Eighty-five percent of Hispanic Americans are Catholic. Most of the others are members of Protestant denominations, and some fewer follow the religious traditions of *espiritismo* and *santerismo*.[31] So the vast majority of Latino people are influenced by a church. LGBTQ Latinos and Latinas have a rough road to travel since almost all of their church affiliations will teach them that living openly as an LGBTQ person is sinful, excludes you from family, and jeopardizes your eternal soul. Rejection by one's family is especially debilitating to LGBTQ Latinos/as because of the key importance of the family relationship to the identity of the individual and its general place of honor and reverence in the culture.

Especially for members of the Latino communities, loyalty to the family is highly valued. *Compadres* is a significant category and often includes close friends, godparents, and others by choice. They are often considered to be as close and important as family. Probably through the historic influence of the Catholic Church, Latinos have a strong sense of the direct connection between the events of life and the power of God, which may appear at times as fatalism.[32]

Many Asian Americans (the Asian minority identity often includes Filipinos and Pacific Islanders) are influenced by the values and teachings of Confucianism, Buddhism, and Taoism as well as Christianity. Thus values that are common in many Asian cultures are harmony, emotional restraint, and indirect communication, the latter being a trait that the more blunt and direct style of the West misses and of which effective pastoral caregivers will be especially aware. Tao spirituality, for example, emphasizes the balance of yin and yang, the female and male, the dark and the light, the passive and the active.[33]

For Asian Americans, the needs of the group often take precedence over the needs of the individual, and thus their religious identity or affiliation

30. Wanda M. L. Lee, *An Introduction to Multicultural Counseling* (Philadelphia: Accelerated Development Group, 1999), 78–79.

31. Statistics are from Advocates for Youth, 2000 M St. #750, Washington, DC 20036; Web site: *www.advocatesforyouth.org/index.htm* (accessed November 2006).

32. Lee, *Introduction to Multicultural Counseling*, 92.

33. Ibid., 104, 108.

will tend to be favored and followed, even at times when it might be in the person's benefit that it not be favored.[34] The Confucian ideal of filial respect and obedience to authority is strong in many. Some LGBTQ Asian Americans also may remain in the closet within their ethnic identity while being very open and out in all of the other parts of their lives. The power of the possible stigmatization by rejection is strong, especially with parents of LGBTQ persons. Some parents — and this would seem to apply to *all* parents — may well know about an LGBTQ identity in their child but expect it never to be named explicitly. This of course sets up a different kind of pressure and stress in the LGBTQ child, but no less strong.

In many of the bands of Indians of the Americas and First Nations of Canada, general acceptance of homosexual behavior may or may not be somewhat more historically accepted than in most other cultural identities. Thus, members of this ethnic minority who are aware of this tradition may have fewer inhibitions to live the LGBTQ life. The Berdache tradition would seem to be an affirming LGBTQ identity among North and South American ethnic minorities, although many among the First Nations and native Indians reject the term because of negative and nonnative associations. The Berdache[35] is a person who is born male but lives and is often raised female in all roles, even as a sexual partner to the men of the community. In some Indian nations, but not in all, this practice has been accepted as normal and useful to the community. Possibly a more acceptable term currently among North American Native people is the term "Two Spirit," a term originating in 1990 but generally believed to be based on ancient traditions.[36]

However, many American (North and South) Natives have been deeply influenced by European-based religion and culture, and thus many of the traditions have been largely lost for decades. Recently the Two Spirit tradition has had a resurgence of popularity. There are historical native terms for Two Spirit individuals in several Native American and First Nations languages.[37]

---

34. Ibid., 104.

35. Walter L. Williams, *The Spirit and the Flesh: Sexual Diversity in the American Indian Culture* (Boston: Beacon Press, 1992); Lee, *Introduction to Multicultural Counseling*, 149.

36. See *www.androphile.org/preview/Culture/NativeAmerica/amerindian.htm#12* (accessed November 2006).

37. Ibid.

Frequently ethnic minority cultures will have a different interpretation of gender roles than those operative in the dominant white culture. The stereotype of *machismo* within the Latino culture, and of studiousness among Asians, even though they are stereotypes (which means they are frequently inaccurate), still hold sway to a degree in both the minority and majority cultures. With Asian American care seekers, relationships are often defined by roles, and these care seekers thus may be more comfortable placing the pastoral caregiver in a role of authority and be reticent to express a differing opinion or to correct.[38]

These cultural traits, however, can be almost completely lost within one generation. Careful evaluation and steering clear of any stereotypical assumptions will help you avoid harmful and sometimes insulting attitudes that can mortally damage the pastoral relationship.

In your pastoral care relationships with any grouping of people, ethnic minority or ethnic majority, I believe you will find that they will respond more enthusiastically and cooperatively the more personal and individual and the less bureaucratic and formal your approach.

Double stress. All LGBTQ persons who are part of an ethnic minority are doubly challenged. For the pastoral caregiver, it is urgently important to understand the force of this double stress. There is the stress that comes to one from being a member of the queer community, and there is the stress that comes to one as a member of a minority.

Both of these pervasive life realities produce unrelenting stress. The double becomes triple and beyond when you consider the identity groups to which these individuals have to relate: the dominant culture, their minority culture, the LGBTQ cultures within both.

However, it is fundamentally important to understand that simply being queer and being a member of an ethnic minority are *not inherently stressful states in themselves.* The stress-related problems that people of color and LGBTQ people have to face are the direct result of the racism, heterosexism, homophobia, and transphobia that exist in the culture, *not* of color of skin, sexual orientation, or gender identity. This might seem a subtle or even an obvious point, but one that is often missed.

---

38. Lee, *An Introduction to Multicultural Counseling*, 93, 108–11.

Pastoral Perspectives
Guidelines for Pastoral Caregivers
to LGBTQ Members of Ethnic Minorities

- If you are from the majority culture and your care receiver is from a minority;

- Or, if you are from a different minority from your care receiver;

- Or, if you are from a minority and your care receiver is from the majority culture:

    - Never pretend to "understand" someone's experience within any culture that is not yours. Assuming the "attitude of a beginner" is an asset.

    - At least at first (possibly always), defer to the care seeker's lived experience and understanding of his or her cultural beliefs and customs.

    - Ask the care receiver for any important information about cultural assumptions and so forth that you feel you need to know. There is little wrong with not knowing. There is much wrong with guessing.

    - Consult with professional colleagues of the particular minority in question. Use resources (books, articles, videos, etc.) presented by members of the minority group in question.

    - On the one hand, try not to underestimate the power and influence and difference of the minority experience. On the other hand, it would be irresponsible to play naïve when it comes to being aware of obvious cultural differences.

    - Be very careful of cultural stereotyping. It can be a strong temptation because of the oversimplifications and type-casting of popular culture, but it is very often wrong and offensive, and rarely or never helpful.

This crushing degree of stress often hits the person at adolescence and early adulthood, a most vulnerable time of life even if there are no additional stresses. Jason is an excellent example.

Jason was a young black man, about twenty-four, of gentle disposition and easy smile, college educated, who had just arrived in town from Chicago when he came to the church to register. At first shy, he only slowly and guardedly became part of the church community. As I got to know him, I learned the following things (among others, of course) about Jason: He was gay, was closeted (especially to his family in Chicago), had an "on-and-off" boyfriend twice his age and both of them kept each other hidden from their day-to-day lives, was unemployed and looking for work, was literally terrified of contracting the HIV virus, was brought up in a strict Catholic family but disillusioned with his church, was socially isolated outside of a limited gay scene in the city and formal contact with the church community who were mostly white and older, and when we would talk, he was often in tears from loneliness. Talk about stress. As the caregiver, all I could think about with Jason is *how can anyone, especially so young, bear such pressures?*

From a pastoral caregiver, Jason — or anyone in his situation — needed first and foremost an abiding and involved presence and accessibility, help in integrating the various elements of his life, encouragement, affirmation, and especially insight into arriving at a vibrant, fulfilling faith life within a community to which he can be known and valued for all he is. The affirming and caring presence and accessibility of the caregiver is the essential expression and incarnation of faith; it is the creating of the healing pastoral relationship, which participates in divine grace.

If you are a caregiver from the cultural majority, please do not underestimate the power of ethnic identity on the LGBTQ person. This is, of course, no different than the power of ethnic identity on people of the majority. But simply because the majority is the majority, its members can often miss their common ties with all identities. This influence can be overwhelmingly powerful and reach to the very core of a person's identity, even to the point of allowing the individual to be and do things he or she would never be or do under normal circumstances. Examples often have to do with hiding and covering: a normally honest young man will lie about his sexual orientation; a grandmother will refer to her granddaughter's female partner as a husband when she talks about her; in conversation, a bisexual woman will deliberately omit reference to anything in her life that has to do with same-sex relationships; the brother of a transsexual woman will speak only in the most vague terms about her and avoid pronouns; a middle-aged man who regularly has sex with men would not even think of identifying as gay. All of these subterfuges, and many more, exemplify the basic problem: double lives.

On the other hand, be sure you do not overlook or blind yourself to the positive influences from the ethnic community. Often among them: a strong sense of identity, of belonging, of family; a pride of ethnic origin; customs, rituals, and celebrations that create community. These traits can be called on to support pastoral ministry by acknowledgment and affirmation.

Double lives. This is a reality that *all* LGBTQ people know something about, not just minorities. Probably all of us have spent time keeping our LGBTQ lives separated from the rest of our lives. Because it is not so much separation as hiding, this process, by its very nature, produces shame. Of course, the ultimate goal when dealing with a double life is to evolve both parts into a single, integrated life.

Living "on the Down Low" is currently perhaps the most popularized expression of this double life. Brought to public attention by J. L. King's book, *On the Down Low*,[39] being on the DL is when a man maintains a relationship with a wife/girlfriend/significant other while also maintaining a separate and hidden life that includes sexual/loving relationships with another man or men. The Down Low is a long way from being an exclusive characteristic of any ethnic minority. The current awareness of it, however, has been heightened by King's book, which explores the reality within the African American community.[40]

Insightful pastoral caregivers will see all of these subterfuges as variations on a single theme of the double-bind: a result of what seems to be an irresolvable conflict; an expression of an impossible-to-open closet door;

---

39. J. L. King, *On the Down Low: A Journey into the Lives of "Straight" Black Men Who Sleep with Men* (New York: Broadway Books, 2004).

40. A sequel and a response to King's book are important to consult for a complete understanding of this issue. The sequel: J. L. King, *Coming Up from the Down Low: The Journey to Acceptance, Healing, and Honest Love* (New York: Three Rivers Press, 2006). The response: Keith Boykin, *Beyond the Down Low: Sex, Lies, and Denial in Black America* (New York: Carroll & Graf, 2005).

a way to cope when there seems no other way; a resistance to choose when the choice is between family, friends, and cultural identity on the one hand, and an honest expression of who-I-am on the other. In other words, "Damned if you do — Damned if you don't."

Inter- and intra-ethnic issues. Just as there are issues and disagreements within the LGBTQ family of diversities, so are there differences within and among minorities. Pastoral theologian Archie Smith tells of attending a conference on embracing diversity. It was an "impressive" conference, he reports, but "we failed . . . as pastoral care providers to cross racial boundaries and address the painful issues of inter-ethnic conflicts and violence. . . . None of us addressed the inter- and intra-ethnic pastoral care issues of gay, lesbian, transgendered, and questioning persons in our communities."[41] Ethnic identities clearly have rich traditions of building communities, but many of them have been lost over time. Smith calls for the "recovery of certain traditions of subjugated knowledge (such as practicing non-violence, enacting justice, and showing unconditional respect for persons . . .)."[42]

As a pastoral care provider, you have an opportunity to develop that sensitivity to the subtle signs of lost traditions within the ethnic groupings of your faith community and encourage their development and contemporary expression.

Pastoral care. Human caring in any form is a potent agent for growth, harmony, and peace. It not only says "I care about you," it lives it out in practice, puts its money where its mouth is. *Pastoral* human caring — that is, care springing from the bottomless well of faith, embodied with the most noble values and abundant generosity of faith, and practiced with love and humility within the context of faith — adds not only a new dimension of care, but the immense and mysterious, the gentle and transforming, the glorious and powerful dimension of grace.

Grace, of course, knows no limits and is a strong and wild energy. Thus, there's no telling the wonders it might achieve. Your pastoral healing, sustaining, guiding, reconciling, nurturing, and prophesying with God's

---

41. Archie Smith Jr. and Ursula Riedel-Pfaefflin, *Siblings by Choice: Race, Gender, and Violence* (St. Louis: Chalice Press, 2004), 29.
42. Ibid., 93.

LGBTQ children participates in that force, whether it's to the communities of the world or to the community gathering this evening — and waiting for you — in your basement hall.

A Checklist for Pastoral Caregivers to LGBTQ People[43]

1. Examine your own assumptions

◆ Be aware that being L, G, B, T, or Q may not be the problem that brings the person to seek pastoral care and normally is not a "problem" at all.

◆ Be aware that religion may be the problem.

◆ Be aware that your care receivers may not wish to explore their sexual identity.

◆ Be aware that, because of social pressure and fear, sometimes LGBTQ people avoid identifying themselves as LGBTQ.

◆ Be aware that a person concerned about same-sex attraction may not be lesbian, gay, or bisexual.

◆ Be aware that the meaning your care receiver assigns to words might have different meaning for you.

◆ Be aware that roles in LGBTQ relationships may or may not run along the same lines as heterosexual relationships.

◆ Be aware that bisexuals are just that and not merely or always going through a stage, a phase, or a transition to being gay.

◆ Be aware that because a person is married does not mean that they cannot be lesbian, gay, bisexual, or transgender.

◆ Be aware that getting married to an opposite-sex person is never a "solution" or a "cure" for homosexuality.

◆ Be aware that children are in no more danger from LGBTQ people than they are from heterosexual people — and in fact possibly less.

◆ Assume nothing about lesbian, gay, bisexual, or transgender behavior.

---

43. The items in the "Checklist for Pastoral Caregivers" are expanded and adapted from guidelines presented by the British Association for Pastoral and Spiritual Care and Counseling (APSCC), *www.bacp.co.uk*.

- Be aware that care seekers may expect you (as a "church person") to be homophobic or transphobic and may be looking for signs to confirm this.

- Be aware that a transgender person, both male-to-female and female-to-male, may be gay, lesbian, or bisexual and thus there is an overlap of experience. Be aware that most transgender people hold that being transgender is innate, just as being gay is; one does not "become" transgender.

2. Be Informed

- Be informed about help lines, books, Web pages, films, videos, pastoral and other counselors, and so on.

- Be informed about the teachings and practices of the various churches in regard to LGBTQ issues.

- Be informed about religious resources for LGBTQ people (see the list of resources).

- Be informed in general; consider if there are aspects of any sexual minority about which you need to learn more, and do so.

- Be both informed and cautious in regard to the terms you use, especially in regard to terms referring to transgenderism and trans-sexuality. These terms can change in popular use and are sometimes used differently by different people.

3. Be self-aware

- Monitor your own attitudes and responses, regardless of your own sexual orientation.

- Be aware of your reaction to having a pastoral care relationship with LGBTQ men and women and that there may be different dynamics from what you expect.

- Be clear about the limitations of what you can offer.

- Be clear on ways to quickly identify and contact possible referrals.

- Be clear about your own feelings toward your care receiver.

- Be clear on all the boundary issues in your pastoral care relationship.

4. Respect

- Respect your care receiver's orientation, identity, personal integrity, and cultural assumptions.

- Respect your care receiver's relationship by not asking inappropriate and nonapplicable questions such as "Who's the 'man' and who's the 'woman' in your relationship?"

- Respect your transgender care receiver by not asking inappropriate medical questions pertaining to possible surgery, possible physical changes or characteristics, and so on.

- Respect and acknowledge the pain of those who struggle with their orientation when it conflicts with their religion or belief system.

- Respect and acknowledge the capabilities of your care receivers.

- Remember the possibility of a "pastoral solution." Don't close the door.

Chapter 3

Pastoral Care in the Tough Times

Though LGBTQ people contribute an immense and diverse richness of gifts to the world and to the church, though they commonly carry the gifts of joy and happiness, and frequently bear an active and fulsome faith, here I want to consider the painful and difficult things they carry:[1] shame, anger, fear, isolation, and all the stressful challenges that life presents. During these tough times, queer people will often turn to you and expect to be held in responsible, knowledgeable, and helpful hands.

Shame. Perhaps the most common negative burden that LGBTQ people carry is shame. It is of course a common human burden, but for queer persons it is also a bestowed burden, one given by the cultures in which they have been raised and nurtured. Shame comes with the territory of LGBTQ lives, and for many the struggle to overcome it is lifelong.

Some years ago I read a potent description of shame: Shame does not come when you understand that "I made a mistake"; shame settles in when you know that "I am a mistake." *Something essential is wrong with me,* is the message that creeps into the young LGBTQ soul; *it is something that I might not be able to change, ever.* The effects remain even when shame is conquered and left far behind. By truly understanding this, you will be a more effective caregiver.

If you recognize some serious symptoms of shame in your queer care seeker, your calling attention to the burden of shame might help. Choose your time and place carefully, and perhaps bring up the topic in the context of the shame to which all oppressed people, including LGBTQ people, fall heir. Calling shame by its name and perhaps recommending some reading can go a long way to achieving healing. Shame and internalized

---

1. With a nod to Tim O'Brien's metaphor in his post-Vietnam novel, *The Things They Carried* (New York: Broadway Books, 1998).

homophobia are closely related, the latter being an expression of the former. Carrying the feelings of hurt and anger are invariably companions of shame.

As caregiver, your words and attitude can help heal and transform shame when its signs appear, for example, by reminding someone that *"You are a well-beloved child of God; you are beautiful; your gifts are needed and appreciated; of course you're an integral part of this community, why wouldn't you be?"*

Opportunities to offer these words are far from rare. Imagine: A lesbian member of your church who lives with her nonmember partner, but is not out in any specific way at church, tells you, "Don't worry, Pastor, Alice won't be coming with me to the church picnic." How easy it is to say, "All right" or "Whatever you wish." But how healing are the words, "I wish Alice would come with you. Please bring her!" Of course, a whole set of realities has to be in place within your church community (as well as within your own heart) for you to be able to make such an invitation. The process has to start somewhere; why not here?

Anger. It would seem impossible for LGBTQ people *not* to feel some anger, given their current status in the world's cultures:[2] from being considered deserving of death,[3] to being barely tolerated second-class citizens, or, in limited locations, being simply tolerated. Combine that anger with the free-floating generic anger that many members of the populace feel today about their lives and the institutions which affect them, and you have a recipe for great anger. We all know it is important for well-developed

---

2. The following countries have penalties of either life in prison or death for gay sex: Mauritania, Nigeria, Sudan, Saudi Arabia, Yemen, Somalia, Iran, Afghanistan, Pakistan, Tanzania, India, Bangladesh, Nepal, Myanmar, Singapore, and Sierra Leone; many other countries have prison sentences from one to twenty-five years (reported in *The Advocate*, September 12, 2006, 25). See also the Web site of the International Gay and Lesbian Human Rights Commission (IGLHRC) at *www.iglhrc.org/site/iglhrc/* (accessed November 2006).

3. "Two gay teenagers were publicly executed in Iran on July 19, 2005 for the 'crime' of homosexuality. The youths were hanged in Edalat (Justice) Square in the city of Mashhad, in northeast Iran. They were sentenced to death by Court No. 19." News of the two executions was reported, with photographs, by ISNA (Iranian Students News Agency) on July 19. This is only one example of the killing, incarcerating, and serious mistreatment of LGBT people in many parts of the world. As reported by Indymedia Ireland (*www.indymedia.ie*) and by L.A. *Weekly News* (*www.laweekly.com*) (sites accessed November 2006).

adults to move beyond anger.[4] For some this is a formidable task, especially overcoming anger at religion.

Two recommendations for you, the pastoral caregiver:

• First, learn to recognize underlying anger. When anger is on the surface and expressed with little reserve, it is easier to identify, deal with, and respond to. But when it is in hiding it is more dangerous and difficult to identify, both by the person involved and the observer. Underlying anger is anger indirectly expressed — for example, by passive-aggressive behavior,[5] a surly attitude, intolerance, and inveighing against perceived enemies. Realize that giving up anger will feel like (and is) a loss. Something needs to take its place.

• Second, once you have recognized the anger, try to find some way to help your care receiver channel the anger, something to fill up the void left by anger. Channeling negative feelings into positive actions is the moral person's rule of life; it's what resourceful people do naturally. Ask yourself: toward what creative outlet can I encourage this LGBTQ care seeker to move his or her anger? Here is an opportunity for creative pastoral caring:

> Could they write to express their anger? Maybe letters to the editor, op-ed pieces, articles, or simply journaling? Is there some project in the church that needs a person of strong emotional energy to lead it? Will you help your angry care seeker to redirect their energies by joining an effort that is directed at righting the wrong at which they are angry? Something as simple as classes in art, sewing, yoga, history, genealogy, and so forth can act to channel the energy of anger. Be creative.

Fear. Many queer people are full of fear, some because of violence threatened or done to them personally or to people they know; all of us because we know violence to be an ever-present possibility. Gay-baiting, gay-bashing, gay-killing, and anti-transgender hate crimes happen all the

4. A good book on anger is Ron and Pat Potter-Efron's *Letting Go of Anger* (Berkeley, CA: New Harbinger, 2006).

5. Passive-aggressive behavior can be described (nonclinically) as a pattern of negative attitudes and resistance in interpersonal or occupational situations along with nonacknowledgment of the behavior, or even a claim of its opposite.

time. (See "Violence" below.) Although most of the terms use the word "gay," the violence finds its victims in all the letters: L, G, B, T, and Q.

It is especially the young who carry the fear of rejection simply because of their youth and their age-appropriate lack of confidence that they could survive without their family's support, understanding, and acceptance. This is not paranoia but a reality-based fear, for indeed parents, siblings, and friends regularly reject LGBTQ people when they come out. In particular, for anyone at any age, rejection based on a core identity can be devastating to one's sense of self, one's way of being in the world, and one's self-confidence.

Effective pastoral caregivers will look for opportunities to stop possible rejection before it happens by undertaking sensitive intervention into family dynamics, by family education, by becoming advocates for LGBTQ people within the church community.

For many caregivers, enlightened teaching will necessarily include an interpretation of your denomination's official teaching, which is often LGBTQ-negative. Such "interpretation" is commonplace and necessary. In addition to the churches that are officially LGBTQ-welcoming and affirming, I know of many specific congregations — Lutheran, Presbyterian, Methodist, Catholic, Jewish, among others — that create a safe, positive, and accepting welcome to LGBTQ members, notwithstanding queer-negative public stances or the official profiles of their denominational polities.

Isolation. An understandable result of shame, anger, and fear is social isolation. Notice the member of the church who holds back, about whom no one knows very much, or who is always withdrawn. Train yourself to notice the most unnoticeable and find a way to care. (Chapter 5 explores in more detail how to create welcoming congregations.)

The first challenge for the pastoral caregiver is always to notice. Be on the lookout for shame, anger, fear, and isolation. Especially if you are not LGBTQ, it is understandably difficult to gear your sensitivity toward issues and attitudes that do not naturally come your way. You might try the Queer for a Day exercise on page 89 — or your own variation of it.

You might have noticed something urgently important in all these negative things we carry. The impetus for them originates outside of us; for the most part, we did not bring these burdens on ourselves.

Teach Your Congregations

- Teach them the truths of LGBTQ experiences, after having researched them and learned for yourself, if necessary.

- Weave the experiences of your LGBTQ members into your preaching on such topics as justice, charity, and the universality of God's love.

- Provide for LGBTQ topics in your educational programs.

- Teach by including LGBTQ people in the liturgical, educational, administrative, and spiritual structures of the church.

- Make sure the youth programs include LGBTQ topics that teach understanding and full acceptance, and do not provide fertile ground for bullying.

- Teach about subtle, often nonphysical forms of violence. Emotional violence (rage, degrading, shaming, denigrating, etc.) and spiritual violence (excluding from salvation, naming as sinner, keeping away from church and religion, denying welcome, etc.) are probably more pervasive than the violence inflicted by fists and weapons.

- Finally, teach clearly: Violence is never an appropriate response to people who are simply different!

One often hears about a so-called gay agenda, a term that implies sinister machinations to overtake society and topple all moral values in the process. Such talk mostly comes from anti-gay sources. In fact, the only "agenda" the vast majority of LGBTQ people have is simply to be left alone and allowed to live our lives. Of course, LGBTQ people have as many internally generated problems as any other segment of the population; we carry those in addition to the ones we are handed at birth by the culture into which we are born. The LGBTQ community is not the only one to whom a negative birthday gift is given; life is stressful for each person in different ways.

> ## Queer for a Day
> ### *An Exercise for Non-LGBTQ Caregivers*
>
> 1. Pick an average workday in your pastoral ministry, and in your mind take on the identity of an L, G, B, or T person.
>
> 2. In every circumstance, from the moment you begin work in the morning to when you stop your work schedule at the end of the day, "become" that person in your own mind.
>
> 3. Assume that everyone you meet knows your identity. If practical and appropriate (for example, with colleagues), tell them of your assumed identity.
>
> 4. Notice at every encounter with someone how your assumed identity affects what's happening to you and your sense of self.
>
> 5. Notice other effects on your life: how you might feel differently with different persons, during a meeting, in public, while alone.
>
> 6. How does this identity change your social life? Your spiritual/prayer life? Your emotional life?
>
> 7. Realize that this role playing, this "faking it," is what some LGBTQ people have had to do, sometimes for a lifetime.
>
> 8. How might you integrate your experience into a Sunday homily or Sabbath teaching, or into an article for the congregational bulletin or a local publication?

Stress and Discrimination

Stress is rightly a hot topic in the early twenty-first century, with our stress soaring to levels not imagined in the relatively easygoing decades before and even following the Industrial Revolution.

For each person, stress is generated at a global level (through awareness of global warming, weather disasters, the unknowns of space exploration, and cosmic events), at an international level (through awareness of wars, famines, politics, economics, terrorism), at a national level (through war, politics, party disagreements, deep divisions of values, social and economic limits), at a local level (through politics, lack of affordable housing or jobs or adequate schools, neighbors, keeping schedules), and a personal level (through work, money, and the give-and-take of family life).

Is there a particular type of stress experienced by LGBTQ people? I think the only unique stress is the type generated simply by being LGBTQ in the world. The stress, of course, is not inherent to sexual orientation or gender identity, but rather is the result of the violence and intolerance of homophobic, heterosexist, and transphobic people toward queer people. But that stress is more than enough, especially when you consider that it is added to stress from all the other levels. As a pastoral caregiver, be aware of both the discrimination shown by religion and the civil discrimination shown by inequities in the areas of civil rights, employment, housing, and education.

In addition to the levels of stress a person carries around, people are also particularly affected by the groups or strata of society to which they belong, particularly if society holds their group in negative esteem.

In North America, simply being a member of any of the following categories brings one a significant amount of stress. The more groups you belong to, the more the stress (the categories are presented in no particular order, and of course there are exceptions):

- Female
- Ethnic minority
- Foreign-born (some more than others)
- Single (nonmarried)
- Single (divorced)
- Single parent
- Non–English speaking
- Limited English speaking
- Having a foreign accent (some more than others)
- L, G, B, T, or Q
- Jobless/unemployed

- Chronically ill

- Physically disabled

- Old

- Poor or homeless

- Addicted

- Mentally ill

- Victim of violence or crime

- Perpetrator of violence or crime

A quick perusal of the list reveals that there are many millions of people who belong to two or more of these categories. Indeed, the "person" who remains is native born, white, male, married, mentally and physically healthy, straight, well-employed, young or middle-age, clean living, and lucky. There are many in that group, and reverse discrimination against them is by no means unheard of.

Within the LGBTQ communities. Queer people have their own specific proclivities and challenges when it comes to prejudices and discriminations within their own communities. Racial discrimination within the LGBTQ community has been noted and criticized on many occasions. Misogyny and misandry exist not only in the straight world but in the queer world as well. Some people are "suspicious" or unaccepting of bisexuality, judging that it is merely (or always) a stage in coming out as gay or a way to semi-hide being gay. It seems that Ls, Gs, and Bs share a degree of the same prejudice and misunderstandings toward Ts that the wider society shows. One also hears less than respectful terms glibly used about straight members of society. Like the broader society in which they exist, ageism and lookism are not hard to observe in LGBTQ communities.

Clearly, LGBTQ people are not without challenges when it comes to discrimination and prejudice. One might think that with people who have endured so much discrimination and prejudice these traits would be almost nonexistent. However, it is not atypical for oppressed groups to manifest a type of blindness to the group's own weaknesses. One hopes that the current communities within the larger LGBTQ community are reaching a stage of development that accesses their own deeper wisdom and opens them to self-reflection and the wise and loving criticism of supportive others.

As a pastoral caregiver dealing with stress and discrimination:

- Consider stress reduction programs as ministry.

- Find ways to provide quiet, safe, and peaceful space, especially for members of the above categories.

- Find ways for members of these categories to find each other for mutual support, acceptance, and understanding.

- Some people operate both at staggering levels of stress and within numerous categories of stressfulness. Helping stressed people to recognize and identify those levels and categories can itself bring insight and welcome change.

- Often the most stressed ones among your people will have to be searched out.

- Teach by your example. The caregiver's self-care speaks louder than the caregiver's words.

- Don't hesitate to deal with the discrimination and prejudice you observe within the LGBTQ community. Encourage honest self-criticism and self-reflection, for these are signs that the "movement" has achieved a good degree of maturity and is losing the shrillness of youth and inexperience.

- When dealing with anyone in regard to their prejudices, look first and steadily at your own.

Physical Illness: HIV/AIDS and Beyond

There is probably no pastoral caregiver in North American whose ministry has not in some way included care for people with HIV/AIDS or their families. Please note that I do not provide exhaustive information here for the pastoral caregiver who is dealing pastorally with congregation members who are ill with HIV/AIDS; refer to the list of resources for more information or, better still, contact local agencies and professionals for further insight and training. It seems that the most up-to-date resources are online rather than in book form. One useful book, however, is *AIDS*

Pastoral Care: An Introductory Guide by Sean Connolly. It was published in 1994 and is outdated, but its general principles of care remain useful; I have used them in the information below.

AIDS in the United States is a different disease today from what it was in the beginning of the epidemic in the early 1980s. We have turned a corner, and thus it is now more commonly considered a disease that one can live with rather than a death sentence. People with the illness — at least those with access to health care and drugs — are living longer and enjoying a better quality of life with the current drug protocols. At this writing, however, all responsible sources identify it as a terminal disease, and the statistics are alarming: We are approaching the 50 million mark for infected people worldwide; approximately 25 million have died, and 11 million others have been orphaned.[6]

The pastoral caregiver who is prepared to minister to the community of people with AIDS (PWAs) should be proficient in the following:[7]

- In general, have a knowledge of HIV/AIDS, its current status and future geographic and populace projections, and the most at-risk populations, especially if they fall within your pastoral purview.

- Know how the disease is transmitted, and how it is not.

- Have a general knowledge of the current treatment protocols.

- Understand the psychosocial issues facing PWAs, such as medical issues, family issues, possibly sexual orientation and being out, possibly drug use, psychological issues such as (in North America at least) being straight and having AIDS, finances, finding a system of support, religious stigma and relationship to church/synagogue, and so on.

- Identify ethical issues often involved in pastoral care with PWAs: questions of euthanasia and suicide can arise, although less often than earlier; be familiar with the preparation of a living will and durable power of attorney.

---

6. For facts and statistics worldwide in HIV/AIDS, see controversial and straight-speaking Larry Kramer's *The Tragedy of Today's Gays* (New York: Tarcher-Penguin, 2005); see also Loretta McLaughlin, "After 25 Years of AIDS, the News Only Gets Worse," *Boston Globe*, June 25, 2006. McLaughlin is a senior fellow at the Harvard AIDS Initiative. See also *www.avert.org/worldstats.htm*.

7. Based on principles presented in Sean Connolly, *AIDS Pastoral Care: An Introductory Guide* (Grantsville, WI: Arc Research Co., 1994).

- Have a good knowledge of the process of grief in order to guide and support the PWA through possible stages of loss of health, stamina, and possibly the issues of terminal illness and death.[8]

In regard to pastoral care for LGBTQ people with other physical illnesses, much of what has been mentioned about care of PWAs applies to non-AIDS illness as well. In addition, work toward the following:

- Facilitate access to the ill person by partners and family, especially in hospitals and other care facilities.
- Arrange regular pastoral visits if the ill person desires.
- Seek out the ill among your LGBTQ members who might not be easily visible.
- Make an effort to understand some of the symptoms and characteristics of a person's illness. Your interest will be deeply appreciated and seen as caring.
- Be on hand to be the go-between with the ill person and the family, especially when there is estrangement between the LGBTQ person and the family, divorce, or other common family challenges that create tension. Illness can often be the catalyst to healing family rifts.
- The chronically ill have special needs that can include but are not limited to: depression, discouragement, frustration, need for opportunity to make friends, need of worshiping community, need for transportation, and need for privacy and appropriate surroundings for intimacy.
- Hospital chaplaincies and departments of pastoral care are almost always rich sources of enlightened and experienced pastoral care for the ill and their friends and families. Take full advantage of their services and expertise. For references, see the Web sites of:

  CAPPE (*www.cappe.org*) — The Canadian Association for Pastoral Practice and Education is a national multifaith organization committed to professional education and concerned with a holistic approach to health care and personal development, with a special focus on spiritual and religious care.

---

8. Recommended book on grief: Elisabeth Kübler-Ross and David Kessler, *On Grief and Grieving: Finding the Meaning of Grief through the Five Stages of Loss* (New York: Scribner, 2005).

HIV/AIDS Pastoral Care
General Considerations

- Don't assume anything about a care receiver's HIV status. This means, for example, not assuming that because your care seeker is a gay man he is HIV-positive, or because she is a straight woman, she isn't. Both are frequently not true.

- Assume a no-blame attitude. Especially when dealing with people who are actually ill, assume the reality-based attitude that illness is illness and there is no guilty illness or nonguilty illness. Notions of "lepers" and "pariahs" must be realities of the past.

- When a gay PWA is hospitalized, be especially cognizant of who is allowed or not allowed access to the patient. Frequently partners, significant others, longtime companions, even spouses (married in a religious ceremony or in another jurisdiction) are kept from visiting. This is an opportune moment for creative and caring pastoral intervention to facilitate access by family.

- Be aware of the global reality of AIDS and that it is now especially a disease of the developing world in women, men, and children. While AIDS in the United States was first identified as a "gay man's disease," it no longer is, even though there are urban pockets where unsafe sex, especially among younger gay men, continues to resurface from time to time, increasing the rates of infection. (See "Addictions, Drugs, and Sex" below.)

- Thus, it is extremely important to support the dissemination of information on prevention within the at-risk communities. It is no secret that churches do not like to deal with sex, which has caused many people to go underground with their sexual issues. Work to help all church leaders to deal with sexuality honestly and without fear.

- My final piece of advice is to take care of yourself as a caregiver. Self-care involves getting enough sleep and rest, enough time off and away from work, support from colleagues, a relatively peaceful ambience in your ministering community, and whatever else you personally need to be an effective caregiver. Ministry to the ill and troubled is exhausting.

ACPE (www.acpe.edu) — The Association for Clinical Pastoral Education is a professional association committed to advancing experience-based theological education for seminarians, clergy, and laypersons of diverse cultures, ethnic groups, and faith traditions.

Mental Illnesses

Being LGBTQ is *not* a mental illness (nor an emotional problem nor an addiction), and never has been, despite having been commonly considered such for years. The American Psychological Association (APA) removed gay, lesbian, and bisexual from the list of mental illness over thirty years ago.[9] The presence of LGBTQ people in the categories of illness stems from an era when the ordering of such information, understandably for the times, fell within the realms of both medicine and religion. Today it is clear that there simply are no symptoms present in being LGBTQ that would indicate a diagnosis of a mental illness, an emotional problem, or an addiction.

Unfortunately, transgender people were not included when the APA made its changes, and "Gender Identity Disorder" is still listed in the *Diagnostic and Statistical Manual* (DSM-IV), which is the handbook used most often in diagnosing mental disorders. (See PsychiatryOnline.com.) One anticipates with hope and conviction that T will soon join L, G, and B as free from such categories of illness. LGBTQ people are, of course, subject to the same mental illnesses and emotional challenges that all human beings are, no more and no less. Being LGBTQ simply adds another layer of stress to those illnesses and challenges. Three disorders in particular, I believe, are important to look at when considering the challenges of any oppressed minority at the beginning of the twenty-first century.

Depression. If you see signs of depression in your care seeker, don't hesitate to take action. First of all, recognize the signs of depression (see box). If symptoms are present to a sufficient degree, supportively suggest that the client might be depressed and that help is available. Then

---

9. See the American Psychological Association's Web site online at *www.apa.org/topics/ orientation.html#cantherapychange* (accessed November 2006); also Alice Ogden Bellis and Terry L. Hufford, *Science, Scripture, and Homosexuality* (Cleveland: Pilgrim Press, 2002), 41–45.

encourage and help find appropriate professional counseling such as a pastoral counselor or family therapist and physician. Be sure to see your care seeker through to an established relationship with an appropriate helping professional.

Signs of Depression to Watch for in Your Care Receiver

- Sad mood; irritability
- Negative, distorted thinking
- Feelings of worthlessness or hopelessness
- Low self-esteem
- Inappropriate feelings of guilt
- Repeated thoughts of death or suicide
- Loss of interest or pleasure in activities
- Finding it difficult to concentrate
- Agitation
- Loss of energy, fatigue
- Change in appetite, significant weight loss or gain
- Change in sleeping patterns
- Physical symptoms, including headaches, muscle aches, stomachaches.

If several of these symptoms persist for more than two weeks, assist your care seeker in finding help. Especially with depression, getting help very often brings improvement.

Occasionally queer folks are labeled as being depressed when really they are frustrated, sad, mad, confused, afraid, and so on. It is often difficult to distinguish clinical depression from simply having too much on one's plate. And, after all, many of us get into a bit of a depressed mood from time to time. If in doubt, seek help. Counseling, and often drug therapy, can frequently help.

Obsessive-compulsive disorder (OCD).[10] OCD is in the category of anxiety disorders and seems to be the emotional challenge of our age. The obsessive part has to do with mental activity and consists of recurrent, intrusive, and unwanted thoughts, impulses, or images that cause significant anxiety. The compulsive part is the acting out and has to do with (often ritualized) behaviors that are intended to suppress the anxiety caused by obsessions. Common examples are constant hand-washing, repeatedly checking if an appliance is turned off, overly zealous and unnecessary cleaning, an endless repetition of religious rituals or prayers, and angry or revengeful thoughts that too strongly affect one's life. In some religious traditions, this condition was referred to as scrupulosity.

Just as many of us get a bit depressed from time to time, some too are a bit OC. They are the people who get a lot of things done. That's not the level of emotional challenge you need to be concerned about. It's when you notice that your care receiver's life is negatively influenced by extreme obsessions or compulsive behaviors, when they interrupt the normal functioning of life, that professional help is in order.

Manic-depression,[11] also known as bipolar disorder, is a cognitive disorder that causes unusual shifts in a person's mood, energy, and ability to function. It's different from the normal ups and downs that everyone goes through; the symptoms of bipolar disorder are more severe. The moods fluctuate between the two poles of high energy/excitement (manic) to low energy/depression (depressive). If you notice these symptoms in any of your care seekers, facilitate their seeking professional counseling help.

Addictions, Drugs, and Sex

LGBTQ people are as prone to addictions as any other segment of the population. Often the stress of heterosexism/homophobia and transphobia are the catalysts that propel them into the addiction. Addiction can be defined as an overpowering urge to use a substance or engage in a practice, regardless of its potential or actual harm. Almost anything can

---

10. Robert J. Campbell, *Psychiatric Dictionary* (New York: Oxford University Press, 1989), 493.

11. Ibid., 422.

become an addiction, including religion. There is a large amount of literature on addictions, a condition we have come to understand much more thoroughly in the last twenty years or so.[12]

When you are dealing with people with addictions of any kind — alcohol, drugs, gambling, religious practice, or whatever — the first priority of your pastoral care is normally the addiction itself and not, in most cases, the possibly unrelated issue that the care seeker may want to address. That can come later, unless it's an emergency. The first priority is to get them to a non-using state or into a program of recovery. For example, an older, closeted woman in your congregation approaches you after the morning worship service to ask you about a theological issue that is confusing and upsetting to her, but you notice right away that she is intoxicated. The theological issue can wait. First, find a way to focus on the possible addiction and help her find appropriate treatment. This can require a good deal of finesse as you are changing agendas on your care seeker.

Drugs. The challenge here for the pastoral caregiver is to avoid naïveté, to learn to recognize signs of drug use, to know where to refer, and to have consistent follow-through with people who are often difficult.

Certainly a percentage of recreational drug users are LGBTQ. There is one category of drug use that deserves special attention at this time in history, and that is the use of crystal meth among gay men. Secular statistics as well as pastoral caregivers who have a large percentage of gay members in their communities attest to the crisis that the use of this recreational drug represents.[13] The scientific name of the drug is *methamphetamine hydrochloride,* and it is a form of what used to be called "speed." Other common street names are "ice," "crystal," "glass," "jibb," and "tina." It is relatively cheap and easy (but extremely dangerous) to produce.

In higher doses, methamphetamine, especially if it is smoked or injected, causes the user to experience a rush of intense pleasure that lasts only a

---

12. See Christopher D. Ringwald, *The Soul of Recovery: Uncovering the Spiritual Dimension in the Treatment of Addictions* (New York: Oxford University Press, 2002); Robert N. Minor, "When Religion Is an Addiction" (Fairness Project Lecture Series), Audio CD (ASIN: B000FPE952), 2006: *www.fairnessproject.org/* (accessed November 2006).

13. See the excellent article by Michael Specter, "Higher Risk: Crystal Meth, the Internet, and Dangerous Choices about AIDS," *New Yorker,* May 5, 2005. Also online at: *www.newyorker.com/printables/fact/050523fa_fact* (accessed November 2006).

Recommendations for Pastoral Caregivers in Response to the Use of Crystal Meth

- Leave naïveté, squeamishness, and hesitancy behind, and become proactive in the campaign to fight this severely damaging drug.

- Learn about the drug, its use in your locality, and the damage it does.

- Associate yourself with local secular or religious organizations that have programs, or an interest in creating programs, designed to deal with crystal meth abuse and education of at-risk populations.

- In your preaching and teaching, refer to its use and the damage it causes.

- By the above, become known as a community resource who, at the least, is willing to add the influence of your faith community to fight the severe damage wrought by this drug.

---

few moments. Users can become addicted quickly, needing ever higher doses as the addiction progresses.

Negative effects include disturbed sleep patterns and loss of REM sleep, hyperactivity, nausea, delusions of power, increased aggressiveness, and irritability. Long-term negative effects, in high doses, can include heart, liver, kidney, and lung damage, and it in general can ravage the body.[14]

In recent years, crystal meth has become a drug of choice in some gay men's party scenes. This trend spread from west to east, from San Francisco to New York and from Vancouver to Toronto.[15] At "PNP" parties ("party and play" — meaning drugs and sex), crystal meth increases energy and reduces sexual inhibition. And the superhuman feeling that often comes with a crystal meth high means the sex is often unprotected. Such

---

14. See the Canadian Broadcasting Company's (CBC) Web page *The Fifth Estate* and the article on "Dark Crystal": *www.cbc.ca/fifth/darkcrystal/facts.html* (accessed November 2006).

15. Ibid.

unprotected sex leads to an increase in HIV infection, as the statistics in some specific areas are showing.

Here is an urgent challenge for the effective pastoral caregiver, especially if you work in an urban center where there is a concentration of gay men: be a voice for health, wholeness, and holiness; don't be naïve; don't be afraid.

Yet the gay community is by no means the only one that is being negatively affected by this damaging drug. According to mental health workers, police, and research scientists,[16] the people who use crystal meth also include large numbers of rural and small-town poor across North America, some young people in the rave and dance scene (who also use Ecstasy), and some people who want to lose weight.

So, five recommendations:

1. Know where to get information about drug use.[17]

2. Train yourself to recognize symptoms.

3. If you think you recognize signs of drug use, don't hesitate to approach your LGBTQ care seeker with the challenge — if for no other reason (you might say to your care receiver) than to set *your* mind at ease.

4. Try not to be fooled. This recommendation is one you probably will fail several times because addicts are masterful at concealing their addiction.

5. Try to see the origins of addiction, any addiction, as a spiritual challenge, a desire for God gone wrong, a wish for goodness without the necessary experience and wisdom, and not simply as someone's pathetic weakness and lack of will.[18]

---

16. Ibid. Click on "The Story of Two BC Towns" (accessed November 14, 2006).

17. Jack Drescher, Andrew J. Kolodny, and Milton L. Wainberg, eds., *Crystal Meth and Men Who Have Sex with Men: What Mental Health Care Professionals Need to Know*, 1st ed. (New York: Haworth Medical Press, 2007). See also *www.aids.about.com/od/substanceabuse/a/crystal.htm* (accessed November 2006).

18. See Patrick Moore's exposé and memoir, *Tweaked: A Crystal Memoir* (New York: Kensington Publishing, 2006). Not for the fainthearted. In an interview in the *Advocate* (August 1, 2006), Moore said, "I think addiction is a spiritual disease....Our intention when we use drugs is to communicate with God."

Sex, safer sex, addictive sex. Every religious congregation, those with schools and those without schools, should have a program of sex education adapted to their specific congregational needs. The prevailing ignorance about sexuality at this stage of human history is scandalous. No one should be without the necessary information they need — when they need it — to mature on all levels of human development.

Sexual maturity and integration are essential parts of spiritual maturity. How urgently churches need to know this! How vital is the teaching of sexual information in today's society! And how courageous are the congregation and the pastoral caregiver who take this on!

Since one could credibly argue that the cause of this historical hesitancy, this embarrassment, this shame, is religion, why not suggest that religion take a strong leadership stance in encouraging complete and free access to information about human sexuality? It is certainly appropriate subject matter for religious bodies to foster and disseminate. The spiritual and the sexual shine as different facets of the same gem. Sexuality is the gift of a loving God and (in many ways because of the church's influence) considered a sacred and holy gift. Churches must stop shrinking in fear and shame from the goodness and beauty and joy of the human body and its sexual expression or become burdened with even more blame for their lack of historical wisdom.

Imagine for a moment that you are a twelve-year-old gay boy (yes, many youngsters know their sexual orientation at this age; see "LGBTQ Youth" below) sitting in the congregation of your church or synagogue week after week and attending the religious school classes religiously. Probably sex is never mentioned in this context or mentioned only in very scary and negative terms; maybe sex is mentioned carefully, at a safe distance, and only in a heterosexual context. What is this boy (as well as everyone else who hears) to conclude? How is he to grow? Exactly what does his faith community expect from him?

In regard to safer sex: You must know what is meant by safer sex, what is included in safer sex acts, and what is excluded. If you do not clearly know this information, here is one place to learn: *www.thebody.com/nmai/ safersex.html* (The Body: The Complete HIV/AIDS Resource; site accessed November 2006). Be aware that the categories of safer sex have changed somewhat over the years and may continue to change, so it is important to keep up to date. At the least, you need to be able to refer people in your care to the places where they can get this information.

Be aware of potential challenges your care seekers may have in trying to reconcile their faith communities' teachings on the use of birth control and condoms with their own practice. If a care seeker comes to you with the problem of sexual addiction, or if you suspect it because the person reports OC behavior around sex, I believe it is best to refer the person to a trained professional helper with experience and expertise in this area. Sexual addiction is often difficult to accurately define and diagnose.

In the same vein, if a care seeker approaches you with a problem of sexual abuse in his or her childhood, make a referral to competent, professional help. Still, as pastoral caregiver, you can continue to relate to, encourage, and otherwise sustain and guide these care seekers.

Both of the last mentioned situations, sexual addiction and childhood abuse, can serve here as a reminder to keep your referral list accurate, handy, and up to date.

The Physically Challenged LGBTQ Person

Being LGBTQ adds a significant element of challenge to the physically handicapped. The goal in this section is to encourage you to notice the presence of LGBTQ handicapped people and also to give you several referrals to helpful resources as you deal with them.

In general, the most important task of the caregiver is to notice LGBTQ people, in this case handicapped LGBTQ people, to see them as they are and with the needs and gifts that they ask from and bring to the community.

The place to begin (or deepen) your knowledge of LGBTQ persons with physical handicaps is online. A good Web site to begin with is out of Los Angeles: *queersonwheels.com* (accessed November 2006).

Here is a quotation from the site: "The physically disabled LGBTQ population has existed for generations. . . . Because this community is a mesh of the LGBTQ and the disabled communities, people who are both often have to choose which one they will participate in, negating the importance of this combined identity. This narrow way of thinking does not value a person as a whole, but rather focuses on an aspect of their identity. Queers

On Wheels recognizes that people have multiple identities and that those identities need to be valued and appreciated."

For vision-impaired or blind LGBTQ people, their families and friends, log on to bflag.org (accessed November 2006), the Web site of Blind Friends of Lesbian, Gay, Bisexual and Transgender People. From their Web site: "BFLAG was formed in 1996. We began as a group of persons who are gay and blind, who sought each other out for support and information.

"In 2000, BFLAG received its charter as a special interest affiliate of the American Council of the Blind. The purpose of Blind Friends of Lesbian, Gay, Bisexual and Transgender People (BFLAG) is to provide for the betterment of the lives of those who are visually impaired and who are lesbian, gay, bisexual or transgender."

For hearing-impaired or deaf LGBTQ people, log on to deafqueer.org (accessed November 2006). From their Web site: "The Deaf Queer Resource Center (DQRC) is a national nonprofit resource and information center for, by and about the Deaf Lesbian, Gay, Bisexual, Transgender, Transsexual, Intersex and Questioning communities."

On paraplegic and mobility problems, see the above reference to *queersonwheels.com.* There may be local organizations dedicated to making life better for disabled LGBTQ people. Seek them out on the Internet.

In my searching the Internet I found that none of these Web sites is religiously sponsored, although some of them do deal with spiritual issues. Would it not be propitious if there were a site — or a book or a film — that brought together a religious sensibility with a desire to provide broad information, including the particular challenges of being sexual, to handicapped LGBTQ people? In the meantime, these sites are fulfilling a great need.

Just as non-LGBTQ people who are learning to deal with LGBTQ people tend to be hesitant and lack confidence that they know what to do or to say, so it is with nonhandicapped people dealing with the handicapped. In both cases, ask from your care seekers what you don't know; ask them for help in learning. What's worse than interacting awkwardly with an LGBTQ handicapped person is not interacting with them at all.

Violence: We Get More Than We Give

We queer folks are a peaceful lot in general. "One would be hard-pressed to name another male culture in America — one, that is, outside formal structures of religious orders or intentional communities — whose public realm is so notably free of assault and aggressive violence among peers." So writes David Nimmons[19] speaking of gay men, and he quotes police statistics to back up his statement.

Where LGBTQ people figure mostly in the violence scene is on the receiving end. The 1997–99 NIBRS (National Incident-Based Reporting System of the Bureau of Justice Statistics of the U.S. Department of Justice) data showed that "out of nearly 5.4 million offenses reported to NIBRS agencies in nearly a dozen States, almost 3,000 were identified as hate crimes. In addition, 61 percent of hate crime incidents were motivated by race, 4 percent by religion, 13 percent by sexual orientation, 11 percent by ethnicity, and 1 percent by victim disability.[20] It is important to note that the government agency does not keep track of issues of violence done to transgender people simply because it is not mandated by federal law yet.

I want to focus on the direct and causal connection between the teaching of some religious organizations about LGBTQ people and the violence done to LGBTQ people. The causal connection, although probably not empirically provable nor even measured as far as I know, seems to me irrefutable and scandalous. May these religious voices soon come to comprehend their role in the violence that comes to LGBTQ people as a direct result of their projected attitudes. Their language can be and indeed commonly is interpreted as tacit permission to do violence.

The language which the Catholic church uses in documents issued by the Vatican is indicative: "The homosexual inclination is … objectively disordered,"[21] and "Although the particular inclination of the homosexual person is not a sin, it is a more or less strong tendency ordered toward an intrinsic moral evil; and thus the inclination itself must be seen as an objective disorder."[22]

---

19. David Nimmons, *The Soul beneath the Skin: The Unseen Hearts and Habits of Gay Men* (New York: St. Martin's Press, 2002), 14.

20. U.S. Department of Justice, Bureau of Justice Statistics: *www.ojp.usdoj.gov/bjs/ibrs.htm* (accessed November 2006).

21. "Declaration on Certain Questions Concerning Sexual Ethics," cited in *Homosexuality and the Magisterium: Documents from the Vatican and U.S. Bishops 1975–1985*, ed. John Gallagher (Mt. Rainier, MD: New Ways Ministry, 1986).

22. "Letter to the Bishops of the Catholic Church on the Pastoral Care of Homosexual Persons," cited in Jeannine Gramick and Patrick Furey, *The Vatican and Homosexuality*

The typical (although not only) perpetrator of violence against LGBTQ people ("gay basher") is an adolescent male who is insecure about his sexuality, which is not an uncommon trait of many people in adolescence. I suggest that the tacit but well-publicized criticisms, scoldings, and at times simple rantings by some representatives of many religious bodies can be the energy that fuels the potential and vulnerable criminal to act. "Some people," says Miguel De La Torre speaking of Christians, "encourage violence toward gays and lesbians when they reduce sexual orientation to a disease or sin.... Christians become complicit with the violence they breed due to their attitudes, words, and actions...."[23]

The violence done to transsexual/transgender persons recently has been especially alarming. The incident that seems to have captured the attention of the country and world is that of Gwen Araujo, a young male-to-female transsexual in California who was brutally murdered, but that's only one of many cases involving violence toward trans people.[24] Araujo was murdered *because* she was transsexual. The case has understandably become a rallying point for LGBTQ activists. If you think that there are no members of your congregation who are dealing with their trans identity, I encourage you to do whatever is necessary to take a deeper look.

"Flaunting it." Violence toward LGBTQ people brings up the subject of flaunting. People, often supportive people of good will, frequently say to LGBTQ people, "You talk about it too much," or "You're too obsessed, too impatient and pushy."

Expressing our sexuality as openly and as naturally as heterosexuals do is not flaunting it: holding hands in public, wearing a wedding band, talking about one's partner or boyfriend/girlfriend, celebrating an anniversary, making casual references to other LGBTQ people in our lives. To many it must seem to be flaunting because it is contrasted to the almost complete silence of the past or because most people in our culture are not

(New York: Crossroad, 1988), 2. More recently (November 2006), similar language was used by the Vatican in the document "Ministry to Persons with a Homosexual Orientation," *www.nccbuscc.org/dpp/Ministry.pdf* (accessed November 2006).

23. Miguel De La Torre, *Reading the Bible from the Margins* (Maryknoll, NY: Orbis Books, 2002), 131.

24. For description and history of the Araujo case and links, see *www.transyouth.net/ stories/gwen_araujo.html* (accessed November 2006). For a faith dimension on transgender people, see Justin Tanis, *Trans-Gendered: Theology, Ministry, and Communities of Faith* (Cleveland: Pilgrim Press, 2003).

comfortable talking or hearing (publicly or privately) about personal sex of any kind, even though — amazingly and incongruously — the media is full of it. Maybe it's new, but it's not flaunting — though clearly, like anyone else, LGBTQ people are capable of flaunting their sexuality. The definition of "flaunt" includes: "to display or obtrude oneself to public notice; to wave or flutter showily; to display ostentatiously or impudently; to treat contemptuously."[25] Sometimes it's harmless, sometimes it's not. LGBTQ people flaunt no more than non-LGBTQ people — even though queer flaunting often makes better television.

Be that as it may, there is a tendency of the oppressed to obsess or overstate when in the fervor of overcoming the oppression. That has been and always will be true for any minority fighting for its rights; it's simply the nature of oppressed people. So a little patience and positive, critical feedback can help. There is a lot of understanding, wisdom, and good-natured insight in the words of Canadian author Robertson Davies, who quipped, "The love that dared not speak its name has become the love that won't shut up."[26]

Domestic violence. Unfortunately gays and lesbians are as likely to be both victims and perpetrators of domestic violence as their straight counterparts. And, counterintuitively, men can be victims and women can be batterers.

A standard and basic skill of every pastoral caregiver must be training in recognizing the symptoms or indications of domestic violence. It is one of the most underreported, undertreated, and widespread forms of violence. Nearly one-third of American women report being physically or sexually abused by a husband or boyfriend at some time in their lives, according to a 1998 study, and nearly 25 percent of American women report being raped and/or physically assaulted by a current or former spouse, cohabiting partner, or date at some time in their lifetime.[27] In 2001, women accounted for 85 percent of the victims of intimate partner violence (588,490 total),

25. Definitions of "flaunt" are taken from the Merriam Webster's Online Dictionary: *www.m-w.com*.

26. For the Robertson Davies quote, see *www.en.thinkexist.com/quotation/the_love_that_dare_not_speak_its_name_has_become/175211.html* (accessed November 2006).

27. See the Family Violence Prevention Fund Web site: *www.endabuse.org./resources/facts/* (accessed November 2006).

and men accounted for approximately 15 percent of the victims (103,220 total).[28]

Indeed, domestic violence, perhaps more than any other form of violence, gives the lie to the stereotypes. Many characteristics that most people would assume to be true about domestic violence simply are not, especially in regard to LGBTQ people. (See the box on p. 109.)

Training in recognizing the signs of domestic violence can be self-conducted. (See the list of resources.)

Falling Between the Cracks: Bi and Trans

General awareness of bisexual and transgender persons and their challenges is probably where awareness of gays and lesbians was about twenty-five years ago. Thus, statistics and enlightened understanding for these groups are hard to come by. The estimates of bisexual people in the United States range from the millions to the tens of millions.

The encouragement I would give to the pastoral caregiver is to increase both your awareness and your understanding: awareness of the presence of bisexual and transgender people in your communities, and understanding of their very real and challenging issues.

Here's the experience of one community in downtown San Francisco. From their Web site: "City of Refuge United Church of Christ is a ministry of restoration. We are intentionally radically inclusive, welcoming all persons regardless of race, color, ancestry, age, gender, affectional orientation, and those who are specially abled. We celebrate the Creator's diversity!"[29]

The pastor, Bishop Yvette Flunder, is an award-winning (for her work with the HIV/AIDS community, among others) and popular speaker, author, singer, and teacher. One of the church's ministries, a part of a program called the Ark of Refuge, is the Transcending Program, which provides treatment advocacy, AIDS education and prevention, peer advocacy, individual counseling and referrals, psychosocial support groups, and substance abuse counseling. They offer a three-hour support group weekly.

---

28. Ibid.
29. See online the City of Refuge United Church of Christ Web site: *www.sfrefuge.org/ending.shtml* (accessed November 2006).

Myths and Facts
about Same-Gender Domestic Violence*

Myths

- Only straight women get battered.

- Gay, bisexual, and transgendered men are never victims of domestic violence.

- Lesbians, bisexual, and transgender women do not batter.

- Battering is less common in same-gender relationships.

- Domestic violence primarily occurs among LGBTQ people who hang out in bars, are poor, or are people of color.

Facts

- Men can be victims, and women can batter. Numbers reflect this: An annual study of over two thousand gay men reflects that one in four gay men has experienced domestic violence. These numbers are consistent with research done regarding battering among opposite-sex couples and lesbian couples.

- Stereotypes about gender and sexual orientation are repudiated by the fact that gay men and lesbians are both victims and perpetrators.

- Domestic violence is a nondiscriminatory phenomenon; victims as well as violent and abusive offenders come from all walks of life, ethnic backgrounds, socioeconomic groups, and educational levels.

- Racist, classist, and inaccurate stereotypes about domestic violence are common not just in the LGBTQ community, but also in the dominant heterosexual culture.

---

*Based on information at the Gay Men's Domestic Violence Project Web site: *www.gmdvp.org/pages/myth.html* (accessed November 2006).

General Comments on Bisexuality*

- Bisexuality is a sexual orientation in which an individual feels sexual attraction towards both men and women, although not necessarily to the same degree.

- A bisexual individual may experience conflict with a homophobic society; however, such conflict is a symptom not of dysfunction in the individual but of the society and the confusion of language.

- All sexual orientations (homosexual, heterosexual, and bisexual) are normal and natural for at least a minority of the population. An adult's orientation is not consciously chosen. It is not changeable through prayer, therapy, surgical intervention, and so on.

- Some persons who are sexually attracted to both men and women feel more strongly attracted to one gender than the other. Further, they may identify themselves as homosexual, heterosexual, or bisexual depending upon their primary attraction. So, bisexuals who feel more attracted to members of the same sex might identify themselves as gay or lesbian rather than bisexual. Others, attracted to members of the opposite sex, might view himself or herself as heterosexual.

- Bisexuality describes how people feel, not necessarily how they act:

  People can feel attractions to both men and women, decide to remain celibate, and still be considered bisexual by themselves and others.

  Bisexuals might make a conscious decision to confine their sexual activity to persons of one gender and still be considered bisexuals by themselves and others.

- Confusion of meaning and terms abounds in regard to sexuality in general, but especially in the area of bisexuality. Be sure that all participants in the conversation agree on the meanings of the terms they use.

---

*These statements are taken from or based on statements offered by the Ontario Consultants on Religious Tolerance at *www.religioustolerance.org/bisexuality.htm*.

Suggested Solutions to Common Challenges for Transgender Persons*

♦ **Names and/or pronouns:** Use the names and/or pronouns appropriate to the person's chosen gender identity. Remember that it is everyone's essential dignity to be called by their chosen name, and it is everyone's right to be recognized as the persons they see themselves to be. Please apologize if you use the wrong pronoun or the wrong name.

♦ **Access to restroom and locker room facilities:** Make sure that everyone understands that transgender people want to use the restrooms that conform to their gender identity. If possible, designate gender-neutral restrooms (toilet facilities that anyone may use, irrespective of gender identity or gender expression).

♦ **Dress code:** Make sure that the dress codes, if there are any in your programs, respect people's rights to dress in conformity with their gender identity.

♦ **Confidentiality:** Make sure that any program you oversee maintains confidentiality with regard to the gender identity, gender expression, sexual orientation, and sexual behavior of *all* the people in the program.

♦ **Role models and accurate information:** Educate others about gender identity. Make sure that everyone you deal with is aware that there is diversity regarding human gender; male and female, of course, but also going beyond these. Search out transgender support groups and LGBTQ-serving organizations in your area. Make sure that these groups and organizations are included on your resource and referral lists.

---

*Adapted from the Advocates for Youth in Washington, DC. See the Web site at *www.advocatesforyouth.org/publications/frtp/transgender_challenges.htm* (accessed November 2006).

LGBTQ Youth

What is the most obvious characteristic of LGBTQ youth? The answer is easy: being young and LGBTQ is much more dangerous and risky than being young and straight. Other than that, I believe queer youth are pretty much like all youth. They, like all youth, need affirmation and understanding, not reprimands and rejection. They need responsible, informed adults to love them, like them, encourage them, educate them, teach them limits and self-discipline and some ways to enjoy life, never abandon them, and include them into an affirming community.

For the majority of LGBTQ youth, the only way they can achieve these values is to keep their core identity hidden in denial, shame, and fear. If they do come out as youths — and more and more are doing so — they can expect trouble. More than four out of five lesbian, gay, bisexual, transgender, and queer students reported being verbally, sexually, or physically harassed at school because of their sexual orientation, reports GLSEN.[30]

Here are a few questions and concerns that probably go through the minds of young LGBTQ people at some time or other — or maybe constantly:

- "So am I gay or bi?"
- "What does it mean to be lesbian?"
- "Some people say it's just a phase . . . ?"
- "But I just wanna be normal!"
- "Was I born gay?"
- "Should I tell someone I might be trans? Who?"
- "Is it possible I did something wrong to make me 'this way'?"
- "Far as I can tell, everyone 'round here hates queer people."
- "I'm not like most of the gay people I see, so how can I be gay?"[31]

Now imagine telling this to a fourteen-year-old with such concerns:

---

30. The Gay, Lesbian and Straight Education Network, GLSEN, is an excellent resource. See their Web site: *www.glsen.org/cgi-bin/iowa/home.html* (accessed November 2006).

31. Based on questions posed on the Web site of AVERT, an international HIV and AIDS charity based in the United Kingdom, with the aim of AVERTing HIV and AIDS worldwide. *www.avert.org/ygmt1.htm* (accessed November 2006).

No one will help you if you have any of these questions. You are totally on your own and cannot expect understanding from anyone, least of all your religious community. In fact, you must not even mention the possibility, because if you do, you can count on being disbelieved, ridiculed, or even punished. So the only person you can talk to, if you're lucky, is your same-age friend who knows as much as or less than you.

Imagine! It's a wonder to me that LGBTQ people get through youth at all, much less get through it in one piece. What might be some helpful and healthy responses and interventions of the pastoral caregiver when dealing with LGBTQ youth? Consider these perspectives:

Pastoral Perspectives
Pastoral Care with LGBTQ Youth

- Make the topic of being LGBTQ available to the community you serve, especially to the young. Make it a topic of conversation that is acceptable and accepted.

- Ask yourself: Am I approachable by LGBTQ youth who seek someone to talk to whom they can trust? What can I do to become so?

- For urban caregivers: Associate yourself with the city's resources that serve street youth and other at-risk youth.

- For rural caregivers: Create safe and affirming space, both physical and psychic, for youths who don't fit the mold.

- For both: Associate yourself with and encourage Gay-Straight Alliances (or their equivalents) in high schools. Volunteer to give presentations or lead activities with them.

- Be on good communication terms with your local branch of PFLAG, and possibly a member or occasional visitor.

- Be aware of GLSEN, the Gay, Lesbian and Straight Education Network, which works to make high schools safe for all students. Enlist their services, support their work: *www.glsen.org.*

Coming out young. The age when persons typically come out of the closet is getting younger all the time. With LGBTQ issues prominently in the news and entertainment media, young LGBTQ people are finding encouragement and permission to reveal themselves to family and friends; some are as young as eleven and twelve. But the path they choose is rough and fraught with danger. They need all the help they can get, including your pastoral care.

Caitlin Ryan, a clinical social worker, spent four years researching LGBTQ youth. She found that the average age of teens coming out was just over age thirteen, slightly younger than the late 1980s when they came out between fourteen and sixteen. In the 1970s, most teens waited until they were adults to come out.[32]

With children (anyone younger than eighteen, or the majority age, or age of consent in your jurisdiction) who come out of the closet and seek your care, or who are simply within the purview of your care, keep the following recommendations in mind:

- Involve the family as soon and as completely as possible. Always acknowledge that the parents, no matter what their reactions or feared reactions, have the authority with the child, not you. In this delicate situation it would at least appear that you are acting *in loco parentis*, and your interventions need to be as transparent and responsible as possible. In reality you are acting to supplement unprovided and urgently needed parental-like care.

- If family involvement is not possible, and often it is not, enlist a knowledgeable and experienced colleague into your pastoral care relationship. This involvement might be simply as a consultant with whom you discuss, in professional confidence, your pastoral relationship or even as an openly involved co-caregiver, depending on circumstances.

- Help your care seeker keep all possibilities open without denigrating their act of coming out. In preteen and even early teen years, one *might* be mistaken about one's orientation, but it's not likely. If it does happen, it will probably be discovered quickly by the individual (they could also

---

32. Caitlin Ryan, *Lesbian and Gay Youth: Care and Counseling* (New York: Columbia University Press, 1998). See also *I Could Not Speak My Heart: Education and Social Justice for Gay and Lesbian Youth* (Regina, SK: Canadian Plains Research Center, 2004). This volume is especially good for educators and for LGBTQ youth.

be dissembling for some reason). Many people report knowing their sexual orientation very early, from eight or nine years old, or even earlier on some level of awareness.[33]

* The primary challenge here will be to engage the family. The next challenges will be keeping a balance between setting clear limits around behavior on the one hand, and affirming the person on the other. In caring for your LGBTQ youth, please don't overlook the primary importance of the family. If all's well in the family, the youngster is more likely to survive and even thrive.

Even with bullying and without family support, the resilience of some young LGBTQ people is remarkable. Take the typical case of Brian, who is from a white, middle-class, divorced, suburban family. He came out to his mother at age eighteen as a freshman in college. He reports struggling for years with his sexual orientation and finally just got tired of the never-ending struggle and pretending he was straight. When he came out to his mother, the result was a yelling match, and he was sent off to live with his aunt and uncle. Brian talks about how his mother denies his being gay, either by avoiding the topic, denying the truth of it, or talking to him about its sinfulness. "At first it was really hard for me. I just wished she'd accept me the way I am." The pain behind those words is evident, but eventually Brian speaks for a growing number of young LGBTQ people when he adds, "but I can't just stop living, put everything on hold for her."

If Brian were in your congregation, how could you see yourself giving effective pastoral care? First of all, would you notice him? That's key. Why might you not notice him — that is, not be aware of what is going on for him and his family? Can you take steps to improve the possibility of noticing such members of your congregation?

Then, might you begin by talking with the mother and trying to understand her vehement stance? Or the father: what is his role with Brian? Are there younger or older siblings who might be torn in their loyalties and have questions? Does Brian need a safe and accepting place to talk about his life? Could he use referrals to LGBTQ-positive church groups, agencies, or organizations?

---

33. While some LGBTQ people realize the nature of their sexuality very early, it is not uncommon for others to recognize it later, even well into adulthood.

LGBTQ Youth and Bullying*

While trying to deal with all the challenges of being a teenager, lesbian/gay/bisexual/transgender/queer teens additionally have to deal with harassment, threats, and violence directed at them on a daily basis. They hear anti-gay slurs such as "homo," "faggot," and "sissy" about twenty-six times a day, or once every fourteen minutes. Even more troubling, a study found that 31 percent of gay youth had been threatened or injured at school in the last year alone! Their mental health and education, not to mention their physical well-being, are at risk.

How is their mental health being affected?

- Gay and lesbian teens are at high risk because "their distress is a direct result of the hatred and prejudice that surround them," not because of their inherently gay or lesbian identity orientation.

- Gay, lesbian, and bisexual youth are two to three times more likely to attempt suicide than their heterosexual counterparts.

How is their education being affected?

- Gay teens in U.S. schools are often subjected to such intense bullying that they're unable to receive an adequate education. They're often embarrassed or ashamed of being targeted and may not report the abuse.

- LGBTQ students are more apt to skip school due to the fear, threats, and property vandalism directed at them. One survey revealed that 22 percent of gay respondents had skipped school in the past month because they felt unsafe there.

- Twenty-eight percent of gay students will drop out of school. This is more than three times the national average for heterosexual students.

- LGBTQ youth feel they have nowhere to turn. According to several surveys, four out of five gay and lesbian students say they don't know one supportive adult at school.

---

*LGBTQ Youth and Bullying is taken from the Web site of the National Mental Health Association at *www.nmha.org*. See their Web site for more information (accessed November 2006).

Bullying. The effective pastoral caregiver will be aware in general of the extreme pain that bullying causes, especially to LGBTQ youth. Here are some suggestions for handling bullying:

+ Be alert to any signs that might indicate bullying: physical wounds, fear of school, social isolation, and so on.

+ Work with public and private schools to have programs on respect for all, school safety, and anti-bullying.

+ Ask school personnel to have a discussion at an assembly or an after-school activity about gay prejudice.

+ Help start a Gay, Lesbian and Straight Education Network (GLSEN) chapter at your local high school. Youth whose schools had these kinds of groups were less likely to have reported feeling unsafe in their schools.

+ Arrange for a group like GLSEN to present bullying prevention activities and programs at your school.

+ Do encourage anyone who's being bullied to tell a teacher, counselor, coach, nurse, or his or her parents or guardians. If the bullying continues, or even if it doesn't, report it yourself.

Suicide. Peer pressure is what drives adolescents. Being different at a stage of development in which conformity is the rule adds insult to injury. LGBTQ youth are different in a way that most young people would name as the biggest — and possibly worst — way possible: they're queer. The tension that is built up in some young people becomes too much for them to cope with, and they resort to suicide or its attempt.

Gay youth are 2 to 3 times more likely to attempt suicide than other young people. They may compose up to 30 percent of completed youth suicides annually. The earlier youth are aware of their orientation and identify themselves as gay, the greater the conflicts they have.

Jay and Young found that 40 percent of gay males and 39 percent of lesbians surveyed had either attempted or seriously contemplated suicide. Bell and Weinberg similarly found that 35 percent of gay males and 38 percent of lesbians in their study had either seriously considered or attempted suicide. Homosexuals are far more likely to attempt suicide than are heterosexuals. A majority of these attempts

---

Recommended Film Resources
for Elementary and Middle School Students

*The Respect for All Project**

- *It's Elementary — Talking about Gay Issues in School* explores how teachers can include discussion about gay people in their classrooms with elementary and middle school students.

- *Let's Get Real* takes an honest look at the epidemic of name-calling and bullying among middle school youth, told entirely from a youth perspective.

- *That's a Family* breaks new ground in helping elementary-age children understand the many different shapes that families take today.

- *Straightlaced* features intimate interviews with teenagers about the pressure to conform to traditional gender roles. Students talk about the toll it takes to live up to gender role expectations.

---

*Respect for All is a program of Women's Educational Media. See the Web site at *www.womedia.org/* (accessed November 2006).

---

take place in their youth. Bell and Weinberg found that 25 percent of lesbians and 20 percent of gay men had actually attempted suicide. A majority of the suicide attempts by homosexuals took place at age twenty or younger with nearly one-third occurring before age seventeen.[34]

---

34. Article by Paul Gibson L.C.S.W., therapist and program consultant, San Francisco, California. Reprinted from "WeAreFamily" on the LAMBDA GLBT Community Services Web site: *www.lambda.org/youth_suicide.htm* (accessed November 2006). Also K. Jay and A. Young, *The Gay Report: Lesbians and Gay Men Speak Out about Their Sexual Experiences and Lifestyles* (New York: Summit, 1977); A. Bell and M. Weinberg, *Homosexualities: A Study of Diversity among Men and Women* (New York: Simon and Schuster, 1978). Some Christian groups have tried to debunk these statistics, claiming they are merely an attempt to foster the "homosexual agenda."

Although statistics in this area are understandably challenging to establish, the fact of a relatively high rate of suicide or attempted suicide by LGBTQ youth is well documented. A recent study from New Zealand indicates that young people of gay, lesbian, and bisexual orientation are at increased risk of mental health problems and suicide. Likely factors in this are homophobia and social discrimination.[35] What are the implications for pastoral care?

Again, the first challenge is to find LGBTQ youth. The best chance of finding them will be by becoming an open and welcoming congregation (see chapter 5), to be approachable by youth, to have some realistic connection with youth. (What children do not tell adults could fill many revealing volumes.)

Next, become aware of the possible signs of suicide:

+ Talking about suicide

+ Statements about hopelessness, helplessness, or worthlessness

+ Preoccupation with death

+ Suddenly appearing happier, calmer

+ Loss of interest in things one cares about

+ Visiting or calling people one cares about

+ Making arrangements; setting one's affairs in order

+ Giving things away[36]

If you hear comments like any of the following, take action:

+ Life isn't worth living.

+ My family would be better off without me.

+ Next time I'll take enough pills to do the job right.

---

35. Christchurch Health and Development Study has studied a group of youths for a quarter of a century beyond their youth. See their Web page at *www.chmeds.ac.nz/ research/chds/* (accessed November 2006). The study was reported in *365gay.com*, August 2, 2005. See also Wanda M. L. Lee, *An Introduction to Multicultural Counseling* (Philadelphia: Accelerated Development Group, 1999), 152–53.

36. Based on information on the Web site of Suicide Awareness Voices of Education (SAVE): *www.save.org/depressed/symptoms.html* (accessed November 2006).

- Take my (prized collection, valuables, etc.) — I don't need this stuff anymore.

- I won't be around to deal with that.

- You'll be sorry when I'm gone.

- I just can't deal with everything — life's too hard.

- Nobody understands me — nobody feels the way I do.

- There's nothing I can do to make it better.

- I'd be better off dead.

- I feel like there is no way out.[37]

What does taking action mean? Ask young people directly, in clear language, if their intention is to commit suicide or otherwise hurt themselves or if they have considered it. If they have, elicit a promise never to do that before talking to you in person. Get in touch with the family if practical and advisable. Get the youngster as quickly as feasible to professional help: a doctor (psychiatrist) or social worker/therapist competent with suicide risk — even, in extreme cases, an emergency room. Follow up soon and often with the professional. Keep your relationship with the young person active and check in often.

Mentors. An excellent goal of pastoral care for LGBTQ youth is to help find mentors for youth within the queer community. This is not as easy as it might sound. I have been part of two such efforts that ended unsuccessfully because of various complications out of our control. There are, however, successful LGBTQ mentoring agencies.[38]

For many, the mentoring process can be casual and local. The key tasks here are to choose mentors who are beyond reproach and totally committed to the process in the long term, and to establish a very proactive system of supervision. Big Brothers and Big Sisters arranges for gay and lesbian

37. Based on information of the Web site of Stop a Suicide Today: Screening for Mental Health, *www.stopasuicide.org/signs.html* (accessed November 2006).

38. For example, see the Web site of the Point Foundation: *www.thepointfoundation.org/index.html* (accessed November 2006); universities often have LGBTQ mentoring groups; examples include the University of Chicago and UCLA.

mentors and could be used in the process.[39] It does not discriminate on sexual orientation of either the youngsters or the Big Brothers/Big Sisters.

Online challenges. Lastly, with regard to LGBTQ youth, is there some way for the pastoral caregiver to have an effect on the use and abuse of the Internet? LGBTQ youth are especially vulnerable to the pitfalls of the Internet precisely because society denies them the normal outlets for peer social contact.

I believe pastoral service in this area is primarily by education: educating parents about the use and abuse of the Internet. Hold information sessions for the congregation's parents and find someone (a trained professional, not one of their kids) to show them the beauty and the beast that is the Internet: how to cope with *myspace.com* and other sites like it; the effective use of parental controls; the easy accessibility to very hardcore pornography; access to a wide array of violence and literally every perversion imaginable; and lastly, the real dangers of deception, entrapment, and worse that continue to happen through the unsupervised use of Internet chat-rooms by children and those who prey on them.

In addition, try exploring the Internet yourself, spending time on sites likely to be visited by kids. (Set your browser to *www.myspace.com* for example.) Then explore Internet sites with queer youth themselves. By acknowledging that responsible adults are aware of all that can happen online, it might give youngsters courage to seek the healthy and helpful and avoid the degrading and dangerous. Can you imagine surfing the Net with members of your congregational youth group? It is an activity that could offer fertile ground for moral teaching, spiritual insights, great conversation, and building trust.

Old Age

Loss. Loss is perhaps the most characteristic attribute of old age; it certainly is the most inevitable. The losses of old age, aside from the constant losses of bodily health and functioning, include the loss of friends and one's place in the community. The astute pastoral caregiver will acknowledge

---

39. The Big Brothers-Big Sisters Web site can be found at *www.bbbs.org* (accessed November 2006).

this and find ways to connect her or his elderly LGBTQ people with others, near or far.

The loss of presence in the world, in the community, in the form of invisibility, often returns to haunt in old age. Old gay men and old lesbians seem to fade into generic old age when, in fact, they remain just as "different" now as they ever were. The challenges for bisexual people also seem to increase with age: their peers will probably be less accepting than the youth-oriented culture they've grown used to; friends, partners, and understanding companions will be harder to find. Many transgendered people face not only the physical difficulties that come with aging, but ongoing social ignorance and specific difficulties in obtaining medical care and admittance to nursing facilities.

Especially for the LGBTQ elderly who live in a care facility or home, please consider the loss of privacy that such living conditions involve. In some institutions I have visited, there is literally no privacy whatsoever. Privacy is not always, or even generally, about sex or sexual expression; it is about feeling able to be who you are, with room for your conversations, with the people with whom you want to spend time, with your photographs, your memorabilia, all the things that represent your life. Being queer manifests itself in all of life's aspects and is expressed in one's ambience, just as it is for everyone.

In older LGBTQ people who were never out — or never fully out — watch for signs again of internalized homophobia. Watch too for what are expressed as regrets, and find ways to encourage conversation about them.

"I don't know why I never really acknowledged who I was; it seems so many young people today do it so easily. Why didn't I do that?" That's a paraphrase of a frustrated comment I heard from an infirm eighty-three-year-old man in a nursing home. He was a very successful businessman, white, married briefly, with no children. He was coming out for the first time, to me, his pastoral caregiver, after four or five visits. In spite of his age and infirmities, he was the live wire of the whole place, but his words carried deep regret. He felt that his popularity would die "if they knew." He needed to be reminded that coming out in the 1940s and 1950s was practically impossible in all but the most unusual circumstances, and he needed to have an ongoing conversation about all that that implied, then *and* now, at this moment of his life. He needed to be affirmed and engaged and acknowledged. Who among us doesn't — especially in old age?

Retirement from the working world is a challenge for many, LGBTQ people not excepted. As they go through the loss of their work or career, many of them feel a bit lost because they no longer fill a clear role and often feel that they have lost a meaningful purpose in life. Many can easily slip into invisibility and isolation. Are there recent LGBTQ retirees in your congregation? A pastoral call might bring great blessings.

From generativity to integration. As your elderly LGBTQ people move from the developmental tasks that serve generativity and avoid stagnation into the final stage of achieving integration and steering clear of despair,[40] they will appreciate your help in remembering and discovering meaning from all the moments of their lives. They will be especially grateful to remember what is deeply meaningful and find ways to continue or deepen that meaning.

The fifteen minutes you spend with an elderly LGBTQ person, simply providing them time and an interested listener for honest, unedited reminiscing, is indeed a rich blessing and far more effective pastoral ministry than it may appear.

It is from the community of the elderly that you might well be able to find the LGBTQ mentors mentioned earlier (under "LGBTQ Youth"). Can you see an expression of pastoral care in bringing together the generations? Who knows what graces might be born of this concurrence?

Dignity. The large majority of old people, those who have fought the good fight and kept the faith, have achieved a high degree of dignity. I believe that a good general rule for the pastoral caregiver working with the geriatric population is to always serve and enhance dignity.

You will find challenges to that dignity at every turn in the lives of the elderly. Ours is a culture that honors youth, not age. Three challenges to dignity that you might encounter with your LGBTQ elderly are sexual expression, keeping partners together, and frailty and death.

- *Sexual expression.* I have heard people in their eighties scoff at the idea of old people engaging in sex. I have heard people of the same age affirming that it is an important part of their lives. A percentage of elderly people have, want, and like a sexual life. Especially for people who live in care facilities or have mobility challenges, how can you

---

40. The last two (of eight) stages of human development of Erik Erikson are generativity vs. self-absorption, and integrity vs. despair.

facilitate desired intimacy? First of all, be aware of the issue; exercise prudence; then never hesitate to delicately inquire.

• *Keeping partners together.* Recall Pastor Leonard (chapter 2) and his intervention that facilitated the coming together of longtime lesbian partners. It is an immense loss of dignity to have someone like an administrator, a politician, or even a younger sibling or family member tell you that your relationship, often of a lifetime, will not be acknowledged, much less honored, by separating partners in old age against their will. Treating an elderly individual like an immature child is insulting. Anything you can do to facilitate elderly LGBTQ partners staying together will add stars to your crown.

• *Frailty and death.* What is unique about frailty, death, and dying for LGBTQ people? Probably nothing, really. I believe we all become very alike when faced with the last moments of life and the door to eternal life. The pastoral caregiver who accompanies the frail old and the dying will be effective simply by adding an LGBTQ sensitivity and awareness to the entire process of the relationship. In addition to pastoral skills required in dealing with anyone who is frail or dying, one might need this sensitivity especially in the following situations:

 – *Memento mori.* Learn to talk comfortably about death all during life, but especially toward the end of life. To talk about one's death in a healthy, honest way and to accept its inevitability are great gifts from a pastoral caregiver.[41]

 – The healing of old relationships, by getting in contact with people for the care receiver, if necessary.

 – Arranging for a pastoral visit (if it is to be done by someone other than you) if desired.

 – Watch for faith issues, past and present; look for resentment against the church as a block to peace; look for self-exclusion from salvation. I was called by the family to visit a frail and dying gay man at a veterans hospital. He said to me when I arrived, "I'm never going to

41. See Peggy Flynn, *The Caregiving Zone: A Unique Guide to Facing the Realities of Illness, Aging, Dying, and Death* (New York: iUniverse, Inc., 2006). See also Flynn's "The Good Death Institute" at *www.tgdi.org* for more information on how to help people face these issues in a healthy, spiritual way (accessed November 2006).

be saved. The church has excluded me from the very beginning of my life, so why concern yourself about me now?" He then threw a glass of water at me. It was a forceful reminder of the pain and anger he carried. Subsequent visits brought some little — but by no means full — reconciliation. It was too late.

– Facilitating access by family, with "family" understood in an LGBTQ way: partners, close friends, and companions.

"Ex-Gay" Ministry and the Question: "Is It a Choice?"

Especially for the pastoral caregiver who is new to this topic, here is some background information. "Ex-gay" ministry is an umbrella term covering programs that attempt to change a person's sexual orientation, through a combination of therapy and religious teaching, from gay or lesbian or bisexual to heterosexual. These are the three categories that "ex-gay" ministry seems to focus on, not transgender. Currently the vast majority of these programs are instituted and supported by Christian organizations. This kind of ministry is also referred to as reparative therapy or sexual conversion therapy.

"Ex-gay" ministry is a logical result of the beliefs about homosexuality by a particularly narrow brand of religion that is popular at present, especially in the United States, and to a lesser extent in Canada. This brand is often referred to as "the religious right" and "Christian fundamentalism," but in truth it can include the whole or a part of many religious bodies, from the Roman Catholic, to Orthodox Judaism, to the independent church on the corner. It holds that homosexuality is not only sinful, but a particular abomination in God's eyes; that it's a free choice by those who engage in this "sinful" "lifestyle"; and that it is their (the religionists') duty to vigorously defeat its acceptance by society.

"Is it a choice?" That is the basic question in the ongoing arguments of religionists on the topic of queer acceptability: do people freely at some point in their lives make a choice to be lesbian, gay, or bi, presumably over the other option of being straight? The vast majority of scientific people and an ever-increasing number of religious people are answering with a clear "no." When the same question is posed to straight people, "When did you decide to become straight?" often the truth hits home.

Evidence also mounts to confirm that there is a genetic and hormonal component involved in being homosexual. "Scientific studies of genetics, brain physiology, and hormones increasingly suggest that for many (if not most) gay and lesbian persons, sexual attraction is not a choice, but an inborn trait."[42] Plus, of course, there is the overwhelming testimony of the lived experience of people: This is the way we were born.

But old contentions die hard, and several widely published religious writers continue to cling to the prescientific religious teachings.[43] They do so, I surmise, because were they to acknowledge that being gay or lesbian (again, these are the two categories most targeted) is a normal variation that has long been identified in human sexuality (as well as in the animal kingdoms),[44] they would have to admit that there is nothing to cure, no addiction to conquer. They contend that being gay or lesbian is a mental illness and/or a moral failing, and thus is the way paved for "ex-gay" ministry.

The exuberance and devotion of the perpetrators of these programs may seem at first astounding. Why such emphasis on the issue of changing gay, lesbian, and bi people into straight people, even to the exclusion of many other pressing issues that might seem more urgent and appropriate for religion?

I believe the urgency comes from the realization that this issue has far-reaching implications for the question of who holds the ultimate authority: religion or science. When the dust settles on this disagreement, the balance of power will likely have shifted a bit. Perhaps no current topic better exemplifies the historically ongoing religion/science disagreements than the legitimacy of queer persons. Who gets to define the question: "spiritual" religion or "secular" science?

To this science-or-religion argument, add the basic disagreement about how the Scriptures are read and interpreted — literally or not — and you have the two bases of the broad and deep divisions among contemporary

---

42. Andrew Weaver et al., *Counseling on Sexual Issues: A Handbook for Pastors and Other Helping Professionals* (Cleveland: Pilgrim Press, 2006), 193; also Quazi Rahman and Glenn Wilson, *Born Gay: The Psychobiology of Sex Orientation* (Peter London: Peter Owen Publishers, 2005); also Alice Ogden Bellis and Terry Hufford, *Science, Scripture, and Homosexuality* (Cleveland: Pilgrim Press, 2002), 14.

43. For example: John F. Harvey's *The Truth about Homosexuality: The Cry of the Faithful* (San Francisco: St. Ignatius Press, 1996).

44. Robert H. Hopke, *Jung, Jungians and Homosexuality* (Boston: Shambhala, 1989), 57.

religions about LGBTQ people in general. The challenge is significant because the way many people read the Bible makes it virtually impossible for them to accept homosexuality as a normal variation of human sexuality; to do so for these people could easily render the whole of Scripture false, thus destroying their faith and often their entire worldview. Thus, for some, the real issue is their scriptural orientation.

However, the reality is that we have to live our lives now. Waiting for religion is not a realistic option. Are queer people to put their lives on hold? To grant authority to any polity to allow or disallow one's validity would be, I believe, deeply irresponsible, both in those who expect it and in those who might follow it.

If the organizations of religion were to acknowledge (as *some* Christian and Jewish ones clearly do) what the scientific world as well as human experience acknowledge — that being LGBTQ for the vast majority of people is an innate quality, not a freely made choice — then religion, as the poet says, would have to be reborn — simply by the power of the beauty of truth. One of the largest "ex-gay" ministries acknowledges, "If we define homosexuality as an identity, and inborn characteristic . . . there is no answer. . . . If, however, we call it . . . a 'struggle with sinful desires and behavior' [quotation marks mine] — then throughout Scripture we're given ways to handle it."[45] My response is, of course, that "there is no answer" because there is no problem, and we already have very healthy ways "to handle it."

Pastoral care. Pastoral care in this area is both individual and systemic. Individually, the pastoral caregiver can inform the care seeker who inquires about the topic of reparative therapy, of the truth and experience as it is available. By their own acknowledgment, reparative therapy is remarkably unsuccessful. Most programs admit that at most they change the individual's behavior for a while. "Changing one's sexual orientation is not simply a matter of changing one's sexual behavior. It would require altering one's emotional, romantic and sexual feelings and restructuring one's self-concept and social identity."[46]

---

45. Rev. John J. Schmid on the Love in Action Web site: *www.loveinaction.org/* (accessed November 2006).

46. American Psychological Association resolution on reparative therapy, August 14, 1997, cited in "Finally Free: How Love and Acceptance Saved Us from 'Ex-Gay'

Also, be aware that some "ex-gay" practitioners unfairly and inac-
curately portray all LGBTQ people as miserable, sad, and isolated or
licentious and wild-living.[47] The percentage of these types of persons is,
of course, the same for LGBTQ and non-LGBTQ.

It is essentially immoral to set oneself as judge and jury in condemning someone who commits no crime and does no harm (*especially* if that
someone considers neither their orientation nor behavior sinful) to a regi-
men of "therapy" that is based on contested and spurious assumptions and
contested and unproven beliefs.

Please understand and help your care seekers to understand that the
"potential risks of 'reparative therapy' are great, including depression,
anxiety and self-destructive behavior."[48] Add to those the frustration of
spending time and money, frequently a great deal of both, on a goal that
is all but unattainable: "Therapy directed specifically at changing sexual
orientation is contraindicated, since it can provoke guilt and anxiety while
having little or no potential for achieving changes in orientation."[49]

Ultimately I believe it is important to do all in your power as pastoral caregiver to dissuade your care seekers from submitting themselves
to reparative therapy or from becoming involved in any way with "ex-gay"
ministry. I hope the four fundamental reasons are clear: It is based on
essentially flawed assumptions about being queer; it is immoral and insulting; its "successes" are extremely rare and almost always partial and
temporary; and it is capable of doing, and regularly does, a great deal of
harm to people already subjected to too much.

Systemically, education is urgently important; our ministry here is to
teach. I believe the role of the pastoral caregiver is to help all who work
in opposition to the harmful attitude that it is wrong to be LGBTQ and
wrong to live out that God-given identity in natural and moral ways.

Ministries." Human Rights Campaign: *www.hrc.org/Content/ContentGroups/Publications1/*
FinallyFREE.pdf; also Bellis and Hufford, *Science, Scripture, and Homosexuality*, 41–45.

47. American Psychiatric Association position statement, December 1998.

48. Ibid.

49. Policy Statement: "Homosexuality and Adolescence," American Academy of Pedi-
atrics, 1993. Quoted on Jeff Ford's Web site, *www.jgford.homestead.com/* (click Reparative
Therapy, Just the Facts [of the APA]); (accessed November 2006). Ford is a former executive with Outpost, an "ex-gay" ministry. Also see Ariel Shidlo et al., *Sexual Conversion
Therapy: Clinical and Ethical Perspectives* (New York: Haworth Medical Press, 2001) for a
broad treatment of the issue of conversion therapy.

At the same time, it is equally important to create welcoming and affirming congregations into which to welcome LGBTQ people. To dissuade people from a welcoming and encouraging "ex-gay" program (which are often attractively packaged, subsidized, and slick) and to offer them nothing in its place is poor pastoral care at best, and morally irresponsible at worst.

Finally, as pastoral caregivers, I believe we must understand and accept people, and that we should not try to force them against their will — having done our best at affirming who they are, encouraging and welcoming them, and teaching wisdom. "People will inevitably make choices with which we deeply disagree and may even cause us great pain," says Joretta Marshall. She goes on, however, to speak of "finding a way to sit at the table with them in the midst of that pain and disagreement...."[50] If a gay man, for example, clearly and for whatever reasons, does not want to *be* who he *is* — the very expression speaks of disintegration — I believe we may not try to force a change in that intention, no matter how self-damaging and ill-conceived we believe it to be. Such an action would be going against the basic rights on which I am insisting. But we can stay at the table with them, keeping the pastoral care relationship open and welcoming.

However, the urgent question here is: What is the primary and ultimate source of the desire to rid oneself of being lesbian, gay, or bisexual? It would be hard to answer anything but "religion." So in a very real way, religion is providing an "answer" (reparative therapy) to a problem that religion itself has created. Religion is trying to repair something that religion has damaged, and continues to damage. Logic, charity, and justice demand that the damaging stop.

It's much more than sex.... In concluding this chapter on your ministry to LGBTQ people as they experience the tough times of life, I want to return to a fundamentally important idea that seems particularly difficult for non-LGBTQ people to understand: being LGBTQ involves much, much more than just the way we are sexual. It really involves all aspects of life: the way we relate to all people, the way we create our homes, the way we raise our children, the way we express our faith and

---

50. Joretta L. Marshall, "Caring When It Is Tough to Care," *www.religion-online.org/showarticle.asp?title=300* (accessed November 2006).

pray, the way we work and recreate, the way we walk and dress, the way we do business, the way we understand God, the way we talk and express our ideas, and so on and so on; in a word, it affects everything.

But this is true of everyone. One's sexuality, no matter what its orientation or identity, has an effect on all aspects of everyone's life. I believe this is challenging for non-LGBTQ people to understand *because* they are the majority. The influence of one's sexuality on all of life is, for the sexual majority, so innate, so intimate, so natural, so normal, and especially so generally accepted by everyone that they really don't have to think about it. For them it's just doing what comes naturally.

Of course, for LGBTQ people it's the same; it's also innate, intimate, normal, and doing what comes naturally.

I make this point here to encourage you, the pastoral caregiver, to contextualize all your dealings with your LGBTQ people, in good times and in bad, to see your LGBTQ people as just that: people — with all the ups and downs, foibles and graces, special needs and common traits of all the children of God in the human family.

Chapter 4

Coming Out

One day last summer, as I walked with my youngest son to the post office in our small New England town, we were approached by two Mormon missionaries. During the course of our conversation it became clear that these young men had assumed that I was married to a woman. This caused my twelve-year-old son to grin broadly. At that moment I realized that I needed to come out as a gay man to the missionaries not only for my own sake, but also because I wanted my son to see me come out. "You know, I'm gay," I offered, "and I have to level with you: I don't agree with the position of your church on homosexuality and queer people." Caught off guard, the missionaries took a few moments to collect their thoughts before launching into an earnest denunciation of homosexuality. I told them that neither I nor my son was interested in listening to their views on homosexuality, and I politely said good-bye. As we walked away from the young men I could sense, in the squeeze of my son's hand, that he was proud that I had come out to these strangers.

As a forty-five-year-old gay man who first came out of the closet in my early twenties, I face the decision daily about whether and to whom I come out. Rarely do I choose not to come out to others, and I am fortunate that, in my work at the Center for Lesbian and Gay Studies in Religion and Ministry, being an out gay person is an asset. As a white, middle-class, college-educated man who now belongs to a liberal religious denomination (Unitarian Universalist), I usually experience coming out as something positive. Although I can "pass" as straight if I want to, I rarely choose that option because I see coming out (and being out) as an important part of my queer identity and an important part of my religious identity. In my own life experience and in the experience of many other LGBTQ people I have met, coming out is a powerful affirmation of oneself as a loving, sexual person. It is also a bold witness to others of the value of living with honesty and integrity.

We devote an entire chapter to coming out because it is a pivotal and ongoing experience for most LGBTQ people. If you are a pastoral caregiver interested in establishing and nurturing a caring relationship based on faith with LGBTQ individuals, then you will want to understand what coming out is so that you can provide them with excellent pastoral care.

What Is Coming Out? Why Do People Come Out?

To come out of the closet is to identify oneself as lesbian, bisexual, transgender, gay, or queer. It is a two-step process that involves acknowledging this identity to oneself and then speaking it aloud to others.[1] For transgender persons, coming out entails embracing a gender identity that is at variance with prevailing cultural norms, and it is important to note that a transgender person may consider him/herself to be lesbian, queer, bisexual, and/or gay, or not.[2] Significantly, coming out is used to refer to the first time that one comes out to self and others as well as to the many subsequent experiences of coming out to others.

People come out of the closet because being honest with oneself and with others about one's sexual orientation and/or gender identity is necessary for a healthy emotional and spiritual life.

• **People come out to leave behind the closet and its many ills.** Rosita came out as queer at the age of fifteen because she didn't want to keep pretending that she was interested in dating boys. She *knew* that she liked girls and that she wanted to date girls. By coming out as queer, she was able to take a stand for herself and live more authentically.

---

1. The Human Rights Campaign provides excellent online resources on coming out. See, in particular, the *Resource Guide to Coming Out* as well as other resources designed for African Americans and Latinas/os: *www.hrc.org.*

2. Justin Tanis, *Transgendered: Theology, Ministry, and Communities of Faith* (Cleveland: Pilgrim Press, 2003), 18, defines transgender people as "those individuals who do not fit comfortably into society's traditional understandings of sex and gender." He also notes that "*transgender* is commonly used as a broad term to encompass a whole range of people who transgress the commonly understood definitions of gender all or part of the time." Transsexuals, transvestites, drag kings, drag queens, and "gender benders," therefore, can be seen as "subsets of the transgender" (19).

• **People come out to reject the lie that an LGBTQ identity is either a mental illness or a sinful condition.**[3] After several years of intensive psychotherapy designed to make him straight, Sanjay began to doubt that the therapy was accomplishing its goal. He also began to question for the first time in his life whether being homosexual was, in fact, evil. Discontinuing therapy, he sought out books that treated homosexuality as something healthy and good. He also met and socialized with other queer people, and, in time, he made a decision to come out to family and friends. His own experiences proved the lie of what he had been taught since childhood, namely, that being gay was a psychological disorder.

• **People come out to express pride and confidence in themselves as loving and lovable sexual persons.** Trevor came out as transgender because he needed to embrace the person whom he had always been inside. He now looks forward to exploring romantic relationships with other people who will know him for who he is. Coming out has opened up the possibility of building a loving relationship with another person. He feels that he is discovering a whole new dimension to his life.

Why Is Life in the Closet So Destructive?

The closet is a place of secrecy, fear, and shame for queer people. As pastoral theologian Larry Kent Graham writes, "Closets deny vitality; they choke creativity."[4] I know this to be true from my own experience: living in the closet prevented me in many ways from leading a productive and satisfying life. Rather than devoting my energies to the life-giving pursuits of rewarding work, meaningful relationships, and an authentic spiritual practice, I was deeply distracted by the secret that I felt I had to keep at all costs. My work life suffered, as did my relationships with other people; my prayer life was hobbled by my inability to be myself before God. In the

---

3. Many queer people remain unaware that the American Psychiatric Association (APA) removed homosexuality as a mental disorder from its *Diagnostic and Statistical Manual of Mental Disorders* (DSM-II) over thirty years ago (in 1973). Religious denominations such as the United Church of Christ, Reform Judaism, and Unitarian Universalism consider queer people as morally equivalent to straight people. None of these religious traditions teach that queer sexuality is sinful or disordered.

4. Larry Kent Graham, *Discovering Images of God: Narratives of Care among Lesbians and Gays* (Louisville: Westminster John Knox Press, 1997), 174.

words of Graham, queer people pay a dear price by seeking safety in the closet and denying their sexuality:

> If we hide our unique sexuality, our capacity to know and name the world truthfully is impaired, and our capacity to reflect God's image is diminished. Creativity is negated and love curtailed. Alienation dominates, oppression prevails, and life withers.[5]

People who live in the closet can suffer the following:

* Poor self-esteem
* Loneliness and isolation
* Eating disorders
* Alcohol and drug addictions
* Sexually compulsive behaviors
* Severe depression and thoughts of suicide
* An inability to build or maintain strong friendships and healthy romantic relationships

For some LGBTQ people of faith, a closeted life leads them to withdraw from their church or synagogue for fear of being discovered or because they feel that they have no place within a community of faith. Gina had been an active member of her parish youth group beginning in her freshman year of high school. Once she decided to come out of the closet as a lesbian, however, she began to withdraw from the group because she knew that homosexuality was forbidden by the Catholic Church. Rather than risk coming out to her friends in the youth group, Gina reluctantly left the group during her senior year in high school without telling anyone why. She deeply missed the companionship of her youth group friends and soon stopped attending church altogether.

Sadly, the shame of the closet causes some people to believe that they have been abandoned not only by other people but also by God.[6] Walter, a twenty-eight-year-old Mormon, realized that he was gay while serving

---

5. Ibid., 174.

6. For a pastoral discussion of the damage done by life in the closet for queer people, see Leanne M. Tigert, "Trouble behind the Door," *Open Hands* 12, no. 1 (Summer 1996): 8–9.

as a missionary in Europe. He understands clearly the choice that he has to make: either continue to hide his homosexuality, or come out and be excommunicated by his bishop and risk ostracization from his family. Up to now he has chosen a life in the closet, but he feels as if he is slowly but surely losing his battle against depression. He has begun to think that his life is not worth living.

How Do People Come Out?

People come out as adults, young people, or senior citizens; they also come out in a variety of life situations. For some individuals coming out is an experience of gradual understanding over a period of many years. Phyllis came out as a lesbian at the age of forty-five when, after many years of living with a man, she fell deeply in love with another woman. She wasn't surprised that she now identified as lesbian nor was she disappointed that she hadn't come out earlier: her long journey toward a lesbian identity felt completely natural to her.

People Come Out

- At various ages
- In a variety of life situations
- Internally and externally
- Sometimes with little or no sexual experience
- Continuously throughout life
- To family and friends
- At work, at synagogue, at church
- When they move to a new neighborhood
- To one person or to more than one person
- And experience acceptance
- And experience rejection
- By being "outed"

Other people come out after a moment of seemingly sudden recognition. Toby, a junior in college, reports that, "It was during one of the many times that I spent with my best friend since high school that I realized how much I loved him. I mean, the love was so intense that right then and there I knew that I was gay."

Some people come out during or shortly after their first relationship with a person of the same gender, while others come out after many years of loving persons of the same gender. One man comes out as gay while married to a woman. A woman comes out as bisexual only after she has come to know other bisexuals. Someone comes out as transgender after being inspired by the story of another transgender person. And, despite the stereotype of queer people as oversexed individuals, some LGBTQ people come out with very little, if any, sexual experience.

Coming out does not necessarily entail revealing one's queer identity to everyone. An individual, for instance, might come out only to a parent, a pastor, a counselor, or a friend. Some people choose to come out to several relatives at once or to a group of friends. Others find that an online community provides them with a safe and comfortable place to come out. Enrolling in school, beginning a new job, joining a faith community, and moving into a new neighborhood are some of the many situations that require an LGBTQ person to decide whether or not to come out to others.

As mentioned in chapter 1, some individuals are forced out of the closet by being outed, that is, having their queer identity revealed without their permission. Actors, politicians, and religious leaders are some of the most common targets of outing. Initially used as a means of defaming a person's character, outing began to be used in the late 1980s by AIDS activists and others in an effort to call attention to closeted politicians who had supported anti-gay legislation or who were viewed as enemies of LGBTQ communities. Whatever the circumstances, outing is frequently a damaging experience that can force a person back into the closet for a period of months or even years; it can also precipitate a personal crisis filled with anxiety and depression.

Coming Out Is an Unpredictable Rite of Passage

In contemporary American society, most LGBTQ people view coming out as an important rite of passage. For many, it is an event to be celebrated and shared with family and friends. In the 1980s hit song "I'm Coming Out," Diana Ross captures the spirit of such celebration when she sings "I'm coming out / I want the world to know / Got to let it show." Soon after its release this song rose to fifth place on the pop charts and was embraced by many queer people as a veritable anthem of gay liberation. No doubt the song became so popular within queer communities because its lyrics proclaimed what an ever-increasing number of women and men were doing in American society: coming out with pride and enthusiasm.

For most LGBTQ people, coming out can be an unpredictable rite of passage because many do not know what to expect from family, friends, and employers until they come out to them. Some people rejoice when they hear the news, while others disapprove of or even reject the person who has come out. Coming out is an experience that mixes joy with pain, certainty with uncertainty, and gain with loss. Consider the following coming-out stories:

- Dylan was sixteen years old when his parents kicked him out of the house because they discovered that he is gay. Finding no support at school, he dropped out and moved to another city where he is now homeless. He has had no contact with his parents since he left home, and he is increasingly depressed. Dylan doubts that he can survive much longer on his own.

- When Corliss and her lesbian partner Anne came out to their minister and to the members of their small Unitarian Universalist congregation, they were met with affirmation and acceptance. Within a few months they were married by the minister in the church's sanctuary, and they are more involved than ever before in the life of the congregation.

- Max admitted to his wife that he is gay, and they divorced within the year. In the divorce proceedings he was denied custody of his two children. While he is relieved that he is finally out of the closet, he is distraught and angry that he no longer lives with his children. He fears losing contact with them.

- After Amanda underwent reassignment surgery and completed her transition from male to female, she was fired from her job as a teacher. Her friends convinced her to contact the Lambda Legal Defense and

Education Fund, which filed suit on her behalf against the school district. While awaiting a court date she has found work teaching in a neighboring district.

- Abby is a young professional who decided to come out as bisexual to her family. Her parents greet the news with anger while her brother says that a person can't really be bisexual. Hopeful that her family will come to accept her sexual orientation, Abby commits herself to fostering a productive and respectful dialogue with them.

These stories indicate the range of responses that queer people encounter when they come out. While some high-school queer youth are fortunate to have a Gay-Straight Alliance or other queer support group in their schools, many young people, like Dylan, have no such resources on which to draw; some young people are even cast out of their homes. Many queer couples are refused welcome and inclusion in their synagogue or church community, but there are others, like Corliss and Anne, who find acceptance and support.

Increasingly, LGBTQ people who come out of the closet while in heterosexual marriages reach amicable solutions with their ex-spouses about child custody, but many judges still consider homosexuality, bisexuality, or a transgender identity to be sufficient grounds for denying custody. Like Amanda, many transgender people face employment discrimination when they come out because most states do not protect transgender people from being fired. The good news is that organizations like Lambda Legal help fight discrimination against LGBTQ people in the workplace.

Coming out for many bisexuals reveals deep-rooted prejudices (sometimes even within queer communities) about the legitimacy of a bisexual identity. As Abby discovered in her brother's comments, some people believe that bisexuals are individuals who have not made up their mind about whether they are queer or straight. Bisexuals can face not only rejection from others when they come out, but also denial that bisexuality is a genuine sexual identity.

Coming Out Is a Graced Opportunity for Pastoral Care

Family, friends, work colleagues, and members of one's faith community can provide valuable support for a person who is coming out. In fact, loving and lasting support from others is the single most important ingredient in coming out successfully. LGBTQ friends who have come out themselves are an added blessing because they can demonstrate through personal experience that life outside of the closet is good.

For LGBTQ people of faith, a pastoral care relationship can provide an excellent context in which to explore coming out. This is because a pastoral care relationship offers a unique environment in which a person of faith can connect more deeply with self, form stronger relationships with others, and build a more honest relationship with God. In the remaining pages of this chapter we look at some specific ways in which you, the pastoral caregiver, can provide care to a person in the various stages of coming out.

Pastoral care and the stages of coming out. Effective pastoral caregiving with an individual in the process of coming out as queer requires the following basic pastoral skills:

- Deep sensitivity

- Active listening skills

- An understanding of the most common aspects of the coming-out process

- Openness to learning about LGBTQ sexualities and queer identities

- The ability to speak comfortably and knowledgeably about issues relating to faith and sexuality

- An awareness of the deep alienation that many LGBTQ people feel from churches, synagogues, and other communities of faith

- A willingness to recommend appropriate resources and support systems

Coming out is certainly a life-changing experience for most LGBTQ people, and it can also be transforming for you, the caregiver, as you work with a person coming out. You may find, for instance, that some of your preconceptions or misperceptions about LGBTQ people and queer sexuality need to be modified or discarded altogether. Your faith might be challenged as you come to appreciate more fully the deep-seated homophobia, heterosexism, and transphobia that exist in our culture and in many religious traditions. Your appreciation for the strength and resilience of the human spirit in the face of adversity may also grow as you journey with an LGBTQ person who comes out in the face of considerable odds.

The Five Stages of Coming Out

Eli Coleman, professor and director of the Program in Human Sexuality at the University of Minnesota, offers a flexible "Five-Stage Model of Coming Out" that is particularly useful for pastoral caregivers working with LGBTQ people:[7]

The Five Stages of Coming Out

1. Pre–Coming Out
2. Coming Out
3. Exploration
4. First Relationships
5. Integration

Coleman's model helps caregivers understand that many LGBTQ people experience coming out in similar ways and that coming out is a lifelong process of healthy identity development. Based on the psychologist Erik Erikson's view that a person must meet the challenges of one developmental stage before moving on to the next, Coleman's model describes coming out as a process that begins in the closet and culminates, ideally, in an integrated way of living. In each of these five stages, therefore, an individual has important developmental tasks to undertake and significant issues to resolve before addressing the tasks and issues of the next stage.

These stages should not be used as an inflexible gauge for assessing the mental health or psychological maturity of a person because many people

---

7. Eli Coleman, "Developmental Stages of the Coming Out Process," in *A Guide to Psychotherapy with Gay and Lesbian Clients*, ed. John C. Gonsiorek (New York: Harrington Park Press, 1985), 31–43. I make extensive use of Coleman's article in this chapter, and I apply his five-stage model to include bisexual, transgender, and queer people.

may not fit neatly into this five-stage model. Nor does everyone move through these stages in the given order since there is great variation in how people express their queer identities. Some individuals move between these stages as the changing situations of life demand and then return at times to an earlier stage to work on particular issues. In addition, a person might live, at least for a period of time, in more than one stage at once. Finally, the model does not presume that everyone reaches the last stage of integration.

1. Pre–Coming Out

The developmental task for an individual during this first stage is to face and resolve the internal crisis brought about by the realization that one is different from others because of one's sexual desires or gender identity. Resolution of this internal conflict, according to Coleman, can happen in one of three ways:

1. An individual may hide her sexual feelings (that is, stay in the closet).

2. An individual may attempt suicide (and perhaps succeed).

3. An individual will achieve a healthy resolution to this crisis of difference by acknowledging his same-sex feelings or gender identity.

We live in a heterosexist world. Among other things, this statement means that all of us are taught from an early age that everyone is, or should be, heterosexual and that everyone must subscribe to the gender norms as currently constructed in our society. Growing up LGBTQ in a heterosexist world can be not only hazardous to one's self-esteem, but also dangerous to one's psychological and spiritual health and well-being.

Psychologists tell us that sexual orientation and gender identity are fixed at very young ages for most people.[8] Once LGBTQ individuals realize, however unclearly or subconsciously, that their sexual orientation or gender identity is different from the norm, many spend considerable amounts of energy working to hide their differences from others. Trying to hide

---

8. Current estimates of the average age at which a person identifies as LGBTQ in our culture vary, but many individuals come to see themselves as queer sometime during their teenage years or in their early twenties. See Dustin Tamashiro, "Coming Out," in *glbtq: An Encyclopedia of Gay, Lesbian, Bisexual, Transgender, and Queer Culture,* ed. Claude J. Summers. *www.glbtq.com/social-sciences/coming_out_ssh.html* (accessed October 3, 2006).

one's queerness in a straight world leads many LGBTQ children to suffer persistent low self-esteem and feelings of intense loneliness. In fact, long before children are able to identify themselves as LGBTQ, this sense of being different from others may lead to a wide range of negative coping mechanisms. Some people become intensely shy and withdrawn; others become unhealthy perfectionists in an attempt to compensate for the confusion and shame that they feel about being different; still others live with a hidden, but very real, despair that their place in their families, schools, and religious communities would be jeopardized if they acknowledged their queerness to others.

> Rachel is a twenty-year-old woman who has recently shared with her rabbi, David, a secret that she has told nobody else: she fantasizes about having sex with another woman. Over the course of several meetings with her, David learns that Rachel believes that homosexuals are "dirty and perverted" people who should learn how to suppress their sexual desires if they wish to live holy lives. She tells the rabbi that she has come to him for help in getting rid of these fantasies because she is afraid that she might soon act on them.

Rachel is clearly dealing with internalized homophobia, which can be especially damaging for LGBTQ individuals because it often prevents them from accepting in a healthy way their sexual desires or gender identity. If Rachel is ever to embrace her lesbian identity and come out of the closet, she will need to decide whether or not she can accept her differences as something good and holy.

What should you do if, like Rachel's rabbi, you meet an individual who is unable to come out because she is dealing with internalized homophobia? Perhaps the most important thing to remember is that people need to claim for themselves and on their own timeline a queer identity if that is who they feel that they are. It is never the job of a pastoral caregiver (or anyone else, for that matter) to drag a person out of the closet; people have the right to decide for themselves how they will live their lives, and whether, to whom, when, and how they will disclose personal information about themselves. If a care receiver is unable or unwilling to embrace an LGBTQ identity (either temporarily or for the long term), then you, as caregiver, must respect this choice. Some people, for instance, stay in the closet because they fear that coming out will mean rejection from family or friends, discrimination in employment or housing, or ostracization from their synagogue or church community.

Since Rabbi David believes that embracing one's homosexuality or transgender identity is a good and life-giving choice, he lets Rachel know this, so that — if and when she is ready to come out — he can be an affirming resource and reliable support for her. In fact, he realizes that she has come to him because she is struggling with the decision of whether or not to embrace her lesbianism. In talking with him about her desires, she may be signaling a readiness to reevaluate her internalized homophobia.

Many individuals on the threshold of coming out seek out a caregiver who seems supportive of LGBTQ people. Such individuals have often also begun, however tentatively, to dismantle their internalized homophobia and take the first steps in coming out.

After a few weeks of attending a new church, Damon heard the pastor, Rev. Linette, preach a rousing sermon of welcome for queer people. Knowing that she read the gospel as a text of liberation and affirmation for LGBTQ people, he felt that he had at last found someone with whom he could speak about coming out as a gay man. In their pastoral care meetings Damon was in good hands with this minister. Rev. Linette had worked before with queer people, and she understood how one's Christian faith could be a powerful tool in overcoming internalized homophobia and external oppression.

Like Pastor Linette, you can help a person to experience coming out as something positive and life-giving. Indeed, as a pastoral caregiver you may be an important authority figure whose assistance to a person coming out can be a valuable sign of God's caring love. Over time, a positive experience of pastoral care can contribute significantly to a process of healing for a person who has found hurt and alienation in the closet.

2. Coming Out

Two developmental tasks need to be accomplished by a person at this stage of coming out:

1. Acknowledging one's homosexual feelings or transgender identity

2. Telling others that one is LGBT or Q

Internal acknowledgment does not necessarily mean that a person has it all figured out with regard to being queer, because such understanding comes only with self-reflection and lived experience. It may take time, as well, for individuals to label themselves as LGBT or Q after internally acknowledging same-sex desire or transgender identity. Similarly, the move from internal acknowledgment to public disclosure of a queer identity is not always immediate; some people take months while others may take years.

As a pastoral caregiver you will want to convey to the care receiver your conviction that an LGBTQ identity is wholesome and good and that coming out of the closet is the best way for queer people to live with integrity. By affirming the care receiver's sexuality or gender identity you make clear that she has your support as she embraces more fully her queer identity. Such affirmation also demonstrates that you are a valuable and affirming ally in her coming-out process.

As with any pastoral care relationship, establishing a comfortable rapport with a care receiver is an important first step. By focusing early discussions on how the care receiver has come to an awareness of homosexual desire or LGBTQ identity and why he has sought out pastoral care, you can come to know the care receiver and understand his unique story. During the first or second meeting you will also want to decide if you feel competent and comfortable working with the person who has requested pastoral care. If not, you should refer the care receiver to another professional who might be a better fit.

Three skills are particularly useful for the caregiver working with a person at the second stage of coming out:

- Attentive listening

- A supportive presence

- A knowledge of available support networks

Through attentive listening, you provide the care receiver with a much-needed sounding board to explore sexual desire and gender identity; skillful listening on your part can also provide a comfortable context for the care receiver to speak aloud the hopes and fears that she has about coming out.

You can demonstrate a supportive presence by celebrating with the care receiver when coming out to others is a positive experience and by offering support and reassurance when coming out proves to be negative. One important goal of pastoral care with an individual is to help her keep in mind the positive aspects of coming out, such as

- The potential for experiencing a healthier psychological and spiritual life
- The promise of forming loving relationships with others
- The joys of living more honestly and openly with self, others, and God

Frank has recently entered into a pastoral care relationship with his parish priest, Father Andrew. At forty-five years of age Frank has decided to come out as gay to his family, but he does not agree with his friends who say that, in order to be out of the closet, he must come out to his colleagues at work.

The priest in this pastoral situation wisely recommends to Frank that he not come out at work until he is ready to do so. He also suggests to Frank that a person can be out of the closet even if he chooses not to tell everyone, including those whom he considers to be good friends. Few people are either completely in or out of the closet. For a variety of good reasons, many individuals choose to come out to some people and not to others. As a caregiver you need to keep in mind that coming out is a personal decision that is shaped by the unique circumstances of an individual's life, and you always need to respect a person's decision not to come out to certain individuals or in certain contexts.

Sometimes a person is forced out of the closet (or outed) by others. In such cases you will first want to explore with a care receiver her understandable feelings of shock, anger, and betrayal. In time she will need to decide how and if she will embrace a public identity as a queer person.

Coming out is easier for most people if they can avail themselves of support networks. Your obligation, as a caregiver, is to have current information on such networks. Local LGBTQ community centers, for example, frequently sponsor support groups for individuals of all ages who are coming out. High-school and college-aged youth should be encouraged to avail themselves of any school-based services available in the form of a Gay-Straight Alliance or other LGBTQ-supportive clubs on campus. The

---

Support Networks for Coming Out

- Local religious congregations that are welcoming and affirming of LGBTQ people
- Local LGBTQ community centers
- Denominational LGBTQ caucuses
- Gay-Straight Alliances
- Queer social clubs
- The Human Rights Campaign Coming Out Project
- PFLAG
- Out & Equal in the Workplace
- "Coming Out Stories" archive on the LOGO TV Network
- Online chat groups and e-mail discussion lists for LGBTQ people of faith

---

Human Rights Campaign (HRC) and PFLAG (Parents, Families & Friends of Lesbians & Gays) have excellent online resources for coming out; local PFLAG chapters have long provided support groups for LGBTQ people and their families; and the International Federation of Black Gay Prides (IFBGP) and the National Black Justice Coalition (NBJC) have teamed up on a program to encourage black LGBTQ people to come out. Out & Equal Workplace Advocates offers support resources for individuals coming out at work, and for people of faith, LGBTQ denominational caucuses and local congregations that are welcoming and affirming of queer people can offer valuable support.[9]

An individual's first experiences of coming out to others are particularly critical because queer people have much at stake when they disclose their queer identity. As Coleman points out, if a person's first experiences of coming out are positive, then they can provide an important confirmation of the decision to come out. They can also offer a valuable boost to one's self-confidence and become a solid foundation for coming out

---

9. See the list of resources for additional resources.

to others. Negative experiences, on the other hand, can shake a person's self-confidence and make him or her less certain about coming out to others in the future.[10]

While many people have a good idea about who will react positively or negatively to their coming out, nobody knows with certainty. The pastoral care relationship offers an excellent opportunity for you to talk with the care receiver about the potential risk factors involved in coming out to various individuals. For example, a person might realize that she is not yet ready to come out to others in her family because she is quite certain that they will react negatively to the news that she is bisexual. This same individual, however, may decide to come out to her closest friends because she feels that they will react positively and support her.

Role-playing with the care receiver can allow him to practice coming out to others and, in the process, consider some important issues, such as:

- Has the care receiver thought about where and when to come out to his family?

- How would the care receiver handle rejection from her parents? What would she say or do? Where would she go for support?

- Does the care receiver feel shame about his queer identity, and, if so, how might such shame influence the experience of coming out to others?

- What are the pros and cons of coming out to one friend versus to a group of friends?

- Would it be a good idea for the care receiver to give her family and friends a book on transgenderism or on being gay or bi when she comes out?

- Are there antidiscrimination policies in place where the individual works so that he cannot be fired for coming out?

- How might the care receiver come out in church or synagogue?

Coming out to family can be an especially challenging experience. The revelation that a child, sibling, spouse, or parent is queer can be met with everything from shock and disbelief to anger and guilt. "Why didn't you

---

10. See Coleman, "Developmental Stages," 34–35.

tell us before?" or "Did we do to something wrong that made you gay?" are two common responses. Emma, a woman in her early fifties, describes coming out to her family in this way:

> I was well into my thirties when I came out to my parents and sisters as a lesbian, and I was surprised by how badly they handled it. My mom was angry and said that I was just confused; my dad begged me not to tell any family friends. My older sister really freaked out and said that I would go to hell if I didn't change. She wanted to help me find an attractive guy who would turn me straight! It was my younger sister, thankfully, who helped all of us deal positively with my coming out. She said that she was not surprised by my news, and she said that she didn't want to lose contact with me. Over the next several months she and I worked hard to keep the lines of communication open among all of us and, in time, my parents and older sister joined my younger sister in accepting me as a lesbian.

While there are families who react positively when a relative comes out, more typical is the response that Emma received from her family: anger, denial, and even rejection. It is often said that when a person comes out to family, family members go into the closet in order to avoid admitting to themselves and to others that they have a child, parent, spouse, or sibling who is queer. For many people, these negative emotions are conquered in time by love and acceptance once they come to know and accept their relative as LGBT or Q. Other individuals, however, face long-term opposition from family members who seem unable to accept their queer identities.

You can be especially helpful to care receivers by acquainting them with resources designed for families struggling to accept a relative who is LGBT or Q. Be sure to have on hand contact information for your local PFLAG chapter (which will have information on support groups for families of queer people) as well as a list of other resources.[11]

3. Exploration

Once individuals have begun the lifelong process of coming out to others, they enter a stage of exploration in which they learn how to interact

---

11. You can find a local PFLAG chapter online at *www.pflag.org*.

socially and sexually as a queer person with other queer people. For many individuals this stage is similar to adolescence because it gives them an opportunity to explore their sexuality and gender identity in ways that they were unable to do during their teenage years when they were either unaware of their queer identity or they lived in the closet.[12]

Coleman lists three developmental tasks for people at this stage of coming out: developing good interpersonal skills, developing a sense of personal attractiveness and sexual competence, and recognizing that one's self-esteem is not based upon sexual conquests. They are helpful guideposts for you in your work as caregiver with individuals at this stage.

Developing good interpersonal skills

A few months after coming out successfully to her family and to her (straight) friends, Donna couldn't understand why she was unable to connect with other lesbians. "What is wrong with me?" she wondered. It was awkward for her to hang out at a neighborhood bar frequented by other middle-aged lesbians because she didn't know how to strike up conversation. She felt as if she didn't fit in with the other lesbians there at all. Donna was beginning to think that her life out of the closet might be as lonely as her life in the closet.

If Donna decides to seek out pastoral care, her caregiver would do well to work with her on improving her interpersonal skills. For instance, it may be helpful for Donna to call to mind those unique qualities that she brings to a relationship and to list those qualities that she is looking for in a friend or a lover. Her caregiver might also urge her to consider a variety of venues for meeting other lesbians: frequenting a local LGBTQ community center or volunteering for a local queer organization might be more comfortable settings than a bar. Joining a group of other newly out queer people might be another way in which she can learn how to become more at ease in queer social situations. She might find that an online dating service is a good way to meet suitable women to date. If she

---

12. According to Coleman, "Developmental Stages," 35, the specific developmental challenge of this stage is to "interact with others who are open and honest about their sexuality [which, in turn] furthers the development of a positive self-image."

is a person of faith, Donna might try attending a welcoming congregation that provides social events and other programming for LGBTQ people.

Since our society attempts to socialize everyone as a heterosexual person, some people, like Donna, may need to sharpen their interpersonal skills in order to relate more authentically to others who are queer. The good news is that such skills can be learned and, typically, the more comfortable a person is with her own queer identity, the easier it is for her to develop these skills.

Developing a sense of personal attractiveness and sexual competence

Noah, a thirty-year-old gay man who has been in pastoral care with Andrea for several weeks, has recently come out of the closet. He has not been able to find suitable dating partners, however, because he believes that he is not handsome enough. He also worries increasingly that his lack of sexual experience will be a hindrance when and if he does find someone to date. Maybe, he says, he is not meant to find a boyfriend.

Like many gay men, Noah did not date other boys as an adolescent; therefore, he never developed a strong sense of his own personal attractiveness as a gay person. Now that he is out of the closet, he is finding it difficult to enter the dating scene. His caregiver, Andrea, believes that Noah's doubts about his attractiveness, which have contributed to his overall low self-esteem, need to be dealt with if he is ever to have successful dating experiences and, eventually, form healthy romantic relationships. She and Noah talk about how he might improve his self-image, and he has begun to understand that a positive self-image is a necessary first step in finding suitable dating partners.

Growing up in a heterosexist culture teaches many LGBTQ people to feel shame for their sexual desires, their unconventional gender identity, or their physical appearance. For some transgender individuals, feelings of insecurity about their unique bodies may erode their self-confidence and they may wonder if others will find them attractive or "normal enough."[13] Most LGBTQ people devote considerable energy while young to hiding those aspects of themselves that might give them away as queer, and even after they come out, they can still find it difficult to appreciate, much less

---

13. I am indebted to Justin Tanis for this observation.

enjoy, what makes them attractive to others. Like Noah, many individuals need to discover and appreciate their own personal attractiveness before they are able to form healthy romantic relationships with others.

Noah's lack of sexual experience highlights three important skills required of pastoral caregivers who work with people coming out: (1) the ability to speak with genuine ease about sexuality in general and queer sexuality in particular, (2) the ability to recommend good resources on queer sexuality, and (3) the ability to put a care receiver in touch with local LGBTQ support organizations. Since our schools and congregations rarely, if ever, treat homosexuality and transgender issues positively in their sex education programs, many LGBTQ people need positive and up-to-date information on queer sexuality. If you, as a caregiver, are able to speak comfortably and knowledgeably about sex, then you can be an especially valuable resource for a care receiver in the process of coming out.

Recognizing that one's self-esteem is not based upon sexual conquests

Tory, a queer man in his early twenties, has been out of the closet for almost two years. During that time he has enjoyed an active sex life. Recently, however, he has begun to feel an inner emptiness in connection with some of his sexual relationships. Tory asks Stuart, a longtime confidant and youth minister at his church, if they can meet to talk.

Tory and Stuart decide to enter into a formal pastoral care relationship and explore what it means to live and love responsibly as a sexually active adult. They begin by discussing how Tory might draw upon his religious beliefs to construct a sexual ethic that affirms his queer identity and helps him to live out his values in his sexual relationships. This values-clarification work proves to be invaluable for Tory, helping him to realize that he has sometimes engaged in sex with others primarily as a way to bolster his own ego.

Many queer people enter into intense and adolescent-like periods of sexual activity after they come out. This is not surprising since most closeted queer people were never afforded the opportunity during their teenage years to explore openly their sexuality. Making up for the lost years of adolescence, which is what Tory has attempted to do, can be a healthy and productive experience for queer people who may be able to repair much of the damage done by having suppressed their sexual desire and avoided healthy youthful sexual experimentation. Indeed, several psychological researchers have concluded that homosexuals (and I would add all queer people) "may benefit from permission to explore and experiment with their sexual identity."[14] However, some individuals, in their attempt to make up for lost time in the area of sexual exploration, may lose sight of ethical considerations with regard to sexual activity.

The pastoral care relationship can be an excellent context for an individual to explore the ethical dimensions of sexual exploration after coming out. As caregiver you can talk with your care receiver and help him to gain a clearer understanding of his personal values with regard to sex and respectful interpersonal relationships. Such discussions can also help an individual to integrate more maturely his sexual behavior with his moral convictions and religious beliefs. The following questions are some possible "discussion starters" for you and your care receiver:

- What defines ethical and meaningful sexual activity with another person?

- Is it OK to be in sexual relationship with more than one person at a time?

- Are anonymous sexual encounters ethical?

- Is sexual activity OK within a relationship that is not loving?

- Is sexual activity OK within a relationship that is not long-lasting?

- How can I work to make my sex life reflect my personal values and beliefs?

You will certainly need to challenge a care receiver if you learn of sexual behaviors that are compulsive or health-threatening; abusive sexual behaviors should also be addressed immediately and named as serious obstacles to healthy psychosexual development and interpersonal relationships. If necessary, you will want to refer the care receiver at once to a professional who can help her conquer compulsive behaviors and/or put an end to abusive relationships.

For some LGBTQ people, substance abuse (discussed more thoroughly in chapter 3) can interfere seriously with a successful resolution to the

---

14. Coleman, "Developmental Stages," 37.

development tasks of the exploration stage of coming out. This is because some individuals misuse alcohol and other drugs in an attempt to anesthetize the emotional pain that can accompany the challenges of learning how to relate to other people as an out queer person. Every pastoral caregiver, of course, should be well versed in detecting signs of substance abuse; in addition, you will want to have on hand information on support groups for LGBTQ individuals dealing with such abuse.[15]

4. First Relationships

Coming out of the closet is an inherently relational process because it means that the out person is now free to interact with other people (queer and nonqueer alike) with greater honesty and integrity than before. Freed from the shame and fear that typify life in the closet, a person now faces the exciting challenge of building relationships that can enhance life in previously unimaginable ways.

For most people, romantic relationships are a wonderfully worthwhile and necessary aspect of life. Part of the insidious damage done to closeted LGBTQ people, however, is that it leaves many of them questioning their ability to sustain romantic relationships. In a culture that often hides, trivializes, or denigrates queer romantic relationships, a person can come out of the closet with precious little self-confidence about finding and sustaining a healthy relationship.

> After a year of living with her partner Alice, Elena has sought advice from her minister because she worries that her relationship is floundering. "We don't seem to be as much in love as we once were," she reports. "Is this normal? Does it mean that we're not going to survive as a couple?"

The developmental task for the fourth stage of coming out is learning how to function maturely in one's first romantic relationship with another queer person in our heteronormative society. Whereas sexual and social experimentation was the development task of the third stage, the individual in this stage seeks to develop intimate relationships that are

---

15. See chapter 3 for discussions of addictions, drugs, and sex, and same-gender domestic violence.

longer-term and demand more significant commitment. Of course, individuals at this fourth stage may have previously enjoyed enduring romantic relationships with other queer people, or they may be currently involved in a relationship that began in an earlier stage of the coming out process. The defining emphasis of a relationship at this stage of coming out, however, is on building and sustaining one's first romantic relationship as an out person.

The pastoral care setting can be an especially productive and supportive environment for the care receiver to reflect on a first relationship. Elena and her minister, for instance, have chosen to explore Elena's goals for her relationship with Alice and to help her normalize the strains that they are experiencing after their first year of living together. As a caregiver you might consider some of the following questions when working with an LGBTQ person who is struggling with a first relationship:

* What expectations do you and your partner have for the relationship? Have you shared them with each other? Are these expectations realistic?

* Do you talk openly with each other about the challenges you face in your relationship?

* How do you resolve conflict in your relationship?

* Which aspects of your relationship are healthy, and which need to be improved?

By discussing some of the common pitfalls of first relationships you can help the care receiver to put into perspective the challenges of his own relationship. For example, Coleman lists "intensity, possessiveness, and [a] lack of trust" as typical strains in most first relationships.[16] In a culture that so often equates "first love" with "perfect love," you may need to remind a care receiver that such challenges are normal for any relationship, that they are opportunities for growth, and that they are not necessarily harbingers of the relationship's demise.

You should also be aware of the unique challenges that LGBTQ people face in their first relationships. Perhaps most significant of these is the general lack of social, religious, legal, and familial supports for queer people

---

16. Coleman, "Developmental Stages," 38.

in relationships. LGBTQ youth, in particular, are rarely supported in their first relationships with one another, and most of them grow up with few, if any, role models of successful queer relationships. In addition, the fact that we live in a country that criticizes LGBTQ people on the one hand for their supposed inability to build committed relationships and yet refuses to let them enter into civil marriage on the other hand can serve as an unsettling but potent reminder that queer relationships are not only devalued but attacked outright in our culture.

> Tyrone and Jacob have been together for two years, and theirs is the first serious relationship for each of them. Jacob worries that their relationship is in trouble because Tyrone still seems uncomfortable when they are out together in public and he has not yet introduced Jacob to his family or to his work colleagues. "Is he ashamed of our relationship?" Jacob wonders.

For some individuals, being in a first relationship with another queer person means adjusting to a higher level of public visibility and, therefore, embracing a greater degree of outness than when one was single. This may be uncomfortable for some and strain the relationship, as is the case with Tyrone and Jacob. Not coming out to family members and friends can pose a serious challenge for many LGBTQ people in their first relationships because it can lead to feelings of isolation, especially when times get difficult.

You may find as a caregiver that individuals need to work through a variety of internalized negative stereotypes about queer relationships that can seriously undermine or even jeopardize their relationships. A few of the more common misperceptions and stereotypes include the following:

- The only genuine relationships are those that imitate straight relationships.
- Gay male relationships are inherently unstable and short-lived.
- A relationship between two people will end when one of them makes a gender transition.
- Bisexuals are incapable of making lasting commitments.
- Long-lasting lesbian relationships eventually become sexless.
- LGBTQ people are promiscuous.

Finally, be open to exploring other issues that may arise for individuals in their first relationships, especially those that involve the often unspoken expectations that all individuals bring into a relationship. For instance, you may be called on to discuss with a care receiver the normal ebb and flow of sexual desire and the challenge that this may pose to a romantic relationship. Issues relating to sexual monogamy; living together; disparity of income; class, racial, and/or ethnic differences; and deciding whether and when to meet the family members or friends of one's partner are other issues that many queer people deal with in their first relationships. Keep in mind that lessons learned in a first relationship can be valuable for an individual in any future relationships.

5. *Integration*

In this final stage individuals strive to "incorporate their public and private identities into one self."[17] Having acknowledged queer desire and shared with others the truth of their LGBTQ identity (stage 2), individuals have come to know themselves more deeply through sexual and social exploration (stage 3). They have also begun to learn how to love others in romantic relationship (stage 4). In this fifth stage of coming out, which usually takes several years to reach after an individual first becomes aware of same-sex desire or begins to question his or her gender identity, the LGBTQ person is able to draw upon a mature confidence born of life experience. This final stage of integration is obviously not static; rather, it encompasses the rest of a person's life with all of its challenges, especially those related to interpersonal relationships and loss. Coleman paraphrases social science researcher J. Grace to describe this final stage as

> open-ended, [and] an ongoing process of development that will last for the rest of the person's life. New feelings about self will continue to emerge, new labels and concepts will be discovered, new social networks will be identified and explored, and new relationships and intimacies will be enjoyed.

As a caregiver working with persons engaged in the ongoing work of integration, you may be called upon to offer them support and encouragement on ways to deal with a wide variety of issues relating to family,

---

17. Coleman, "Developmental Stages," 39.

interpersonal relationships, career, illness, aging, and the death of loved ones. You will need to continue to educate yourself, of course, about the circumstances of queer people's lives since they are different in many ways from the lives of nonqueer individuals.

Coming Out as a Spiritual Journey

Coming out of the closet is "deliverance from oppressive structures to liberating values, from self-hatred to communal love and support. It is a sacred journey because it involves courage and steadfast faith in God."[18] These words of Antonio Salas remind us that coming out can be a marvelous experience of liberation as well as a lifelong journey requiring stamina and fortitude. Coming out is similar in many ways to the journeys from oppression to freedom that countless women and men of faith have taken throughout history. It is also an ongoing experience with many ups and downs along the way. Clearly, coming out is not for the faint of heart.

If you are not queer, I invite you to take just a moment — right now — to imagine what it might be like to come out. Keep in mind that you have grown up in a culture that presumes that you are straight. At some point in your life you come to identify queer desire or an LGBTQ identity within yourself, but you retreat, out of fear, to the safety of the closet. After much soul-searching, however, you come out to yourself and then to others.

By coming out you have arrived at a summit in the journey of self-acceptance. Hopefully you have arrived with a sense of relief and joy. If you are fortunate, you have had help in the climb to this summit — your faith has sustained you, and there have been other people who have supported you and will continue to support you on the lifelong journey of coming out. Nevertheless, as you look out from your perch and survey the landscape of your future, you see that there are many more mountains, some quite formidable, to climb: perhaps ostracization by family and friends, discrimination in housing, loss of employment, and, if you are Jewish or Christian, possible rejection from a synagogue or church community that condemns LGBTQ people and their sexuality. By imagining yourself

---

18. Antonio Salas, "My Journey of Deliverance," Center for Lesbian and Gay Studies in Religion and Ministry Web site: *www.clgs.org/7/7_1_1.html* (accessed October 3, 2006).

as queer, you, as a caregiver, can begin to understand some of the many unique challenges that face an LGBTQ person of faith who comes out.

The story of Exodus in the Hebrew Bible offers a wonderful biblical metaphor for understanding coming out as a sacred journey. Long a favorite of queer Jews and Christians who identify with this profound example of divine deliverance from human oppression, the Exodus story reminds us of the power of faithful risk-tasking in the face of overwhelming odds. After years of suffering at the hands of the pharaohs, the Hebrews courageously followed Moses out of the land of their bondage. Once they had escaped into the desert they began the arduous and dangerous trek to a promised land that they had never seen. These desert years were filled with doubt and despair for the Hebrews, but God never abandoned them. Quite to the contrary: God led this journeying people back home to the land of their ancestors.

LGBTQ people of faith understand what it is like to journey with God from an old life of oppression to a new life of freedom. As gay Episcopal Bishop Gene Robinson has written, the Exodus story can be seen as the "greatest coming-out story in the history of the world":

> Queer people know what it's like to be slaves in Egypt. We know what it's like to hear of the promise of freedom in the Promised Land; we know how scary it is to step out and leave Egypt [by] leaving the closet; and we know what it's like to wander in the wilderness for forty years and wonder why it's taking so long.[19]

The good news, of course, is that many LGBTQ people of faith also know that the promise of the Exodus *was* fulfilled by a God who led his people from a barren wasteland into a land flowing with milk and honey. And LGBTQ people know from personal experience that the Exodus promise *is* realized every time that a person embraces her queer identity after years in the closet. LGBTQ people of faith know, as well, that the experience of coming out is an experience of coming home: to oneself, to others, and to the God who has called them to be the beautiful queer people that they are meant to be.

---

19. V. Gene Robinson as quoted in Julia Duin, "Gay Bishop Dismisses Anglican Report," *Washington Times*, October 11, 2004; available online at *www.washingtontimes.com/national/20041010-113559-1206r.htm* (accessed October 3, 2006).

✍ Chapter 5

Creating Communities of Care

Baptist minister Jacki Belile recommends a threefold task for congregations seeking to welcome LGBTQ people: (1) "take into account the depth of people's betrayal and pain at the hands of the institutional church in all the dimensions of fellowship, preaching, teaching, and pastoral care"; (2) offer "significant opportunities for LGBT[Q] people to have visibility, voice, and leadership roles in the life of the community"; and (3) ask this question: "to what are we welcoming folks?" In addition, Belile believes that members of a welcoming congregation "must reckon with the realities that they may be called to go places which push the envelope of respectable Christian doctrine or moral teaching...that seeks to 'main-stream' LGBT[Q] folks."[1]

In this chapter I explore how congregations can become communities of care for LGBTQ people by welcoming and including them in all aspects of congregational life. This is no small task given the fact that queer people have experienced significant alienation and outright discrimination from churches and synagogues. For centuries religious institutions of all kinds have persecuted queer people because of their sexual desires and sexual activity and, despite the fact that several Christian denominations now affirm LGBTQ people and their sexuality, most, in fact, still teach that homosexual activity is sinful and that transgenderism is somehow disordered.[2]

---

1. Jacki Belile, "Building Well-coming Communities of Faith," *Chicago Theological Seminary Register* 92, no. 2 (Summer 2002): 4–5.
2. For a description of Christian positions on transgender people, see Justin Tanis, *Transgendered: Theology, Ministry, and Communities of Faith* (Cleveland: Pilgrim Press, 2003), 85–114. On Judaism and transgenderism, see Charlie Anders, "Transformed before God: Welcoming Transgendered Jews," *Tikkun Magazine, www.tikkun.org/magazine/tik0509/article.2005-08-10.3345465137* (accessed July 10, 2006).

LGBTQ people have long been present and active in congregations of every religious tradition and denomination, however closeted many have been in order to survive in their local faith communities. To speak of straight people "welcoming" LGBTQ people into congregations, therefore, can cause us to ignore this longtime presence of queer members and attenders. Perhaps more accurate terms for congregations that seek to become communities of care for LGBTQ people would be "recognizing," "acknowledging," and "embracing" congregations. Whatever terms are used, however, it is important to recognize the fact that "welcoming" LGBTQ persons may mean beginning with those who are already present within the congregation.

A congregation that commits itself to becoming a community of care will necessarily be transformed by the queer people who are invited to live as out and full-fledged members of the congregation. In fact, I believe that a congregation whose members fear such transformation is not yet ready to become a community of care because it is unable to incorporate and celebrate LGBTQ people who bring unique gifts, talents, and needs to the religious community. The process of creating a welcoming community may challenge straight individuals in profound ways. For instance, open displays of affection between queer people, recognition of LGBTQ families, the preaching of sermons based on queer readings of Scripture, and calling LGBTQ individuals to positions of visible leadership — these may cause discomfort for some straight members of a congregation.

To welcome queer people into congregations of faith is risky precisely because it is an invitation that involves change on the part of those who have the power to do the welcoming. We know that people were deeply unsettled by demands from the Jewish prophets and from Jesus to welcome and love the poor, the stranger, and other outcast persons. In similar fashion, people today can be shaken up by calls to welcome queer people into congregational life. And yet, just as many people in the Hebrew and Christian Scriptures were blessed with unexpected gifts when they heeded a call to embrace the marginalized and the outcast, so too can congregations today expect spiritual growth and a revitalization of community life when doors of welcome are opened to LGBTQ people.

There are a variety of ways in which a congregation can realize the three steps described below. The recommendations are not offered as fail-safe

instructions for every religious congregation wishing to welcome and provide care for queer people. Rather, they reflect some of the most important
ways in which congregations have successfully accomplished this.[3]

Three Basic Steps to Building a Community of Care for LGBTQ People

1. Create a Genuine Welcome
2. Integrate Queer People into the Life of a Congregation
3. Build Alliances with Queer Communities outside the Congregation

---

Create a Genuine Welcome

Everyone can distinguish a genuine welcome from one that is half hearted,
and it is not difficult for LGBTQ people to realize whether they are welcomed or not in a particular congregation. Merely posting a welcome sign
or publishing a statement of acceptance does not prove, of course, that
a congregation is actually welcoming and inclusive. Signs and statements
can certainly be important indications of welcome and inclusion, but they
must be backed up by reality, that is, by a congregational commitment to
an ongoing process of learning how to become a community of care.

A church or synagogue that cares for queer people is one that honors
them as morally complete human persons, invites them into full membership, and celebrates their life experiences in all aspects of congregational
life. Building a community of care requires reversing age-old prejudices
and doing away with insidious practices of exclusion, however unintended
they may be. Building a community of care also calls upon the leaders
and members of a congregation to expand their notions of community in
ways that are countercultural because they violate the heterosexist norms

---

3. See my study of twenty-one San Francisco Bay Area churches and synagogues
that provide high levels of pastoral care for their queer members: "With Open Arms:
Gay Affirming Ministries in Bay Area Faith Communities," *www:clgs.org/5/open_arms.html*
(accessed July 10, 2006).

of our society and call into serious question the anti-queer theologies and practices of many of our religious traditions.

A congregation that seeks to open doors of welcome to LGBTQ people may face disapproval from some members who believe that they do not have a legitimate claim to membership in the community. A congregation may also face censure from denominational officials who oppose any change in belief systems and policies that marginalize queer people. To become a community of care may, indeed, mean that some members will leave the congregation or that a congregation's institutional affiliations will be jeopardized or even terminated. For the congregation that feels called to welcome and include all people, however, these risks are worth taking because they are outweighed by the opportunity to grow as a community that welcomes, loves, and includes all of God's children.

A Genuine Welcome Is

- Educated
- Stated
- Transforming

A genuine welcome is an educated welcome. A congregation interested in becoming a community of care should begin with education and compassionate dialogue. The leaders and members of a church or synagogue will need to educate themselves about sexual orientation, gender identity, and the most genuine and effective ways to integrate LGBTQ people into the life of the congregation. Throughout this process a congregation needs to make a commitment to engage in open and honest conversation with queer people about their lives.

Many congregations have found it helpful to form a welcoming task force to facilitate the process of deciding how to become welcoming and inclusive. Composed of laity and clergy, queer and nonqueer people, congregational staff members and perhaps individuals from outside of the congregation, this task force should be commissioned at a Sabbath or Sunday worship service. The primary duties of the task force include exploring current congregational attitudes toward homosexuality and transgenderism and working to educate the congregation on how to build a community of care. The ultimate goal of this task force should be to draft a statement of welcome for the congregation's consideration.

The task force will also want to consult resources on building welcoming congregations, including curricula that have been developed within the congregation's own religious tradition. Soon after its formation the task force should engage the entire congregation in a process of learning and dialogue by means of weekly classes, panel presentations, reading materials, or discussion groups that explore the following important questions and issues:

• How do nonqueer members feel about welcoming and including queer people in the life of the congregation?

   Take a survey of congregants to understand better their current attitudes on homosexuality, transgenderism, and bisexuality.

• In many congregations, discussions about sexuality can be highly charged and potentially contentious.

   Be prepared for potentially heated discussions and work to create a safe environment for individuals to disagree with each other. State clearly that differing points of view are welcome, and emphasize that all opinions expressed in a spirit of love and respect will be heard.

• What does the congregation's faith tradition have to say about human sexuality in general and homosexuality, bisexuality, and transgenderism in particular? How have queer and nonqueer individual theologians, clergy, and laity (from inside and outside the congregation's particular tradition) dealt with issues relating to sexuality and LGBTQ people in the past thirty years?

   Offer education nights or weekend classes on homosexuality and LGBTQ issues for your congregation. Have your minister or rabbi preach on homosexuality and queer people. Mention frequently in congregational worship the congregation's journey toward welcome.

• What do psychologists and other medical professionals have to say about sexual orientation, gender identity, bisexuality, and homosexuality?

Provide accessible reading materials on homosexuality, bisexuality, and transgenderism that have been written by respected doctors and psychologists.

- Listen to the experiences of queer people of faith.

  Host a panel discussion with queer people, recommend books and articles by queer theologians and spiritual writers, and include writings by queer people of faith in your congregational newsletter. Invite any LGBTQ individuals, couples, or supportive relatives or friends of queer people who are already in your congregation to speak about their life experiences.

- What can the congregation learn from other congregations that provide excellent pastoral care for queer people?

  Invite lay members and clergy from nearby welcoming congregations as well as representatives from denominational LGBTQ groups to share their knowledge of how to build communities of care. Visit welcoming congregations to see firsthand how their members welcome and include their queer members.

A genuine welcome is a stated welcome. LGBTQ people understand from years of experience that they are unwelcome in most congregations. Since our culture is saturated with the anti-queer rhetoric of religious leaders who claim to represent the only authentic Jewish and Christian positions on homosexuality, a congregation that seeks to become welcoming needs to state clearly and publicly its welcome in order to be heard. A public statement of welcome, therefore, is the best way for queer people in search of a religious community to know that a congregation is welcoming. It also reassures those LGBTQ people already present in a congregation that they are not excluded or relegated to second-class membership.

When the members of the welcoming task force, in concert with congregational leadership, believe that their congregation is ready to decide if it will become officially welcoming, they should draw up a statement of welcome and present it to the membership at large for its consideration and approval. In many congregations the governing board may need to approve such a statement before the congregation as a whole votes on the matter. Some congregations may decide to vote after several months of education and discussion, while others may need more time. Many congregations celebrate the passage of their welcoming statement in a worship service that ritualizes the decision and confirms the congregation's ongoing commitment to build a community of care. Print your statement frequently in your church newsletter, in your weekly Order of Service, on your congregational Web site, and in your local news media.

A well-crafted statement of welcome is brief but clear in its message. It is also one that makes specific mention of LGBTQ people. While some congregations choose to model their statements closely after those written by denominational advocacy groups, others write their own. Keep in mind that your statement serves not only as a welcome to queer people but also as an ongoing reminder for your entire congregation of its ideals and as a gauge to assess its growth over the years. Below are four examples of welcoming statements from a variety of religious traditions:

- "We are lesbian, gay, bisexual, transgender and heterosexual Jews, together with family and friends, both Jewish and non-Jewish. We come from a wide range of religious, ethnic, class and cultural backgrounds to worship God with egalitarian, feminist and gay-positive Jewish liturgy."[4]
  — Congregation Sha'ar Zahav, San Francisco

- "We proclaim that all people are created in the image of God and affirm that each person, regardless of age, economic status, faith history, ethnicity, gender, mental or physical disability, marital status, sexual orientation or lifestyle, is a beloved child of God and worthy of God's love and grace."[5]
  — First United Methodist Church, Duluth, Minnesota

- "As a Welcoming Congregation, [our church] welcomes bisexual, gay, lesbian, and transgender people into our community."[6]
  — The Auburn Unitarian Universalist Fellowship, Auburn, Alabama

- Our church "is committed to the full participation of all persons in our church community without regard for sexual orientation, personal

---

4. Congregation Sha'ar Zahav, *www.shaarzahav.org/* (accessed July 10, 2006).
5. First United Methodist of Duluth, *www.fumcduluth.com/* (accessed July 10, 2006).
6. The Auburn Unitarian Universalist Fellowship, *www.auuf.net/welcoming.html* (accessed July 10, 2006).

background, or human condition. Our More Light Committee works on ways to make all of us more aware of the contributions Presbyterian lesbian, gay, bisexual and transgender persons are making and could make to further God's Commonwealth."[7]

—Third Presbyterian Church, Rochester, New York

Of course, a welcoming statement does not mean that a congregation has completed its work of becoming a community of care for LGBTQ people; such work is continual. However, a statement does send an important and bold message that a congregation has begun to educate itself about queer people and is eager to welcome (more) queer people into all areas of its life.

A genuine welcome is a transforming welcome. By genuinely welcoming and integrating LGBTQ people into a congregation, all members experience transformation. When individuals who once were unwelcome and perhaps even unnamed are brought into a community of faith, new perspectives are gained on what it means to live as people of faith. When individuals who have been marginalized for so long enter into congregational life, they also are transformed because they have been freed, perhaps for the first time ever, to live as out queer people of faith.

Following are some ways in which a congregation can be transformed by welcoming out queer people into its midst:

◆ *Visibility.* As word of a congregation's welcome and inclusivity spreads there will be an increase in the number of LGBTQ people who attend worship services and other congregational programming. Some individuals in your congregation may begin to recognize for the first time the presence of queer people in their midst, some of whom, of course, may have been present for a long time. If a church or synagogue feels genuinely welcoming, some queer people with children may begin to attend events designed for families, queer couples may be present at programs designed for married couples and feel comfortable expressing their affection for one another by holding hands during a service. Some longtime members and visitors may come out as transgender, while new transgender individuals may begin to attend.

---

7. Third Presbyterian Church, Rochester, *www.thirdpresbyterian.org/outreach-service/ morelight/morelight.shtml* (accessed July 10, 2006).

- *The emergence of new perspectives on faith.* The inclusion of out LGBTQ individuals as board members, ushers, worship leaders, and religious education teachers will contribute to the richness of a congregation's faith life. The learning experiences of children in a congregation's religious education program, for instance, will be enriched by the personal and age-appropriate life stories offered by their out lesbian teacher; participants in a Bible study group may hear for the first time how a transgender or bisexual person interprets a particular biblical story; and the public celebration of a union ceremony of two gay men may expand some congregants' notions of love and family.

- *A growing diversity.* Welcoming LGBTQ people is a progressive act of faith that often attracts other individuals who have felt alienated from faith communities for a variety of reasons. People who disagree with the beliefs and practices of the congregation in which they were raised, couples and families in search of a diverse faith community, and young people eager to experience a congregation that encourages questioning and exploration will be attracted to check out a synagogue or church known for its welcome of queer people.

- *An expanded consciousness of social justice issues.* Building a community of care for LGBTQ people may spur the members and leaders of a congregation to address other social justice issues such as fair housing, immigrant assistance, antiracism work, environmental protection, and world peace. Many of the skills and processes that the congregation has employed in creating a community of care for queer people can be useful in welcoming and including other marginalized people, including those who are separated, divorced, other-abled, unemployed, or recovering from substance abuse or domestic violence.

- *An ethos of welcome.* Hospitality is wonderfully contagious. Welcoming a diversity of people into congregational life expands a congregation's sense of itself. As previously marginalized people are welcomed into full membership, the members and leaders of a congregation begin to realize that the best way to ensure vitality and growth is to continually broaden their hospitality. Building a community of care is an ongoing project that includes welcoming everyone but especially the outcast in our society.

Integrate LGBTQ People
into the Life of a Congregation

Once a congregation has publicly declared its welcome, it needs to work toward including and integrating queer people more fully in all aspects of congregational life. Since a community of care assumes, accepts, and celebrates the presence of queer people within its midst, the day-to-day life of the congregation should reflect this. Renovating congregational life so that it speaks its welcome and inclusion loudly and clearly is a process of trial and error. It is also a process that requires effort, time, and patience since most congregations naturally and often unconsciously reflect the larger heterosexist biases of our culture, which have been in place for decades and which can take years to change.

Relatively simple changes in three important areas of congregational life can help begin the process of making a congregation more welcoming. By using inclusive language, creating inclusive space, and celebrating inclusive rituals a congregation can become a more effective community of care for queer people.

Use inclusive language. With the rise of feminist consciousness and the women's movement in the 1960s and 1970s, many congregations began to understand that the language of worship (that is, biblical translations, liturgical prayers, and hymnody) reflected deep sexist biases. In similar ways, the rise of a queer presence in local communities of faith has raised the awareness that LGBTQ people are often rendered invisible by language with a heterosexist bias. There are several simple, but important, ways in which congregations can address the issue of making language inclusive:

• *Formulate an inclusive language policy* that reflects the congregation's commitment to welcome all people. Since language mirrors and reinforces our view of the world, making a conscious decision to include LGBTQ people in a congregation's vocabulary can help to remind everyone that the words they use can be an important means of welcome and inclusion.

• Undertake a *thorough review of the language* used in all congregational publications — including worship and hymn texts, educational curricula, and other program materials — so that those texts that presume a straight audience are expanded to include queer people. For example, after his church developed an inclusive language policy, Robert, a religious education director, became aware that every example of a family in the congregation's religious education textbook series included a mother and a father. He began to encourage his teachers to add examples of families with two moms, two dads, or a single parent in an effort to reflect the congregation's commitment to inclusion.

- Be sensitive to *transgender language issues.* By keeping in mind that the use of highly gendered language can exclude those who do not think of themselves as belonging to one gender, a congregation can speak its welcome to transgender individuals. Ask the advice of a transgender person in your congregation or local community on how to speak in ways that welcome transgender people. In terms of addressing individual gender-variant people in the congregation, a good rule of thumb is to ask people how they would like to be addressed rather than make assumptions and risk offending an individual by using the wrong name or pronoun.[8]

- *Transform language* that excludes into language that includes. Language, of course, can include the visual as well as the aural. For example, when Melinda, a leader of her church's youth group, pointed out to other members that a recent poster advertising their upcoming dance had photographs of only straight couples, they decided to issue a new version of the poster that included images of same-gender couples.

Create inclusive space. Congregational space can be exclusive space, especially with regard to transgender individuals. For instance, most congregations do not provide restroom facilities that are accessible to gender-variant people, and this omission can be a considerable barrier for transgender persons who belong to, attend, or visit your congregation. Providing at least one accessible unisex restroom is an important sign of welcome, because many transgender individuals encounter hostility from nontransgender people when they attempt to use a single-gender restroom.

---

8. Tanis, *Transgendered,* 119, writes that "calling transgendered persons by pronouns and names that do not represent their current gender presentation or identity" can be a devastating experience. It is better to ask someone how to address him/her than to assume. Instead of the terms "sister" and "brother," Tanis recommends the use of the word "sibling" to avoid using gendered language.

(Such restrooms, incidentally, are also particularly useful for a parent with an opposite-gender child and for people with caregivers.)

Your congregation will also want to consider how educational and social programs restricted by gender can create exclusive space. This does not mean, of course, that women's groups or men's groups no longer have a home in the congregation, but that such groups should be encouraged to consider the fact that the congregation is striving to become a community of welcome and care for transgender people. Each group should be asked to discuss and explore how they can include transgender individuals who may want to take part in the group's activities.

Celebrate inclusive rituals. A congregation that is a community of care not only includes LGBTQ people as leaders and participants in its rituals and liturgies, but it also celebrates their lives, their relationships, and their families through worship.[9] Most important, worship in a congregation that welcomes and includes queer people takes account of their presence and recognizes their needs. For instance, the vocabulary of worship should be sensitive to the fact that there are families in your midst with two mothers or two fathers. Recognition of married couples in congregational worship should include queer couples who may not be accorded the civil right of marriage. When planning a memorial service with the survivors of a gay man, ask them who should be invited to play special roles in the service and, in particular, who should be asked to offer words of eulogy. Forms of prayer that divide a congregation into women and men may alienate some transgender people who don't identify as either one gender or the other. Developing sensitivity to the presence and needs of queer people in worship can be a positive learning experience for the entire congregation. One way to facilitate such learning is to include LGBTQ individuals as members of the congregation's worship committee or as ad hoc members of a group planning a particular service.

In addition to making all worship inclusive, congregations can celebrate those events that are unique to queer people. Below are a few examples of the ways in which a congregation can do this through worship and ritual:

---

9. Kelly Turney, ed., *Shaping Sanctuary: Proclaiming God's Grace in an Inclusive Church* (Chicago: Reconciling Congregation Program, 2000) is an excellent resource for planning Christian worship services. For Jewish rituals and liturgies that celebrate queer people, see *Ritualwell: Ceremonies for Jewish Living, www.ritualwell.org/* (accessed July 10, 2006).

• *Coming out services*: Since coming out is a pivotal event in the lives of many queer people, your congregation might consider devoting one worship service a year to celebrate people in your congregation who have recently come out as LGBTQ. Recognition of individuals who have recently come out can also be celebrated as one part of a larger Sabbath or Sunday worship service.

• *LGBTQ pride services*: Celebrate gay pride and honor the LGBTQ civil rights movement sometime during June, which is recognized the world over as Gay Pride Month. Special prayers, sermons, and songs can be especially effective ways of celebrating LGBTQ pride and raising awareness within the congregation about queer history and culture. Decorating the interior worship space with rainbow colors, the traditional colors of queer pride, or hanging a rainbow flag outside the church or synagogue are other ways to highlight your congregation's pride celebrations; they will also be especially meaningful to many queer people.

• *Same-sex marriage and holy unions*: Make your congregation a place of welcome for LGBTQ couples who want to marry or enter into covenants of commitment or holy unions. Congregations of many religious traditions have been celebrating the marriages and unions of LGBTQ couples for many years now, of course, and they remain uniquely powerful opportunities for the recognition of the love and commitment of queer people within the context of a faith community.

• *Rituals marking gender transitions*: Several events in the lives of transgender people can be recognized and celebrated within the context of congregational worship, including the decision of an individual to change gender, the choice of a new name, and the preparation for and completion of surgical procedures for a person who is transitioning. Of course, planning for a worship service or ritual moment within a larger service should be done with the transgender person(s) involved; several resources are now available that provide creative models for ritualizing important moments in the lives of transgender persons.[10]

---

10. For resources on Jewish liturgy and rituals for transgender persons, see the Web site "trans Jews" at *www.transjews.org/index.html*. See "A Liturgy of Re-Naming for Transgender Persons" in Turney, *Shaping Sanctuary*, 204–5; and "Liturgical Resources" in Tanis, *Trans-Gendered*, 187–93.

- *Celebrations to honor queer families*: Your congregation can honor the lives of LGBTQ people and their families in many ways. The adoption of a child by a queer individual or couple, the reconciliation between parents and their queer child, and the celebration of wedding/holy union anniversaries provide opportunities for celebrating LGBTQ lives, loves, and families.

- *AIDS liturgies*: While AIDS is a disease that does not discriminate on the basis of sexual orientation, living with HIV/AIDS is a continuing reality for many queer people. The annual recognition of World AIDS Day in December provides an excellent opportunity for your congregation to pray for everyone throughout the world who is living with the disease and to remember those who have died from it. Consider hanging AIDS quilts in your sanctuary as a way of reminding congregants of the ongoing reality of HIV/AIDS in our local, national, and international human community.

- *Recognition of LGBTQ religious leaders*: Your congregation can celebrate in worship an LGBTQ person whom it has supported, sponsored, or called to the ordained ministry. Supporting an LGBTQ member who has entered the seminary or calling an out queer person to ordained ministry are some especially appropriate events to celebrate in spoken prayer and ritual.

In addition to renovating language, space, and rituals to reflect a commitment to welcome and include LGBTQ people, a congregation that strives to become a community of care needs to devote itself to increasing queer membership and queer leadership in every area of congregational life. Being explicit in welcoming and accepting queer people into all facets of a congregation can help individuals realize that being a community of care entails the full integration of queer people. Advertise in the local (queer and straight) press that your congregation is welcoming of LGBTQ people. Programming that includes queer people will prove to be an especially effective way to let the world outside your congregation know that you are serious in your efforts to build a community of care for all people.

The best way to increase the presence and involvement of LGBTQ people in congregational life is to continue the process of education and dialogue begun in the early stages of building a welcoming community of faith. Many congregations find that a standing committee on LGBTQ persons and their concerns can help advance the process of building welcome by offering educational programs and fostering continued dialogue between queer and nonqueer people. By serving as a catalyst for learning and conversation, this committee can help to model and foster increasing trust between LGBTQ persons and non-LGBTQ persons.

- Specifically mention in your congregational brochures that LGBTQ persons are welcome not only to become members of the congregation but also to join the various groups and committees that make up the congregation; do not limit your invitation to groups and committees that deal with queer issues.

- Invite the LGBTQ people in your congregation to form a social or support group that might include as one of its works the welcoming of new queer members into the congregation.

- Review your congregational policies on membership, hiring of staff, and recruitment of clergy to be sure that these are aligned with your congregational statement of welcome.

- Support and join a denominational LGBTQ advocacy group.

- Offer education nights with queer instructors and panelists. Topics might include explorations of heterosexism, transgenderism, the Bible, LGBTQ parenting, and the history of LGBTQ people within your denomination.

- Create opportunities for continued dialogue between queer and nonqueer members of your congregation.

- Explore how all programs within your congregation might be transformed by your welcoming and inclusive stance. Remember, the goal is to weave queer people and issues into all aspects of congregational life.

- Encourage your clergy to preach occasionally on issues related to the welcome and inclusion of queer people; invite a local queer clergyperson to preach.

- Celebrate June as LGBTQ Pride Month in your congregation with educational events and a special pride worship service.

- Provide educational opportunities for your clergy to develop skills in the pastoral care of queer people and their families.

Build Alliances with LGBTQ Communities

Once your congregation has made the decision to welcome and include LGBTQ people, don't keep the news of your welcome within the walls of the congregation — rather, spread the word! There are many effective ways of doing this, including regular congregational advertisements in the gay and straight press, postings on the main page of your church or syn-agogue Web site, and listings in the local telephone book and wherever your congregation is mentioned in local community calendars or denom-inational publications. Find as many ways as possible to proclaim your welcoming and inclusive stance and make visible your commitment to queer people. Most congregations also post a sign of welcome, a pink triangle, a rainbow, or a denominational symbol of welcome on their build-ings. Stories abound of individuals who have chosen to visit a local faith community because they saw a sign of welcome in front of a synagogue or church.[11]

Perhaps the most important external work of a welcoming congregation is finding opportunities to become an ally to the larger LGBTQ com-munity. Through outreach to individual LGBTQ people and by building alliances with a variety of queer groups and social justice organizations, a congregation can walk its talk of living as a genuine community of care. People of faith can be valuable allies not only inside congregations, but also out in the community where there is often discrimination against queer people and their families in employment, housing, and educational oppor-tunities. Your congregation might consider some of the following ways to become an ally:

• Find opportunities to educate your local community about religion and queer people. By speaking from a progressive faith perspective you can demonstrate that not all people of faith consider homosexuality a sin or seek to restrict the rights of LGBTQ people and their families.

• Find ways to work with PFLAG (Parents, Families & Friends of Lesbians & Gays), GLSEN (the Gay, Lesbian and Straight Education Network), your local LGBTQ community center, and other organizations whose missions are to advance the rights and well-being of queer people.

---

11. See Faith-Based LGBTQ-Affirming Resources on page 225 below.

- Host a weekend workshop or retreat at your church or synagogue for LGBTQ people of faith and their allies. Organizations such as the Center for Lesbian and Gay Studies in Religion and Ministry, the Institute of Welcoming Resources, and other national LGBTQ religious organizations offer such workshops as a way of educating and energizing local faith communities around issues relating to queer sexuality and religion.

- Pay attention to local, state, and national legislation that affects queer people, and educate your congregation about ways they can become agents of political change. Organizations such as the National Gay and Lesbian Task Force (NGLTF) and the Human Rights Campaign (HRC) serve as valuable civil rights watchdog organizations for queer people, and they also work with progressive people of faith who are eager to take part in public debates and undertake political activity in support of LGBTQ people.

- When the civil rights of queer people are being threatened, speak up! The leadership and membership of congregations can offer vital support when a municipality is debating whether or not to include LGBTQ people in nondiscrimination policies, enact trans-inclusive legislation, write laws to prevent hate-motivated violence against queer people, or remove queer-positive materials from local libraries. In state debates over marriage, progressive people of faith can offer valuable testimony of support for civil marriage rights for all persons.

- Make available congregational space at low or no cost for local queer and queer-friendly organizations. Organizations (especially those with small budgets) greatly appreciate free or inexpensive space for their meetings.

- Celebrate LGBTQ cultural events such as Queer Pride Days, Coming Out Day in October, and World AIDS Day. Your congregation might consider marching in the local gay pride parade or hosting interreligious worship services that are open to members of the local community.

Embracing the Challenge of Care

Building a community of care for queer persons is an exciting, challenging, and rewarding experience for congregations that choose to welcome and integrate LGBTQ individuals into all aspects of their congregational life.

Most people of faith need supportive and dynamic religious communities within which to explore and express their faith. Queer people, like other marginalized people, often feel a heightened need to connect spiritually with others in a community of faith, given the fact that congregations have excluded them for so long. I dream that some day every faith community will welcome, include, and care for LGBTQ people as full and equal members. The only way to make that dream a reality is by rolling up our sleeves and building those communities of care, one congregation at a time.

Chapter 6

Caring for Relationships

Am I Prepared to Offer Care?

Engaging in pastoral care with LGBTQ people means that you will be invited to work with them as they explore, wrestle with, and take joy in their interpersonal and family relationships. Like all persons, queer people experience life-giving satisfaction as well as significant challenges in their relationships with friends, loved ones, and family members. The ministry of providing effective pastoral care to LGBTQ people, however, is unique in many ways, and it requires that caregivers be honest about their willingness and their abilities to offer high-quality and effective care.

First and foremost, the pastoral caregiver needs to deal with any inner conflicts that she or he may have regarding queer people. Joretta Marshall writes that "pastoral care specialists who want to offer the most appropriate and genuine care to women in lesbian partnerships must work conscientiously to discover the biases, prejudices, or internal fears that they carry into their praxis."[1] This advice is equally valuable for caregivers who work with gay men, transgender persons, and bisexuals, because the best pastoral care for LGBTQ persons is that which affirms their sexuality as a gift from God.

If you are ready and able to take on the exciting and rewarding challenges of caring for queer people in their relationships, I encourage you to continue reading this chapter in a spirit of openness and humility, because, to be frank, many LGBTQ people within our Jewish and Christian faith communities bring questions, concerns, and life situations to pastoral caregiving that often require a bold rethinking and reevaluation of current Jewish and Christian models of relationship and family. Such rethinking and reevaluation does not mean, of course, that a pastoral caregiver need

---

1. Joretta L. Marshall, *Counseling Lesbian Partners* (Louisville: Westminster John Knox Press, 1997), 131.

set aside her beliefs or moral principles when working with LGBTQ people. However, it does mean that you, as caregiver, should be prepared to weave together the relational and familial experiences of queer people with the moral teachings of your own religious traditions in ways that truly honor the people in your care and also maintain fidelity to the best and most life-giving aspects of your own traditions.

Some Ways of Understanding LGBTQ Relationships

Over the past thirty years or so, several Christian and Jewish theologians have written creatively on lesbian and gay understandings of relationships; in an effort to offer constructive theological grounding for this chapter's discussion of pastoral care and LGBTQ relationships, I would like to include here a few ideas from some of this work. My goals are to provide an introduction to some ethical dimensions of queer relationships and to pique your interest in how the experiences of many LGBTQ people have been understood in theological terms.

Given the long Jewish and Christian theological traditions of denigrating homosexuality and condemning queer people and their relationships as sinful, it is no surprise that many pastoral caregivers know little, if anything, about the varied ways in which LGBTQ people build and sustain their relationships. For instance, a caregiver may be unaware that while some couples desire to enter into monogamous unions or partnerships that closely resemble the ideal of heterosexual marriage, not all do. Many queer people have extended networks of friendship that may include former lovers; some couples may view sexual involvement outside of their main relationship not as a violation of the relationship but rather as an agreed-upon and life-giving aspect of their main relationship. A queer person who is single may find deep meaning in her singleness and have no desire for a live-in companion with whom to share her life. Assuming that every LGBTQ person desires to marry or condemning every person who does not restrict his sexual involvement to one other person are mistakes for the caregiver who is interested in working effectively and productively with LGBTQ people.

Even though many religious leaders and theologians continue to teach that lifelong celibacy is the only morally permissible option for LGBTQ people, most queer people of faith have learned from experience that they, like most nonqueer people, are not called to a life of permanent celibacy. Moreover, many Americans, including those who are people of faith, are beginning to see that the varied ways in which many queer persons structure and negotiate their relationships are worthy of appreciation and even emulation. In some of our congregations and seminaries LGBTQ people of faith are speaking out as morally responsible individuals whose relationships, while often significantly different from the model offered by heterosexual marriage, are valid expressions of love. Queer theologians have taken the lead in reflecting theologically and ethically on the nature of LGBTQ relationships, and it is upon their work that I principally draw in my discussion below. Not only is such a consideration of queer (and feminist) theological reflection on relationships necessary for effective pastoral care, but it also can expand Jewish and Christian understandings of the goodness and beauty of all human relationships.

Five Characteristics of Queer Relationships

1. The foundation of friendship
2. Hospitality and community building
3. Celebration of embodiment
4. Liberation as a shared experience
5. Queer love as generative

The above five interrelated characteristics of LGBTQ relationships are worthwhile for you, the pastoral caregiver, to consider as you prepare to work with queer people in relationships. These five items represent ideals, of course, but they are ideals that are rooted in the real-life experiences of many queer people.

The Foundation of Friendship

Friendship is the most important characteristic of queer relationships. As gay theologian Robert Goss has stated, "Friendship serves as the primary paradigm for understanding [queer] individual, coupled, and extended re-lationships."[2] In my own experience I have found this to be true: friendship best describes the broad variety of relationships that I, a gay man, enjoy with other queer people, from my twenty-five-year relationship with my partner to my relationships with a variety of other LGBTQ people in my life. It was to queer friends, significantly, that I first turned when I began to acknowledge my gay identity, and it was among queer friends that I celebrated when I came out of the closet. Since then I have continued to delight in the friendship that I share with other LGBTQ people, and I know that life without these friendships would be arid and colorless. It is they who have made it possible for me not only to feel so at home in queer culture but also to thrive as a well-adjusted gay man in the larger straight world.

Lesbian Roman Catholic theologian Mary Hunt argues convincingly that friendships constitute "the central relational experience for women," and I would argue that the same is true for many gay, transgender, and bisexual people as well.[3] With a common experience of loneliness and isolation that comes from living in the closet and as people who have suffered discrimination from family, civic institutions, employers, and our faith communities, LGBTQ people have long turned to each other in friendship as a way to endure and bring meaning to their suffering.

Hunt's theology of friendship also stresses that healthy and well-functioning friendships rest on the important foundations of equality and mutuality, and that these two elements give rise to genuine empowerment for each person in the friendship. To be empowered means that an individ-ual makes her own choices about how to live her life and decides what is best for herself and for those in her care. To be empowered also means that friends work to shed those harmful relational dynamics that grant power

---

2. Robert E. Goss, "Queering Procreative Privilege: Coming Out as Families," in *Our Families, Our Values: Snapshots of Queer Kinship,* ed. Robert E. Goss and Amy Adams Squire Strongheart (New York: Harrington Park Press, 1997), 17.

3. Mary E. Hunt, *Fierce Tenderness: A Feminist Theology of Friendship* (New York: Crossroad, 1991), 91. Hunt, 87–106, also posits that traditional Western philosophies of friendship, with their exclusive focus on male relationships, are simply inadequate in helping us understand friendships between women. Her own model of friendship consists of four key elements: love, power, embodiment, and spirituality.

to one friend at the expense of the other(s). In the ideal, queer individuals are sensitive to the widespread damage done to friendships because of poisonous patriarchal notions of dominance and subservience that still infect so much of our culture. Having been marginalized by others because of their queerness, LGBTQ people have the opportunity and obligation to fashion their friendships along more egalitarian lines. And indeed, queer people throughout history have a long-standing tradition of building such relationships.

By valuing friendship rather than heterosexual marriage as the most important of human relationships, the pastoral caregiver can begin to understand and appreciate the variety of ways in which LGBTQ people form their relationships with one another. The deep and ongoing relationship with a current or former partner or lover, the camaraderie of a few close intimates, and the supportive network of a large circle of friends — each of these counts as genuine friendship for queer people. Viewing friendship as the key relational experience in life dethrones marriage (whether straight or same-sex) from its problematic place in our culture as the best kind of human relationship for each and every person. Friendship is something, as Hunt stresses, that every person can enjoy; it is also something that takes many innovative and life-giving forms, as we see in the friendships that queer people create and sustain with one another.

You may find it helpful to call to mind and share with your LGBTQ care receivers the high regard in which same-sex friendship is held in the Hebrew and Christian scriptures. Ruth and Naomi share an intimate friendship, as do David and Jonathan; Jesus and the apostle John are portrayed as particularly close friends. The Gospels stress time and again Jesus' message that the greatest love of all is that which friends have for one another. In fact, Elizabeth Stuart reminds us that "the only model of relating that we can definitely see operating in the life of Jesus, as presented to us by the Gospels, is friendship. One could say that the essence of Jesus' ministry was simply befriending — the forming of mutual, equal, loving, accepting, and transforming relationships."[4]

---

4. Elizabeth Stuart, "Just a Perfect Blendship: Friendship and Sexuality," in *Our Families, Our Values*, 171.

The scriptural emphasis on friendship should offer hope to LGBTQ people of faith who may find themselves overwhelmed by and under siege from those religious and political leaders of our day who insist that marriage between a woman and a man is the highest form of a loving relationship, that a wife and husband are the only suitable parents for children, and that our society should retain its preferential option for married straight people. The Christian biblical record certainly reminds us that marriage (understood, as it is today, as the romantic partnership between two people of different genders) was not held up as the highest form of life for Jesus' followers, and the great value it places on friendship can encourage LGBTQ people of faith to treasure more dearly the delightful variety of friendships that they create and sustain.[5]

Hospitality and Community Building

Hospitality is another biblical value that imbues the relationships of many queer people who have a keen personal understanding of what it means and how it feels to be an outsider. At an early age, many LGBTQ individuals come to realize that their differences make them unwelcome in families, communities of faith, and society at large, and therefore, they understand how important and life-saving it can be to welcome the outcast and the stranger. Perhaps this sense of being an unwelcomed minority hints at why so many queer people throughout history have been particularly drawn to work in education, religious ministry, medicine, the arts, entertainment, the travel industry, and social work — endeavors that require a high level of skill in hospitality and building community.

Pastor Nancy Wilson recalls the value of hospitality in the desert cultures of the Hebrew Bible when she proposes a queer theology of sexuality that joins this biblical value of hospitality with the experience of LGBTQ people who have such a strong desire to welcome others. "Perhaps our neediness or loneliness," she writes, "has made us almost 'promiscuous' in our desire to provide hospitality. Being shut out has made us want to

---

5. See Mary Ann Tolbert, "Marriage and Friendship in the Christian New Testament: Ancient Resources for Contemporary Same-Sex Unions," in *Authorizing Marriage? Canon, Tradition, and Critique in the Blessing of Same-sex Unions*, ed. Mark D. Jordan with Meghan T. Sweeney and David M. Mellott (Princeton, NJ: Princeton University Press, 2006), 41–51.

include with a vengeance."[6] Wilson suggests that the biblical notion of hospitality, which calls everyone to welcome the stranger into one's home, is key to any queer sexual theology because queer people understand how sex can be a way to extend welcome to others — not in the sense of relating sexually with strangers but rather in the sense of viewing our sexual relationships as unique opportunities for welcoming our lovers into our lives and into our very selves: "To share sexually with someone is literally to *make room* for them in our body and in the space surrounding our bodies."[7]

Community building is another talent of many LGBTQ people and one that informs the ways in which they relate to one another. For many years now, queer people have formed and maintained vital communities of support (be they neighborhoods, social service agencies, synagogues, churches, clubs, or other organizations) that continue to provide safe spaces in which they can socialize, find mutual care, and gain political power in democratic societies. One could say that the art of forming community is the making of friends writ large, and queer people are indeed true masters of this art.

In a fascinating analysis of contemporary gay male culture in the United States, David Nimmons writes of the remarkable communal sensibilities of gay men that are evident in high rates of volunteerism, altruistic practices of caretaking for the sick and infirm, and unique bonds of deep friendship with straight women. Nimmons urges his reader to consider the lessons that such community-mindedness offers for American society as a whole, and he likens these "gay enclave cultures" to intentional communities of service that have appeared in various guises throughout history:

> Gay experiments in affection, the norms and rituals of our intimacies, echo ethics taught by a wide variety of religious traditions. These values are strikingly consonant with Judeo-Christian ethics of communalism and social liberation. They sound a lot like what Jesus preached. The innovations in love and community we are crafting today have previously been seen primarily in religious orders, secular communes, utopian settlements, intentional communities, and fraternal brotherhoods. Our habits of diffuse bonding and support,

---

6. Nancy L. Wilson, *Our Tribe: Queer Folks, God, Jesus, and the Bible*, 1st ed. (San Francisco: HarperSanFrancisco, 1995), 233. Her emphasis.

7. Ibid., 249. Her emphasis.

voluntary caretaking, and service recall practices of the first Christian apostles. They recall values espoused by spiritually constituted
brotherhoods from early Christian practice, to medieval monasteries,
to modern-day religious orders.[8]

Pastoral caregivers who work with LGBTQ people in relationships
should keep in mind the gifts that many queer people possess in the areas
of hospitality and community building because such networks of care and
support, both formal and informal, can be of immense help for LGBTQ
care receivers. Queer support groups of various kinds are an excellent
example of a community resource that can provide individuals with a
quality of care that is comfortable, safe, and rooted in queer experience.
By encouraging your care receivers to take advantage of these existing
networks of care, you, as pastoral caregiver, can help them benefit from
the hospitality and community of other queer people.

A Celebration of Embodiment

Embodiment means being at home both in the macrocosm of nature and
in the microcosm of one's own body. Embodied persons feel connected to
and genuinely comfortable with their physicality because they understand
that the human body is a great good and not, as many schools of Jewish
and Christian theology have taught, a dangerous beast that must be tamed
if one is to live a holy life. To be embodied means that one does not see
the desire for or enjoyment of sensual or sexual pleasure as necessarily evil
or inherently sinful; rather, it means that one delights in one's body and
revels in bodily pleasures because they are an integral and healthy aspect of
human existence. Many LGBTQ people are "embodied knowers," Carter
Heyward suggests; they feel at home in creation and in their bodies in
such a way that they value what they experience through their senses and
their emotions, and they enjoy the physical pleasure mediated by their
bodies.[9] Such an embodied understanding of human nature has no use for
dualistic philosophies, theologies, or ethical systems that equate the body

---

8. David Nimmons, *The Soul beneath the Skin: The Unseen Hearts and Habits of Gay
Men* (New York: St. Martin's Press, 2002), 139.

9. Carter Heyward, *Touching Our Strength: The Erotic as Power and the Love of God*
(San Francisco: HarperSanFrancisco, 1989), 7.

with fallen human nature, chaos, and evil while glorifying the soul as the uniquely spiritual, dispassionate, and redeemable part of the person.

Judith Plaskow, a feminist theologian in the Jewish tradition, has proposed a sexual theology that is based on an embodied understanding of human existence. Rejecting traditional patriarchal theologies that view women's sexuality as something that must be brought under control by men via the institution of marriage, she constructs a theology that posits sexuality as crucial to our capacity for feeling and as an essential means through which we communicate with God and other persons. In this view, sexuality is not some evil force that needs taming but is rather a good and essential aspect of who we are as embodied persons.[10]

Many LGBTQ people treasure and celebrate the gift of their sexuality and gender identity because they have risked much in naming and claiming their gender identity and sexual desires as an integral part of who they are. Put another way, many queer people bring a hard-won and keen appreciation of their embodiedness and a celebration of that embodiedness to the sexual relationships that they have with other persons. Elizabeth Stuart suggests that "perhaps because we are defined by our sexuality, lesbian and gay people are more acutely aware of the part sexuality plays in all our relationships — that it is our embodied passion that incarnates itself in every friendship, although the level of intimacy and its expression will vary."[11]

As a pastoral caregiver, you can help your LGBTQ care receivers appreciate their embodiedness and begin to recover from years of living in social and religious environments that bombard queer people with toxic messages about their bodies and their sexual desires. You may find, in fact, that many LGBTQ people in relationships have internalized highly negative views of their own bodies and absorbed understandings of their sexual desire as displeasing to God. More broadly, your pastoral care of LGBTQ persons may also teach you and your care receivers that embodiment is a Jewish and Christian virtue that all humans are called to practice.

---

10. Judith Plaskow, "Toward a New Theology of Sexuality," in *Twice Blessed: On Being Lesbian, Gay, and Jewish*, ed. Christie Balka and Andy Rose (Boston: Beacon Press, 1989), 141–51.

11. Stuart, "Just a Perfect Blendship," 173.

Liberation as a Shared Experience

In chapter 4 we explored some of the ways in which coming out of the closet is an experience of profound liberation for most LGBTQ people. Acknowledging one's true gender identity to self and others, embracing a queer identity, and proudly naming oneself as bisexual, transgender, lesbian, or gay is like crossing a threshold into a new world filled with the promise of living more authentically. For LGBTQ people of faith the experience of coming out calls to mind stories of liberation from the Bible in which the people of Israel are set free from the bondage of slavery and the followers of Jesus are liberated by his healing words and actions.

This shared experience of liberation shapes queer relationships in many ways. Knowing what it is like to live in oppression and then taste the sweet freedom that comes from accepting one's queer identity, many LGBTQ people feel a common bond with others who yearn to be liberated from oppressive systems and structures of all kinds. There are many queer people who are able to draw upon their own experience of liberation from the closet as they do the lifelong work of building and tending relationships with others, queer and nonqueer alike. To live as a liberated person includes being in right relationship with others in ways that honor and respect the freedom and integrity of every person.

Pastoral care with queer people in relationship involves understanding, validating, and honoring this profound experience of liberation that requires that one act ethically and justly in one's relationships with others. Given their own experiences of oppression and liberation, LGBTQ people can be especially effective agents of justice making and peace building in their own lives and relationships in ways that help to heal the whole human family.

Queer Love as Generative

All human relationships (including those of queer people) are potentially generative, meaning they can be life-giving both for those who take part in the relationship and for those outside of the relationship. For example, the fruits of an equitable and well-functioning friendship are often enjoyed by the many individuals who come into contact with the persons who make up the friendship. The love and generosity found in any healthy human relationship often overflow the relationship and contribute positively, often in unrealized ways, to the lives of countless others in our families, our faith communities, our workplaces, and, in fact, in our entire world. LGBTQ relationships, of course, are no different in this regard, despite the fact that they are often portrayed as selfish, hedonistic, and of little or no use to others or to society at large.

Generativity is often narrowly understood as the ability to procreate. Some traditional Jewish and Christian systems of morality continue to condemn queer sexual relationships precisely because they cannot lead to biological reproduction. And yet, the experience of many people — queer as well as nonqueer — testifies to the wonderfully creative nature of many forms of sexual activity that are not linked to reproduction. Despite the insistence of those who demand that all sexual activity must be open to the possibility of conceiving children or that heterosexual sex alone is good because it is tied to procreation, LGBTQ people in relationships that are sexual *do,* in fact, experience their sexual activity as healing, uniting, expressive, loving, and creative. This understanding that sex between same-sex persons can be as procreative as sex between opposite-sex persons is expressed well by Bob Goss: "*Procreativity* may refer to the literal renewal of the earth through human reproduction or reproductive strategies, or it may also refer to the contributions made for renewal and transformation of society. Both opposite-sex and same-sex couples have an equal opportunity to express literally and metaphorically the procreativity of the Creator God."[12] Blessed by God with bodies that are good and holy, queer people share with all other human beings the ability, and indeed the responsibility, to enjoy sex as one of the many goods of creation.

Good pastoral care of LGBTQ people in relationships helps them to understand that their relationships can be as procreative and generative as any other form of human relationship. Well-functioning friendships, partnerships, civil unions, and marriages between queer people provide positive testimony to this conviction. LGBTQ people in healthy relationships do indeed partake in the work of a creative and creating deity, and one important goal of pastoral care with queer people is to help them

---

12. Goss, "Queering Procreative Privilege," 12. His emphasis.

understand that their relationships are needed to spread love and justice throughout the world.

Pastoral Care for LGBTQ Persons in Relationships

As a pastoral caregiver who is committed to providing the best possible care to LGBTQ people in relationships, you need, first and foremost, a genuine willingness and the proven ability to listen with an open mind and an understanding heart to the life stories and faith journeys of those who come to you for care. Since an individual's past and current relationships are an important part of what shapes him, you should familiarize yourself with and become comfortable discussing the various kinds of relationships that queer people form with one another. Educate yourself and keep current on issues in the field of LGBTQ theology and pastoral care, and commit yourself to exploring new ways of applying Jewish and Christian ethics in your work with LGBTQ persons in relationship. Like everyone else who comes to you for care, an LGBTQ person in relationship needs you to be a knowledgeable, empathetic, and affirming caregiver.

What you offer your care receivers is the wisdom you have gained from your own life experience, your education and pastoral training, and the faith tradition(s) that have shaped you. The teachings of your own faith tradition(s) may, in fact, support the condemnation of LGBTQ people and their sexual relationships, while your pastoral care with queer people demands that you find affirming ways to care for them. Your ongoing relationships with these care receivers may also lead you to interrogate with renewed intensity established theological positions that pathologize LGBTQ people so that you can provide them with a constructive and true-to-life ministry of care and ethical assistance that they will expect (and deserve) from you.

Since the Hebrew and Christian scriptures and moral theologies have been used for centuries to denounce and demonize LGBTQ people and their relationships, you may be the first pastoral caregiver that a particular queer person has ever approached for care. You may also be a person's last hope for receiving pastoral care that affirms queer sexuality as a gift from God and values LGBTQ relationships as holy and healthy forms of human love. You carry a heavy responsibility here: you are called to bring a message of hope and healing to those who have long been marginalized by faith communities because of how and whom they love. Certainly Jewish and Christian religious and ethical traditions can be of help to LGBTQ people of faith in terms of their relationships, but a serious rethinking on your part of some important aspects of those traditions as they have developed over time is required. Perhaps most important, you will need to take seriously the lives and loves of queer people themselves despite the fact that these lives and loves have often been dismissed as immoral and therefore not worthy of even a hearing by many religious leaders and theologians. An exciting pastoral challenge? Without a doubt.

Grounded in the conviction that pastoral caregivers learn best by listening intently to and sincerely honoring the experiences of their care receivers, the exploration of caregiving that follows is based on the real-life experience of LGBTQ individuals and couples of faith who have freely chosen to enter into pastoral care in order to find support as they build and maintain loving and supportive relationships with other queer people. I share the conviction of lesbian minister Sally Boyle that "pastoral care has as its ultimate goal the empowerment of people to live in just and loving relationships";[13] therefore, the focus in this section is on pastoral care with LGBTQ people who seek to build just and loving as well as healthy and mature relationships with each other.

The six vignettes that follow are composites of real-life situations, and they will be used as case studies according to the following schema:

- I present a succinct case study of an LGBTQ person in relationship who is seeking pastoral care.

- Next I briefly consider some theological and ethical considerations relating to the case.

- Finally, I discuss some courses of action, based on sound pastoral care practices that are informed by faith considerations, for helping the care receiver(s) and caregiver address the issue(s).

These case studies are necessarily brief, and the theological viewpoints offered are intended as touchstones for your further reflection. The theological considerations following each case study are rooted, of course,

---

13. Sally M. Boyle, *Embracing the Exile: A Lesbian Model of Pastoral Care* (Dundas, Ontario: Artemis Enterprises; Etobicoke, Ont.: United Church Publishing House, 1995), 15.

in the conviction that lesbian, transgender, bisexual, and gay persons, their identities, and their desires are God-given and, therefore, good. A second conviction is that the yearnings of LGBTQ people for intimate relationships are healthy, life-giving, and necessary components of a life well lived.

Remember that your first task when entering into a pastoral care relationship with LGBTQ people is to assure them that you offer them a safe environment in which to talk about themselves. Once this has been established, you, as caregiver, have three main goals to accomplish, as Larry Kent Graham has written:

- Discern their need in clear terms.

- Validate it pastorally and communally.

- Help evaluate theologically and ethically the quality of life it makes possible in relation to self, God, and neighbor.[14]

Let's see what that looks like when applied to particular individuals in relationship. As you read these case studies, put yourself in the position of the caregiver and consider how you might best serve your own care receivers with sensitivity, understanding, and an open heart.

Lenore and Dixie: Same-Sex Marriage

Lenore, thirty-five, and Dixie, thirty-nine, have come to you for pastoral care because they are trying to decide if they should marry each other. Having lived together in a monogamous relationship for almost four years, they feel ready to commit themselves in marriage to each other in the presence of their family and friends, who have, over time, come to support their relationship. Raised as conservative Christians, they have never attended church together as a couple, but you learn that they have an interest in finding a congregation

---

14. Larry Kent Graham, *Discovering Images of God: Narratives of Care among Lesbians and Gays* (Louisville: Westminster John Knox Press, 1997), 185: "To provide strategic care, then, is to help lesbians and gays — as well as straight persons — discern their sexual orientation in clear terms, validate it pastorally and communally, and help evaluate theologically and ethically the quality of life it makes possible in relation to self, God, and neighbor."

where they might not only get married but also become active members. They are uncertain about how to go about planning a Christian wedding ceremony for two women.

As you get to know Lenore and Dixie, you learn that they are a couple who undoubtedly have a deep and mature love for one another. They also are two people who approach the question of marriage with appropriate gravity and typical nervousness as they move toward a lifelong commitment with each other. After only a few pastoral care sessions with them, you come to realize that what they are seeking from you is assistance in determining whether or not they are ready to make a marriage commitment. Before referring them to a minister who can offer them marriage preparation classes and perhaps preside at their marriage in the context of a welcoming congregation, you agree to work with them for several sessions so that you might come to know them more fully and offer them your pastoral opinion on their readiness to marry.

Given their four-year relationship of living together as a couple, Lenore and Dixie have grown in love and navigated successfully a few crises, including Dixie's extrarelational affair. They tell you that they received counseling two years ago from a marriage and family therapist to help them work through issues relating to Dixie's affair, and it appears that they have come to a healthy resolution of the problems that the affair caused. Lenore says that she feels that their relationship emerged from the therapy stronger than before, and Dixie agrees with her.

You find that much of Dixie and Lenore's uncertainty over entering into a Christian marriage has to do with their similar experiences of having been ostracized by their parents when they first came out in their early twenties and leaving behind congregations whose ministers strongly disapproved of homosexuality. Understandably, Lenore and Dixie want to be sure that they are respected as lesbians and that their relationship is honored in the congregation where they marry and become members.

Your relationship with this couple spurs you on to further reading in the area of pastoral care with lesbian couples, and you discover Joretta Marshall's insightful writing on the covenantal models that many lesbians use in their relationships. Upon your suggestion, Dixie and Lenore read Marshall's book on lesbian partnerships, and the three of you decide to use it as a study text for your remaining pastoral care sessions. Despite

Marshall's preference for the terms "lesbian relationships, covenants, or partnerships" instead of marriage (due to the patriarchal history of the institution and the many heterosexist notions associated with it), Dixie and Lenore articulate clearly their own reasons for preferring the term "marriage" for their relationship. They do identify deeply, however, with Marshall's discussion of love, justice, and mutuality as the key components in many lesbian partnerships and, given their experience of Dixie's affair, they ask to discuss with you in further detail Marshall's description of what "fidelity" means in covenantal lesbian partnerships, which reads as follows:

> In the lesbian and gay community, the meaning of monogamy and fidelity is questioned intensely. Monogamy and fidelity have traditionally been defined by the heterosexual community as sexual faithfulness to one's primary relationship. However, in the lesbian and gay communities it is seen as important not to simply employ the heterosexist definition of fidelity in relation to lesbian covenantal partnerships. Instead, fidelity in lesbian relationships centers on how women covenant mutually about the boundaries of their external friendships, accepting responsibility and accountability for maintaining clarity about the agreed-upon emotional and sexual perimeters for relationships with others.[15]

Your ongoing discussions with Dixie and Lenore about the meaning of fidelity help them to clarify what a monogamous commitment means to them as a couple. They tell you that their understanding of monogamy is based on an agreement to be open and honest with each other and to strive to respect the boundaries that they mutually set for their relationship. They thank you for bringing Marshall's views into your discussions with them because they value an understanding of women's committed relationships from the perspective of a lesbian expert on pastoral care.

You encourage Lenore and Dixie to get in touch with several denominational LGBTQ advocacy groups to learn which churches in the area welcome queer people. With their permission you contact a minister at one of these churches and learn that she offers marriage preparation classes for same-sex couples; she has also married several lesbian couples in the past

---

15. Marshall, *Counseling Lesbian Partners*, 60–61.

two years. Lenore and Dixie begin to meet with this minister and eagerly sign up for her next marriage preparation course. In your final meeting with this couple you offer them a bibliography of Christian worship resources for LGBTQ couples who are considering marriage.

Jacob: Claiming a Transgender Identity

Jacob makes an appointment to see you. In your first meeting he tells you some of his story: now nineteen years old, he changed his name from Rebecca when he was fifteen and refused to wear women's clothes any longer. Since then Jacob has had a very stormy relationship with his parents, who don't understand his transgender identity but have recently come to accept grudgingly his decision to identify as male. For the past year or so he has been attending a dynamic Reform synagogue as an out "transman," and the rabbi there has been, in Jacob's words, "supportive but really clueless when it comes to trans people." Jacob wants to find other trans youth for support and friendship. He says that he is especially eager to date another trans person.

After this first meeting with Jacob you return to some of the books on transgender identity and transgender spirituality that you have in your library in order to refamiliarize yourself with the stories and experiences of transgender people. You also decide to search on the Web for more information and discover a list of resources recommended by the National Center for Transgender Equality and the World Congress of Gay, Lesbian, Bisexual, and Transgender Jews. Keenly aware that nearly all queer youth are in desperate need of peer support when they are newly out, you also contact an area parent from the local PFLAG chapter who tells you of a monthly meeting for trans teenagers in the area. During your second pastoral care session with Jacob, you share these resources with him. He is clearly happy to have this information.

After a few meetings, you and Jacob establish a relationship of trust and mutual learning, and he discusses with you what he is looking for in a person to date. You learn that is he open to dating either an FTM ("Female-to-Male") or an MTF ("Male-to-Female") individual, and he begins to talk about the possibility of someday undergoing gender reassignment surgery. Once again, you recommend several resources on the topic, including those available from the Harry Benjamin International Gender Dysphoria Association (HBIGDA), which maintains an international directory of physicians, lawyers, psychologists, and other professionals who work with transgender individuals.[16]

In your last pastoral care session with Jacob you are happy to hear that he has taken the lead in organizing some educational events at his synagogue on queer issues. Although he was initially reluctant to suggest such an event to his rabbi, Jacob was pleasantly surprised when the rabbi introduced him to several lesbian, gay, and queer members of the congregation, including another trans teenager, who are eager to work with him on developing a series of educational nights on queer people and the Jewish faith.

Yolanda: Polyamory

A local minister whom you know asks if she might refer to you for pastoral care a middle-aged lesbian in her congregation who revealed to her a month ago that she is living in a long-term polyamorous relationship with two other women. This minister tells you that she disapproves of polyamorous relationships. Her congregant, an out lesbian, is a beloved member of the church community who currently serves on the church's board of trustees. You accept the referral.

Yolanda, a fifty-six-year-old lawyer, appears ill at ease when you meet her in your office for the first time. She asks you if you have ever met a person in a polyamorous relationship, and you respond that you haven't. You tell her that you are a person with an open mind who would be happy to work with her as a pastoral caregiver if you both decide that this is a good idea. Upon hearing this, she breathes a sigh of relief and smiles. You ask Yolanda what she hopes to gain from pastoral care. She says that she needs to talk with someone about the turmoil she is experiencing since coming

---

16. The World Professional Association for Transgender Health Inc., *www.hbigda.org/* (accessed October 6, 2006). HBIGDA also publishes the "Standards of Care for Gender Identity Disorders," which contain the association's "professional consensus about the psychiatric, psychological, medical, and surgical management of gender identity disorders."

out to her pastor as a person in a polyamorous relationship. Yolanda is considering leaving this church where she has belonged for almost ten years and "taking a break" from Christianity altogether because of her minister's disapproval of polyamory, which, she understands, reflects the long-standing teachings of the Christian faith.

Are polyamorous relationships moral? This is a question you find yourself asking as you reflect upon your first meeting with Yolanda. You realize that in order to offer her good pastoral care you need to understand polyamory in greater depth and explore how some progressive theologians are approaching it as a moral issue. Your reading to date has made you aware that both straight and queer individuals enter into polyamorous relationships, but that there is little reliable statistical data in the psychological or pastoral literature on how common such relationships are today. Nevertheless, the opportunity to care pastorally for Yolanda leads you to read about polyamory and to consider those frameworks of pastoral care that might be helpful to Yolanda.

In your second meeting with Yolanda you both agree to meet regularly and work through her dilemma about whether or not she will stay in her congregation. After mentioning that she has not gone to church since her pastor told her that she did not approve of her polyamorous relationship, Yolanda tells you about her deep love for her partners Therese and Abigail. Together for fifteen years, the three of them met while working together in the same law office one summer. Now all in their late fifties, these women own a house together and see themselves as a loving family made up of adults whose love for another is life-giving; they have chosen not to be sexually active with anyone outside their relationship. Neither of Yolanda's partners belongs to or attends a faith community, but she is a lifelong Presbyterian who finds great joy and meaning in Sunday worship and in the service she provides the congregation as a board member.

Following your second meeting with Yolanda, you decide to talk with a few of your closest pastoral care colleagues about polyamory. You learn to your surprise that one of them has had considerable experience working with individuals in polyamorous relationships. This colleague shares with you his own "conversion" to an understanding that polyamorous relationships can be healthy and ethical. He has come to know well three gay men who live together in a polyamorous union, and he believes that theirs is an example of a relationship that blends love, equality, and mutuality.

This same colleague also lets you know of the existence of Unitarian Universalists for Polyamory Awareness (UUPA), a group that is working to create greater understanding and acceptance of polyamory. You find this organization's definition of polyamory particularly helpful as you prepare to work further with Yolanda:

> [P]olyamory [is] the philosophy and practice of loving or relating intimately to more than one other person at a time with honesty and integrity. We advocate for any form of relationship or family structure — whether monogamous or multi-partner — which is characterized by free and responsible choice, mutual consent of all involved, and sincere adherence to personal philosophical values.[17]

You share this document with Yolanda, and she states that it mirrors her own position on polyamory. She also says that she finds the traditional Christian prohibition of polyamory wrong because of her own experience with her two partners. "Our relationship is ethical," she tells you, "because it is between consenting adults and is based on mutual love, real equality, and genuine respect."

In your subsequent meetings with Yolanda the two of you continue to talk about whether or not she will retain membership in her current congregation. You encourage her to consider meeting with her pastor again, but she decides against this course of action because she feels that this minister has "slammed the door shut" to any further discussion. As Yolanda reflects on why she has hidden her polyamorous relationship over the years from everyone in her congregation, she realizes that she needs to find other polyamorous people of faith for support. She locates and joins an online support group, relieved to know that there are others who share her experience and understand her values.

Yolanda thanks you often for the opportunity to meet with you in a safe environment to talk about her relationship. During your fifth, and final, pastoral care session with Yolanda, she says that she has decided not to return to her congregation. Rather, she has chosen to "take a break" from

---

17. Note: Unitarian Universalists for Polyamory Awareness is an independent organization with no official connection to the Unitarian Universalist Association. The UUPA mission statement: "to serve the Unitarian Universalist community of polyamorous people by providing support, promoting education and encouraging spiritual wholeness regarding polyamory," *www.uupa.org/index#mission* (accessed October 6, 2006).

church for a while and begin the search for a different faith community. "My hope is to find a community," she says, "in which I can be open and proud about who I am and whom I love."

Cecil: Constructing a Meaningful Sexual Ethic

A bisexual man in his mid-twenties, Cecil possesses enormous energy and a winning personality. Since graduation from college a few years ago he has become active in a local Christian congregation with a reputation for progressive theology and a diverse membership. Cecil e-mails you and asks if he might meet with you sometime. He says that a friend recommended you as a caregiver who has a reputation within the queer community as an empathetic and easy-to-talk-with caregiver. You arrange to meet with him the following week.

Bounding into your office just a few minutes late, Cecil says hello, shakes your hand, and sits down ready to talk. Within a short amount of time he tells you some of his story: he has identified himself as bisexual ever since he was fifteen, and he has enjoyed several sexual relationships with both women and men. He is not yet ready to settle down with one other person, and he says that a "healthy sex life" is one that offers him the richest and most rewarding way to live. Having left the conservative Christian denomination in which he was raised, he searched during his college years for a church that preached a progressive gospel of justice, equality, and peace. He eventually found such a congregation that did not demand that he live a celibate life until marriage.

"Thanks for telling me a bit about yourself, Cecil," you respond with sincerity. "So, tell me: what brings you here today?"

"Well," he answers, "I want to talk with another person of faith about my sexual relationships. Sometimes I feel empty inside about them . . . and I guess I wonder why."

As your first meeting with Cecil comes to a close, you suggest that he and you explore, over the course of several sessions, sexual morality within a Christian context. You ask him to think about his own value system in the coming weeks and consider how he decides which sexual relationships are good and which are not. He leaves the session full of energy, ready to carry out his "assignment."

Over time the two of you establish a comfortable and productive relationship of care. You listen intently to what he has to say, and in return, he is eager to hear your comments. After a few sessions he says that he has come to realize more clearly that those sexual relationships not rooted in a genuine concern for the other person often leave him feeling empty inside, and that most of those one-night stands with someone he has just met turn out to be disappointing in the end. What he had yet to figure out was *why* this was so since, in his words, "I never accepted those rules about sex that I had been taught as a kid in Sunday school." He simply couldn't agree that the only morally permissible sexual relationships were between a man and woman who had committed themselves to each other in marriage. You suggest to Cecil that he read a couple of articles by the Christian ethicist Kathy Rudy on sex outside of monogamous heterosexual marriage.

Rudy writes that the nonmonogamous sexual mores of gay male culture offer Christians valid ethical standards for evaluating their sexual relationships. Although the nonmonogamous sexual practices of some gay men have long been viewed by religious authorities as promiscuous and nonrelational, Rudy believes that they can be highly ethical and, in fact, authentically Christian because of their communal nature.[18] Noting that everyone has a deep yearning for connection with others, she suggests that the morality of sexual activity is best judged by whether it unites persons in meaningful ways:

> We are all, I believe, trying to escape meaninglessness in our lives. ... We want to escape the hurt that accompanies not belonging anywhere. Some of us do this with people of the same sex, others with people of the opposite sex. Some of us do this by having long-term, monogamous relationships, others by living in communities where love and support and belonging exist in different patterns. In any case, the pertinent question is not which kind of partner or pattern is the only ethical one, but rather which kinds of sexual interventions change our lives and make us part of one another, which acts unite us into one body, which contexts fight meaninglessness.[19]

18. Kathy Rudy, *Sex and the Church: Gender, Homosexuality, and the Transformation of Christian Ethics* (Boston: Beacon Press, 1997), 77.
19. Ibid., 83.

The "progressive sexual ethic" that Rudy calls for is one that has people evaluate their sexual relationships not in terms of monogamy but according to the standards of unitivity and hospitality. That is, those relationships that bring us into communion with others and with God and that also help us to care for one another are good relationships.[20]

In your remaining discussions with Cecil he says that Rudy's theology of sexuality is helping him to formulate a sexual morality that aligns his Christian faith with his own experience of sexual relationships. Cecil shares with you his growing conviction that sex with other persons is indeed good when it helps him make and sustain meaningful connections with other people. He says that he is coming to understand that sex which is devoid of such connections, on the other hand, is much less rewarding because it risks treating other people as objects and not as persons. Cecil also shares with you his growing appreciation that good sex for him is much more than the search for mutual pleasure with another person. Following Rudy, he agrees that good sex is that which contributes positively to relationships of genuine care. As the two of you bring your pastoral care sessions to a close, you feel confident that Cecil has made real progress in living more reflectively and more ethically in the world.

Derek and Lionel:
The Challenge of an Open Relationship

Ten years into a monogamous relationship and three years after civil and church marriage ceremonies in Massachusetts, Derek and Lionel are in crisis: Lionel wants "to open up their marriage" so that they are free to have outside sexual relationships. Derek, however, is opposed to this because he believes that monogamy is required of all married Christian couples. He also believes that nonmonogamous marriages eventually lead to divorce. Their minister has recommended that Derek and Lionel consider entering into a pastoral care relationship with you.

In your first session with Derek and Lionel it is clear to you that their relationship is at a crossroads. Derek is angry and resentful because "Lionel is

20. Ibid., 127.

unfairly changing the rules of our relationship after ten years." In response, Lionel says that he still loves Derek as his lifelong partner, but that he has come to realize, over the past few years, that a monogamous relationship is not what he wants in life. He says that he isn't interested in anonymous sex but rather in keeping open the possibility of sexual relationships with good friends. When you ask them what it is they hope to get from working with a pastoral caregiver they respond in unison, "Help!"

After learning more about the history of their relationship you understand that these two men care deeply for one another and that they seem to have weathered well many of the challenges that come with a ten-year relationship, including the death of parents, job losses, and a recent move across the country. You also discover that Derek and Lionel have recently joined a local Metropolitan Community Church where they feel very much at home. It is, in Lionel's words, "the first congregation where we can be Christian and gay — with no hiding who we are from others."

Your challenge in this pastoral situation is to help Derek and Lionel work through their current impasse and, by encouraging them to reflect and talk about their values, come to an agreement about how to move forward in their relationship. At the end of your first session the three of you decide to meet weekly for the next couple of months. Derek and Lionel express gratefulness that they share a Christian identity with you, their caregiver, and as they leave your office, you realize that you will be exploring with them in considerable depth issues of fidelity and monogamy. After they are gone you continue to think about the role of monogamy in the relationships of Christian couples.

There are many couples who embrace monogamy as the best way for them to build a committed relationship of love and fidelity. For many Christian LGBTQ couples who have modeled their relationships on heterosexual marriage, sexual monogamy is a given. They share the view of theologian Virginia Ramey Mollenkott when she writes that "there can be little doubt that the biblical ideal for sexual experience is a monogamous lifetime or at least long-term relationship."[21] In addition, many straight

---

21. Virginia R. Mollenkott, "The Sex-Love Connection in the Hebrew and Christian Scriptures," in Mollenkott, *Sensuous Spirituality: Out from Fundamentalism* (New York: Crossroad, 1992), 117.

Christian supporters of same-sex marriage insist that such marriages be monogamous.[22]

On the other hand, there are LGBTQ couples who value nonmonogamy as a vital dimension of their relationships, including Christian couples who have married or entered into civil unions or other forms of partnership. These couples permit sexual activity outside of their primary relationship, albeit usually within certain limits and according to agreed-upon rules. Whereas a pastoral caregiver can easily draw upon traditional Christian teachings on marital monogamy when working with LGBTQ care receivers, are there any sound theological principles for supporting nonmonogamy in queer marriages or partnerships?

Carter Heyward, a lesbian Episcopal priest, has written on the connections between Christian spirituality and lesbian sexuality, and she argues that nonmonogamy is not necessarily synonymous with promiscuity. Indeed, in her "ethic of erotic friendship" for adults, which stresses the goodness of human sexual pleasure, the importance of mutuality, and the requirement that we not harm others in our sexual relating, Heyward speaks of nonmonogamy as a legitimate way of relating sexually to others in friendship:

> To be nonmonogamous is not necessarily to be, in the pejorative sense, "promiscuous" — wanton and nondiscriminatory — in our sexual practices and choices of sexual partners. It may be rather a way of participating in the embodied fullness of different special friendships. Gay men, more than either lesbians or heterosexual persons in our society, seem to have developed ways of being honest and open in relation to two or more lovers over a single period of time. Often, in these cases, a primary commitment to a particular lover is sustained.[23]

Your reading of Heyward has given you some theological context for understanding that Lionel's desire for an open relationship may reflect a desire for experiencing friendship more deeply. However, as you come

---

22. See, for instance, Sidney Callahan, "Two by Two: The Case for Monogamy," in *Commonweal* (July 15, 1994), *www.findarticles.com/p/articles/mi_m1252/is_n13_v121/ai_15682146* (accessed October 6, 2006).

23. Heyward, *Touching Our Strength*, 136–37.

to know this couple better, you realize that Derek's attachment to a monogamous relationship is firmly rooted in his beliefs.

In subsequent sessions with this couple you work on facilitating conversations in which each of them can state clearly his own views and work toward understanding better the other's views. The goal, of course, is a mutually agreed-upon resolution to their dilemma, but in the meantime it is important that each of them clearly articulate for himself and then for the other his own point of view. You share with them the views of Hunt and others that the best relationships are those that embody equality, mutuality, and individual empowerment, and you compliment them often on their willingness to be honest with one another about their disagreements. You acknowledge that this is hard work for any couple and, quoting Carter Heyward, tell them that the "vital work of 'taking care of the relationship' requires negotiating the conflicting feelings, needs, desires, and expectations that are present, to some extent, in all relationships."[24]

During one of your sessions with Lionel and Derek you bring up the issue of fidelity in relationships, and this proves to open an especially fruitful discussion that enables them to explore more deeply a value that each of them says is vital to their relationship. While Derek says that he understands sexual monogamy as the deepest sign of fidelity within any marital relationship, Lionel sees a commitment "to be there for the other person through everything" as the core meaning of fidelity.

After several weekly meetings with Derek and Lionel you agree to their request to continue meeting with them. Clearly, this couple is committed to deepening their dialogue and finding a way to come to an agreement about their sexual relationship and, in the process, save their marriage. You look forward to continuing pastoral care with them.

Mary Margaret: Celibacy and an LGBTQ Identity

For forty of her sixty years Mary Margaret has been a member of a Roman Catholic religious order. Entering the convent right out of high school, she tells you that she had wanted to be a nun since she was a little girl. She says that she has lived her life with a high degree of satisfaction and, in particular, that she has found college teaching

24. Ibid., 130.

to be a ministry that has sustained her throughout her many years as a religious. What brings her to pastoral care at this moment in her life, however, are some nagging questions about her own sexual desires. Lately, she finds herself yearning deeply for the company of other lesbians.

Sister Mary Margaret tells you in your first meeting with her that she loves being a nun and that she has never regretted her decision at the age of twenty to enter the novitiate and begin her training for the religious life. She enjoys communal living, daily prayer, a shared apostolate with other women, and the lifelong opportunity to work as a minister of the gospel. You are genuinely impressed with how satisfied Mary Margaret appears to be with her life, but when you ask her about her desire to seek companionship with other lesbians, her facial expression changes to one of weariness. She speaks with less assurance in her voice.

"When I was in my mid-thirties," she tells you, "I fell in love with another nun in the convent, and it was an earthshaking experience because I had never felt that way about another person before." You learn that, after much struggle, the two nuns decided that they could not live in the same house if they were to remain true to their vows of chastity. Mary Margaret tells you that, although this relationship never became sexual, it was a genuine relationship of love. Following their "breakup," she worked hard to sublimate her sexual feelings, and she decided to devote herself ever more diligently to her teaching and community responsibilities. Of particular help in this difficult time was another sister in her community who served as Mary Margaret's spiritual director; together they read *The Sexual Celibate* by Donald Goergen.

Over the course of several sessions you and Mary Margaret explore her current desire to be with other lesbians. She emphasizes repeatedly her deep and ongoing commitment to her religious vow of chastity and says that she is afraid that becoming emotionally involved with other lesbians might lead her to break this vow. "I need to spend time with other lesbians, but I'm afraid that I might fall in love again with a woman. And then what might happen?" she asks.

Mary Margaret's mention of *The Sexual Celibate* leads you to suggest that the two of you reread this book and see what, if anything, might still be of value to her as she works on understanding more deeply the nature of her call to a committed life of celibacy as a religious sister.[25] It turns out that this book provides a helpful framework for your pastoral care sessions with Mary Margaret because of its frank and theologically based discussions of vowed celibacy. She calls to mind how much she appreciated, in her earlier reading of the book, the author's claim that celibate religious women and men are sexual beings who, like everyone else, need to love others if they are to be well-integrated and fulfilled.

After four months of pastoral care, Mary Margaret comes to the point of realizing that she needs the friendship of other lesbians to be happy. Shedding many of her earlier fears that socializing with lesbian women will lead her into a sexual relationship, she says that she now understands that living in fear of intimacy is an unhealthy way to live. She looks forward to learning how to enjoy the friendship and support of other lesbians as she continues to value her vocation and vows as a nun.

Pastoral Care and Queer Families

LGBTQ persons typically belong to two types of families: families of origin and families of choice. A family of origin refers to the biological family into which one was born and raised or the family into which one was adopted and raised. Families of choice, on the other hand, describe those families that a person creates on the basis of love and friendship. A family of choice may or may not entail a sexual relationship between the adults in the relationship and it may or may not include children.[26] For the many LGBTQ people who have experienced alienation and rejection from their families of origin, their families of choice have been a saving grace, providing them with the love and acceptance that has sometimes been tragically withheld by members of families formed on the basis of blood or legal ties. Many queer people, of course, eventually reconcile with and find support from their families of origin around issues relating to their gender identity and sexual preference, but for most LGBTQ people their families of choice continue to hold an essential place in their lives and their hearts.

---

25. Donald Goergen, *The Sexual Celibate* (New York: Seabury Press, 1974).

26. See Kath Weston, *Families We Choose: Lesbians, Gays, Kinship* (New York: Columbia University Press, 1991), 38–41, 118.

Some queer families of choice may resemble the conventional modern nuclear family with two parents and their children. Most, however, take decidedly different forms. Whatever their makeup, these families come in many and varied configurations that reflect the wonderful creativity with which LGBTQ people create family. Here are just a few examples:

+ Five lesbian women who live together as friends
+ A group of men living with HIV who form an extended, nonresidential network of mutual care and support
+ A longtime queer support group at a local Christian congregation
+ A transgender couple raising their adopted children
+ A group of LGBTQ college students who live on the same floor in a university dormitory
+ A lesbian couple who co-parent their son with a gay male couple
+ Three men who live together in a polyamorous relationship

Given the discussion above on queer relationships without children, I focus here on issues that arise in connection with queer families that include children: the choice to bear or to adopt children, seeking support as a queer parent with children, issues of isolation for children in families with queer parents, and creating a supportive religious community for queer youth.[27]

Marissa: Choosing Biological or Adoptive Parenthood

Marissa is a thirty-year-old lesbian and grade school teacher who has decided to become a single parent. She has lived in a large house with two other lesbians and a gay man for six years now. They consider themselves a family, and everyone in the household is happy about and supportive of Marissa's decision to have a child. A committed Christian who is active in her congregation's religious education pro-

---

27. On issues relating to LGBTQ people and their families of origin, see chapter 4, "Coming Out."

gram, Marissa is having difficulty deciding whether to have a child biologically or to adopt an infant from a local social services agency.

During your first pastoral care session with Marissa you learn a good deal about the love, care, and support present in her household, which she describes as both a "co-housing community" and "a real, honest-to-goodness family." As co-owners of the house in which they live, she and her three adult friends share a close common life that includes meals and frequent socializing together. Although nobody is romantically involved with another household member, they are a family that hopes to remain together indefinitely. You learn from Marissa that her decision to have a child has come after years of personal reflection and discussion with her family members. In fact, she would like to share some of the parenting responsibilities with her housemates, whom she hopes will be "like aunts and an uncle" to her child.

In your subsequent pastoral care meetings you explore more deeply with Marissa the issue of whether she should have a child through artificial insemination or adoption. On the one hand she would love to have the experience of pregnancy and childbirth; she also likes the idea of having a biological connection to her daughter or son. On the other hand she knows that there are thousands of children awaiting adoptive families through public and private foster care and adoption agencies. "How am I going to decide which is the best thing for me to do?" she wonders.

You encourage Marissa to pray about her questions and to talk with other queer people who are parents. She joins a local support group for LGBTQ parents-to-be that you recommend to her, and she begins to talk regularly with a lesbian couple in her congregation who have adopted children. In time she discovers that she wants to adopt a child.

José, Michael, and April:
A Queer Family in Search of Community

José and Michael, each in their late forties, have been together for fifteen years. They have one daughter, April, who is now four years old, and a year ago they moved from their urban neighborhood with few children to a suburban neighborhood with many children. José and Michael have begun to feel isolated, however, in this new setting because they are the only gay parents.

This couple has been referred to you by their minister, who has no experience working with gay couples with children. Her congregation has a few lesbian and gay couples who are members, but none of them are parents. After speaking briefly with Michael on the phone you agree to meet with him and José the following week.

In your first meeting with this couple you understand how deeply isolated they feel as gay parents. Their move to a neighborhood with no other gay or lesbian couples has proven uncomfortable for them because, as they report, they are a shy and rather introverted couple with little experience making friends with straight couples. They worry in particular that their daughter April will grow up with few friends because they are so disconnected from the families who live around them.

As you get to know this couple you realize that their isolation is causing significant problems within their relationship. With little understanding of the challenges of gay parenting, their family and friends seem unable to provide them with much support. Clearly, this couple is showing signs of stress, and they are feeling increasingly inadequate and ill-equipped as parents. Realizing that they need to find networks of support for themselves as a couple and as gay parents, you point them in the direction of local resources, including a queer parenting group at the LGBTQ community center and a nearby PFLAG chapter. In addition, you suggest that José and Michael consider some ways in which they might get to know their neighbors in order to discover which of them might be supportive of them as a family and help them feel more at home in the neighborhood.

After several sessions with this couple you learn that they are disappointed with the lack of support they feel as members of their current congregation. Since church involvement has always been an important part of their life together, they say that they are coming to realize that they need to find a faith community with at least a few other gay or lesbian parents. They also realize they need to become more involved in their daughter's preschool by serving on a school committee (in order to meet other parents) and by helping out in the classroom. You applaud this realization and suggest that their occasional presence in April's classroom can be an important way of normalizing for her and her peers the fact that she has two fathers. Finally, they decide to hold an open house so that they can begin the process of making friends in their neighborhood.

By encouraging José and Michael to make connections with other gay and lesbian parents in their area and to take the lead in meeting their neighbors, you have helped them to understand that *they* need to be more proactive in creating the kind of community in which they want live. After a few weeks of visiting other local congregations they find a church with an active LGBTQ social and advocacy group. Although this church belongs to a different denomination than their current congregation, they realize that it will offer them a supportive spiritual home for their family. You wish José and Michael luck as they get to know their neighbors and prepare to join a new faith community. Based on the newfound enthusiasm with which they are approaching this task, you expect that they will meet with success.

Damon, Clare, and Abby: Building Support for a Queer Family in a Community of Faith

Damon is the only child of Clare and Abby. Now nine years old and in the fourth grade, he recently came home from Sunday school upset because two children had called his moms "dykes and lesbos." After working successfully with their son's Sunday school teacher on ways to address the issue of teasing, Clare and Abby decided to begin a conversation with you, the pastor at their church, about making the congregation more welcoming of children with LGBTQ parents. You say that you are eager to help educate the entire congregation about ways to welcome families with gay and lesbian parents.

In your first meeting with Clare and Abby you talk with them about some ways in which they might work with their church leadership to build a congregation that welcomes and affirms all children, including those with LGBTQ parents. Clare and Abby have been active for a few years in a local chapter of COLAGE (Children of Lesbians and Gays Everywhere), and they believe that their experience as effective advocates for children of queer parents in the local school system has prepared them to help foster a productive conversation at their church about LGBTQ people and their families.

You suggest to this couple that one of the most effective ways for a church to become welcoming to and inclusive of all families is through its educational programs. Given the increasing number of LGBTQ-welcoming resources designed and produced by individuals and groups representing various Christian denominations, you recommend that Abby and Clare explore the Institute of Welcoming Resources Web site.[28] You also encourage them to contact the UCC Coalition for LGBT Concerns, a national organization for LGBTQ members and their allies in the United Church of Christ, the denomination to which their church belongs. The coalition has a particularly valuable resource in its Open and Affirming Program, which assists local congregations working to welcome and include LGBTQ people.[29]

Since lifelong religious education opportunities can be a particularly effective way to build acceptance and inclusion of queer individuals and families in a congregation, you suggest that Abby and Clare also check out the "Our Whole Lives" curriculum, a comprehensive sexuality education program intended for church members at various stages of life from kindergarten through adulthood.[30] Written by the United Church of Christ and the Unitarian Universalist Association, this curriculum is based upon the conviction that young people and adults alike make good decisions about sexual activity when they are well-informed about human sexuality in a holistic manner and when they engage in values-clarification processes that are appropriate to their age level. Homosexuality is included in the curriculum as a natural variation of human sexuality, and LGBTQ people are rendered visible in the lessons that make up this program. By normalizing queer people and their sexuality, this curriculum teaches, from an early age, the value of accepting all people. Use of the Our Whole Lives curriculum can also help communities of faith in their work to welcome and affirm LGBTQ people and their families as full-fledged members of a faith community.

Abby and Clare are excited to learn about this new curriculum, and the more they come to understand it, the more they believe that it contains

---

28. "Christian/Denominationally Based GLBT Organizations," *www.welcomingresources.org/links.htm#religious* (accessed October 6, 2006).

29. The UCC Coalition for LGBT Concerns, *www.ucccoalition.org/programs/ona.html* (accessed October 6, 2006).

30. See *Planning Guide for Our Whole Lives: Leader Trainings for Unitarian Universalist Districts and Clusters*, *www.uua.org/owl/planningguide.pdf#search=%22introduction%20to%20our%20whole%20lives%22* (accessed October 6, 2006).

good ideas on how to teach children and adults the values of diversity. Soon these women are on the road to becoming certified teachers of the curriculum. They discuss with their minister and religious education direc-tor how they might incorporate aspects of the Our Whole Lives curriculum into their church's Sunday school program. "I think that we will spark a worthwhile discussion at our church about how to welcome queer parents and their children. We also hope to explore with other members of our congregation how we might include information on homosexuality in our religious education program," Clare says during your last meeting with this couple. "The good news is that folks at our church are open in exploring how we might do this. Who knows? Maybe we can begin to figure out a way to include issues about LGBTQ people and their families at *all* levels of our congregation's educational programming."

Jason and Alice:
Accepting a Transgender Child

Jason and Alice, parents of a twenty-one-year-old, telephone and ask if they might meet to discuss their child. They describe them-selves as "devout Christians" who have not seen their child in more than a year because they have not been able to accept their child's transgender identity. "How can we, as good Christians, embrace a trans child?" they ask. You agree to meet with them the following week.

Alice and Jason are clearly upset as they greet you for the first time in your office. You shake their hands, invite them to sit down and make themselves comfortable, and then ask them to tell you more about their child. Alice begins eagerly:

"Our child used to be called Robert," she says, "but for the past year or so he has insisted on being called Ella. I don't know what we did wrong in raising our son to want to be a woman. We've always been a solid and faithful Christian family, but I don't know how to accept my son as a woman."

Jason continues, "I *do* want to love and accept my son, but I don't know where and how to begin. He is lucky to be in a liberal college environment where evidently he is accepted as a she. To be honest, I'm relieved that our child no longer comes home to visit or attends church with us. I mean, what would we say to other people? How could we explain to the minister that our son is now our daughter?"

As you assess Jason and Alice's situation during your first pastoral care visit with them, you see clearly that this couple not only feels alone in their struggle to accept their child's transgender identity, but that they have not availed themselves of any positive educational information on transgender people. Nor have they found a way to understand their transgender daughter from a faith perspective. You suggest that they join you in learning about transgender people and that they consider joining a support group for parents of transgender children.

In your second pastoral care sessions with this couple you learn that they desperately do want to accept their child and her transgender identity but that they don't see how they can reconcile this acceptance with their Christian faith. "Doesn't God decide before we are born whether we are male or female?" Alice asks at one point. Jordan adds, "I've always been taught that God doesn't make mistakes in making us who he wants us to be."

You invite Jordan and Alice to read and pray about three passages in the Christian New Testament during the coming week: Matthew 19:11–12, Acts 8:25–39, and Galatians 3:28. These biblical references provide important messages of affirmation for transgender persons because they call upon us to reevaluate our understandings of gender variance in the light of faith. Drawing upon Justin Tanis's exegesis of these three passages, you explore with Jordan and Alice the reference to "eunuchs for the kingdom" in Matthew's Gospel as a call for us today to accept transgender individuals as children of God; the message of radical inclusion for gender-variant people contained in the story of the Ethiopian eunuch in Acts; and Paul's profound description of a Christian unity that overcomes all sorts of divisions, including that of gender.[31] Jordan and Alice are deeply moved to read scripture passages that speak positively to them about transgender people.

The medical, psychological, and legal information on transgender issues that you recommend to Alice and Jordan proves to be an essential

---

31. Justin Tanis, *Trans-Gendered: Theology, Ministry, and Communities of Faith* (Cleveland: Pilgrim Press, 2003), 72–83.

ingredient in their journey toward understanding their daughter Ella and her transgender identity. Some of the most helpful resources come from the PFLAG Transgender Network (TNET), the National Center for Transgender Equality (NCTE), and the National Lesbian and Gay Task Force (NLGTF).[32] In addition, a local support group of parents of transgender children puts Alice and Jordan in touch with other people struggling to understand and accept their children; this network of support moves them to start a process of rebuilding their relationship with Ella. They take the first steps toward this goal by welcoming their daughter back into their home.

As your pastoral care relationship with this couple comes to a close, they thank you for your help in bringing them out of the closet as parents of a transgender child. In their last session with you, Alice and Jordan speak of the great distance they have come in embracing their daughter as their beloved child, and they share with you their dream of someday becoming advocates for all transgender people.

What Queer Relationships and Queer Families Can Teach Our Faith Communities

One need only peruse the Hebrew and Christian scriptures to realize that they reveal a wonderful variety of human relationships and family structures that reflect life-giving values of love, mutuality, and equality.[33] In this chapter we have explored a few of the ways in which LGBTQ people structure their interpersonal and family relationships with the goal of understanding how you, as a pastoral caregiver, can support queer people in their interpersonal and family relationships. While the biblical record urges you to be a caregiver who is open to a variety of relationships and family structures, the ministry of pastoral care challenges you to provide excellent care for those who come to you for help in sustaining their relationships and their families. Once again, the hallmarks of such care include an acceptance and celebration of LGBTQ persons and their sexuality, an eagerness to learn from queer people themselves about their

---

32. PFLAG Transgender Network (TNET), *pflag.org/PFLAGs_Transgender_Network .tnet.0.html* (accessed October 6, 2006).

33. See Mollenkott, *Sensuous Spirituality,* 194–97, who lists forty "Diverse Forms of Family Mentioned or Implied in the Hebrew and Christian Scriptures."

relationships and their families, and a commitment to explore theologies of sexuality that creatively apply the healing wisdom of the Jewish and Christian faith traditions to the lived experience of queer people. As we know, caregivers in these faith traditions have often been anything but a source of healing or support for LGBTQ people. Fortunately, however, the growing acceptance and affirmation of queer people in many of our congregations is bringing about a revolution of positive pastoral care. Caring for LGBTQ people may not always be easy, but it is certainly rewarding and an essential ministry of our faith communities.

Epilogue

Thank You and Welcome

We believe that pastoral care with lesbian, bisexual, transgender, queer, and gay people of faith is a challenging, rewarding, and grace-filled experience. As we remarked in the Introduction, "What a time to be in ministry with us!" We now add: "What a gift pastoral care with queer folk can be for care receiver and caregiver alike!"

Clearly, there is an urgent need for compassionate and reality-based pastoral care for the many LGBTQ people who strive to embrace their gender identity, their sexual orientation, *and* their commitment to a spiritual life in a faith community — all in equal measure. No longer content to hide in the shadows of church or synagogue life, queer people of faith are standing up in increasing numbers and claiming their rightful place as daughters and sons of God called to full membership in our communities of faith.

To ignore the pastoral care needs of LGBTQ women and men because they are LGBTQ is unjust; to insist that the sexual orientation, gender identity, or sexual expression of queer people is sinful or disordered is incompatible with the powerfully liberating message of the scriptures; to offer pastoral care that is half hearted or does not speak adequately to the lives and needs of LGBTQ persons is to deny them the love and support that all religions teach is due every person.

In this book we have attempted to provide a practical handbook for pastoral caregivers, especially those in training, who are called to work with LGBTQ people. While we do not claim to offer the last word on any aspect of LGBTQ pastoral care, we do hope that we have provided you, the reader, with some reliable guidance and thought-provoking questions. Most important, we have stressed the importance of listening, with an open mind and open heart, to the experiences of queer persons in your care so that you might know something of their life's journey and build with them a pastoral relationship of genuine respect, effective care, and mutual growth.

It is common knowledge that current debates concerning LGBTQ persons and queer sexuality threaten some denominations, churches, and synagogues with schism and outright dissolution. Your pastoral care with LGBTQ people is indispensable in this tumultuous time because it offers living testimony to the Jewish and Christian belief that everyone is equal in God's sight. Moreover, your ministry can change people's hearts and contribute significantly, probably in ways never fully knowable, to building the beloved community that Martin Luther King Jr. described so eloquently and that we, as committed Christians and Jews, yearn for so deeply.

LGBTQ pastoral care is still in its infancy, and those caregivers who work in this field are true pioneers. We have shared our ideas in this book as one way of giving back to the many women and men who have served us as companions and guides on our own journeys as queer people of faith. We are grateful for your time and attention to our efforts. If you have been a pastoral caregiver to LGBTQ people for a long or short period of time, in our own names and in the names of many, we say, "Thank you! We are honored to be colleagues with you in this vital work." If you are new to this particular ministry or preparing for it, we say, "Welcome to a fulfilling, exciting, and urgently needed field of pastoral care!"

Appendix

Sexual Rating Scales

Research has consistently shown that human sexuality can be understood more accurately as a continuum rather than as a duality, as a fluid and changing state rather than a static one. Without comment on the numbers in each category nor the exactness of the boundaries, the following two scales help to show this continuum in a graphic way.

The Kinsey Homosexual-Heterosexual Rating Scale

The Kinsey Scale attempts to measure *sexual orientation,* from 0 (exclusively heterosexual) to 6 (exclusively homosexual). It was first published in *Sexual Behavior in the Human Male* (1948) by Alfred Kinsey, Wardell Pomeroy, and others, and was also prominent in the complementary work *Sexual Behavior in the Human Female* (1953). Introducing the scale, Kinsey wrote:

> Males [This part of the study deals only with males] do not represent two discrete populations, heterosexual and homosexual. The world is not to be divided into sheep and goats. It is a fundamental of taxonomy that nature rarely deals with discrete categories.... The living world is a continuum in each and every one of its aspects. (639)
>
> While emphasizing the continuity of the gradations between exclusively heterosexual and exclusively homosexual histories, it has seemed desirable to develop some sort of classification which could be based on the relative amounts of heterosexual and homosexual experience or response in each history.... An individual may be assigned a position on this scale, for each period in his life. A seven-point scale comes nearer to showing the many gradations that actually exist. (639, 656)

Heterosexual-Homosexual Rating Scale

0. Exclusively heterosexual with no homosexual
1. Predominantly heterosexual, only incidentally homosexual
2. Predominantly heterosexual, but more than incidentally homosexual
3. Equally heterosexual and homosexual
4. Predominantly homosexual, but more than incidentally heterosexual
5. Predominantly homosexual, only incidentally heterosexual
6. Exclusively homosexual

(Scale is reprinted by permission of The Kinsey Institute for Research in Sex, Gender, and Reproduction, Inc.)

The Klein Sexual Orientation Grid

The Klein Scale attempts to further measure sexual orientation by expanding upon the earlier Kinsey scale.

Because most people had been (and arguably still are) first exposed to sexuality with the binary of heterosexual or homosexual, Kinsey set his scale of sexual orientation with seven intervals, beginning at 0 with "Exclusively Heterosexual" and concluding at 6 with "Exclusively Homosexual."

Fritz Klein refined the scale and somewhat simplified it. It remains with seven intervals, but has added five factors of one's sexual makeup. One is thus asked to make a judgment by applying the seven categories to the following five factors:

Klein's five factors are:

1. Sexual Attraction: To whom are you sexually attracted?
2. Sexual Behavior: With whom have you actually had sex?
3. Sexual Fantasies: About whom are your sexual fantasies?
4. Emotional Preference: Do you love and like only members of the same sex, only members of the other sex, or members of both sexes?
5. Social Preference: With members of which sex do you socialize?

Klein's seven categories are:

1. Other sex only.
2. Other sex mostly.
3. Other sex somewhat more
4. Both sexes equally
5. Same sex somewhat more
6. Same sex mostly
7. Same sex only

To use the scale simply ask the questions posed in the five factors and answer by choosing one of the seven categories. For example: "To whom are you sexually attracted?" (factor 1). Choose an answer from the most accurate category, for example, 6: "Same sex mostly." Or another example: "With members of which sex do you socialize?" (factor 5). The answer may be 4: "Both sexes equally."

In addition, the Klein Scale investigates sexual experience and fantasies in three times: the present (the most recent twelve months), the past (up to twelve months ago), and the ideal (which is as close as one can get to intention and prediction of future behavior). Klein allowed the concept that people's sexuality can change through their lives and gives a more expanded and nuanced picture of one's sexuality.

By considering these other life factors, Klein's categorical scale offers much more in terms of understanding that sexual activities do not necessarily denote *sexual orientation,* and just because two people have the same *sexual identity* does not mean that they have the same sexual practices.

For more information and more detailed graphic representations of the scales, please consult the following Web sites, from which much of the above material is taken:

www.kinseyinstitute.org/resources/ak-hhscale.html

www.members.tde.com/ben/kleingrid.html

www.en.wikipedia.org/wiki/Klein_Sexual_Orientation_Grid

Resources

Activism

Goss, Robert. *Jesus Acted Up: A Gay and Lesbian Manifesto.* San Francisco: Harper-SanFrancisco, 1993.

Kramer, Larry. *The Tragedy of Today's Gays.* New York: Jeremy P. Tarcher/Penguin, 2005.

Parents, Families & Friends of Lesbians & Gays (PFLAG). *www.pflag.org.*

Soulforce. "A network of friends learning nonviolence from Gandhi and King seeking justice for God's lesbian, gay, bisexual and transgender children." *www.soulforce.org.*

White, Mel. *Religion Gone Bad: The Hidden Dangers of the Christian Right.* New York: Tarcher, 2006.

Age, Young and Old

Big Brothers/Big Sisters: *www.bbbs.org.*

Clunis, D. Merilee. *Lives of Lesbian Elders: Looking Back, Looking Forward.* New York: Haworth Press, 2005.

Covenant House is a national outreach to kids who live on the streets. *www.covenanthouse.org.*

Kimmel, Douglas, ed. *Lesbian, Gay, Bisexual, and Transgender Aging: Research and Clinical Perspectives.* New York: Columbia University Press, 2006.

Lambda GLBT Community Services Web site has a useful article on teen suicide: *www.lambda.org/youth_suicide.htm.*

The Point Foundation provides financial support, mentoring, and hope to meritorious students who are marginalized due to sexual orientation, gender expression, or gender identity: *www.thepointfoundation.org/index.html.*

Remafedi, Gary, ed. *Death by Denial: Studies of Suicide in Gay and Lesbian Teenagers.* Boston: Alyson Publications, 1994.

Ryan, Caitlin. *Lesbian and Gay Youth: Care and Counseling.* New York: Columbia University Press, 1998.

Stop a Suicide Today: Screening for Mental Health. *www.stopasuicide.org/signs.html.*

Suicide Awareness Voices of Education (SAVE). *www.save.org/depressed/symptoms.html.*

AIDS

Bartlett, John G., and Ann K. Finkbeiner. *The Guide to Living with HIV Infection* (Developed at the Johns Hopkins AIDS Clinic). Baltimore: Johns Hopkins University Press Health Book, 2006.

Connolly, Sean. *AIDS Pastoral Care: An Introductory Guide*. Grantsville, WI: Arc Research Co., 1994.

Local resources: Use search engines and printed directories to find local AIDS services. Here are two examples: Chicago: APCN (AIDS Pastoral Care Network), *www.accesscommunityhealth.net/services/service.aspx?svcId=16;* Grand Rapids, *www.graceoffice.org/acn*.

Messer, Donald E. *Breaking the Conspiracy of Silence: Christian Churches and the Global AIDS Crisis*. Minneapolis: Augsburg Fortress Publishers, 2004.

Bisexuality

Andrew, Elizabeth. *Swinging on the Garden Gate: A Spiritual Memoir*. Boston: Skinner House Books, 2000.

The Bisexual Resource Center in Boston: *www.biresource.org*.

Kinsey Scale of Human Sexuality: *www.kinseyinstitute.org/research/ak-hhscale.html*.

Klein, Fred. *The Bisexual Option: A Concept of One Hundred Percent Intimacy*. New York: Priam Books, 1978.

Klein Sexual Orientation Grid: *www.biresource.org/pamphlets/scales.html*.

Kolodny, Debra R., ed. *Blessed Bi Spirit: Bisexual People of Faith*. New York: Continuum, 2000.

Celibacy, LGBTQ

Goergen, Donald. *The Sexual Celibate*. New York: Seabury Press, 1974.

Isherwood, Lisa. *The Power of Erotic Celibacy: Queering Heteropatriarchy*. London, New York: T & T Clark, 2006.

Schneiders, Sandra. *Selling All: Commitment, Consecrated Celibacy, and Community in Catholic Religious Life*. New York: Paulist Press, 2001.

Children of LGBTQ Parents

Elliot, Keith. *Zack's Story: Growing Up with Same-Sex Parents*. Minneapolis: Lerner Publications, 1996.

Garner, Abigail. *Families Like Mine: Children of Gay Parents Tell It Like It Is*. New York: HarperCollins, 2004.

Howey, Noelle, and Ellen Samuels, eds. *Out of the Ordinary: Essays on Growing Up with Gay, Lesbian, and Transgender Parents*. New York: St. Martin's Press, 2000.

Newman, Leslea. *Heather Has Two Mommies*. 10th anniversary ed. Los Angeles: Alyson Books, 2000.

Willhoite, Michael. *Daddy's Roommate*. Los Angeles: Alyson Books, 1990.

Coming Out

Austin, Jen. *Coming Out Christian: Finding Wholeness in Faith and Sexuality*. Dallas: Sources of Hope Publishing, 2006.

Bono, Chastity, and Billie Fitzpatrick. *Family Outing: A Guide to the Coming-Out Process for Gays, Lesbians, and Their Families*. Boston: Little, Brown, 1998.

Borhek, Mary. *Coming Out to Parents: A Two-Way Survival Guide for Lesbians and Gay Men and Their Parents.* Cleveland: Pilgrim Press, 1993.

Buxton, Amity. *The Other Side of the Closet: The Coming-Out Crisis for Straight Spouses and Families.* Rev. ed. New York: J. Wiley, 1994.

de la Huerta, Christian. *Coming Out Spiritually: The Next Step.* New York: Jeremy P. Tarcher/Putnam, 1999.

Dickens, Joy, ed. *Family Outing: A Guide for Parents of Gays, Lesbians and Bisexuals.* London: P. Owen, 1995.

Glaser, C. *Coming Out to God: Prayers for Lesbians and Gay Men, Their Families and Friends.* Louisville: Westminster John Knox Press, 1991.

Grever, Carol. *My Husband Is Gay: A Woman's Guide to Surviving the Crisis.* Freedom, CA: Crossing Press, 2001.

Griffin, Carolyn, and Marian Wirth. *Beyond Acceptance: Parents of Lesbians and Gays Talk about Their Experiences.* Rev. ed. New York: St. Martin's Press, 1996.

Likosky, Stephan, ed. *Coming Out: An Anthology of International Gay and Lesbian Writings.* New York: Pantheon Books, 1992.

Mattmann, Urs. *Coming In: Gays and Lesbians Reclaiming the Spiritual Journey.* Glasgow: Wild Goose Publications, 2006.

O'Neill, Craig, and Kathleen Ritter. *Coming Out Within: Stages of Spiritual Awakening for Lesbians and Gay Men.* San Francisco: HarperSanFrancisco, 1992.

PFLAG. *Our Daughters and Our Sons: Questions and Answers for Parents of Gay, Lesbian and Bisexual People.* www.pflagdetroit.org/Publications/Our_Daughters_and_Sons_Final_03.pdf.

———. *Our Trans Children.* www.pflag.org/Our_Trans_Children_-_Intro.otc.0.html.

Schimel, Lawrence, ed. *Found Tribe: Jewish Coming Out Stories.* Santa Fe, NM: Sherman Asher, 2002.

Tigert, L., and T. Brown, eds. *Coming Out Young and Faithful.* Cleveland: Pilgrim Press, 2001.

Diversity

Bell, A., and M. Weinberg. *Homosexualities: A Study of Diversity among Men and Women.* New York: Simon and Schuster, 1978.

Religious tolerance.org: A useful Web site for researching religious tolerance and diversity: www.religioustolerance.org.

Drugs and Addictions

"Anti-Meth Site" contains valuable information about crystal meth. www.kci.org/meth_info/links.htm.

"Dark Crystal" an article on *The Fifth Estate,* Canadian Broadcasting Company. www.cbc.ca/fifth/darkcrystal/facts.html.

Minor, Robert N. "When Religion Is an Addiction" (Fairness Project Lecture Series). Audiocassette. *QuestLiving.com,* 2006 (ASIN: B000FPE952).

Moore, Patrick. *Tweaked: A Crystal Memoir.* New York: Kensington Publishing, 2006.

Osborne, Duncan. *Suicide Tuesday: Gay Men and the Crystal Meth Scare*. New York: Carroll & Graf, 2006.

Ringwald, Christopher D. *The Soul of Recovery: Uncovering the Spiritual Dimension in the Treatment of Addictions*. New York: Oxford University Press, 2002.

Specter, Michael. "Higher Risk: Crystal Meth, the Internet, and Dangerous Choices about AIDS," *New Yorker Magazine*, issue of May 3, 2005. *www.newyorker.com/printables/fact/050523fa_fact*.

Education

Canadian Plains Research Center. *I Could Not Speak My Heart: Education and Social Justice for Gay and Lesbian Youth*. Regina, SK: University of Regina, 2002.

GLSEN: The Gay, Lesbian and Straight Education Network. *www.glsen.org/cgi-bin/iowa/home.html*.

Greenberg, Rabbi Steven. *Wrestling with God and Men: Homosexuality in the Jewish Tradition*. Madison: University of Wisconsin Press, 2004

Isay, Richard A. *Being Homosexual*. New York: Farrar, Straus & Giroux, 1989.

Kundtz, David. "Why Do They Hate Us So Much." *www.clgs.org/5/pdf/kundtz_why_hate.pdf*.

McNeill, John J. *The Church and the Homosexual*. 4th ed. Boston: Beacon Press, 1993.

"The Respect for All Project." A program of Women's Educational Media. Four Films: *It's Elementary — Talking about Gay Issues in School; That's a Family; Let's Get Real* (bullying); and *Straightlaced* (on the pressure to conform to gender roles). *www.womedia.org*.

Ethics and Morality

Balka, Christie, and Andy Rose, eds. *Twice Blessed: On Being Lesbian, Gay, and Jewish*. Boston: Beacon Press, 1989.

Batchelor, Edward, Jr. *Homosexuality and Ethics*. New York: Pilgrim Press, 1980.

Countryman, L. W. *Dirt, Greed, and Sex: Sexual Ethics in the New Testament and Their Implications for Today*. New ed. London: SCM Press, 2001.

Fortune, Marie M. *Love Does No Harm: Sexual Ethics for the Rest of Us*. New York: Continuum, 1998.

Gula, Richard M. *Ethics in Pastoral Ministry*. New York: Paulist Press, 1996.

Jacobsen, Janet R., and Ann Pellegrini. *Love the Sin: Sexual Regulation and the Limits of Religious Tolerance*. Boston: Beacon Press, 2003.

Jordan, Mark D. *The Ethics of Sex*. Oxford: Blackwell Publishing, 2002.

———. *Telling Truths in Church: Scandal, Flesh, and Christian Speech*. Boston: Beacon Press, 2003.

Jung, Patricia Beattie, and Ralph Smith. *Heterosexism: An Ethical Challenge*. Albany: State University Press of New York, 1993.

Kolodny, Debra R., ed. *Blessed Bi Spirit: Bisexual People of Faith*. New York: Continuum, 2000.

Nelson, James B. *Embodiment: An Approach to Sexuality and Christian Theology*. Minneapolis: Augsburg, 1978.

Stuart, Elizabeth. *Just Good Friends: Towards a Lesbian and Gay Theology of Relationships.* London: Mowbray, 1995.

Weaver, Andrew, et al. *Counseling on Sexual Issues: A Handbook for Pastors and Other Helping Professionals.* Cleveland: Pilgrim Press, 2005.

Ethnic Studies and Issues

Boykin, Keith. *Beyond the Down Low: Sex, Lies, and Denial in Black America.* New York: Carroll & Graf, 2005.

EyeBite Productions. *De Colores: Lesbian and Gay Latinos: Stories of Strength, Family and Love.* A film by Peter Barbosa. *www.EyeBite.com.*

Gilley, Brian Joseph. *Becoming Two-spirit: Gay Identity and Social Acceptance in Indian Country.* Lincoln: University of Nebraska Press, 2006.

GRACE. Gay Christian Asians and Allies. GRACE works in partnership with allies to create safe and supportive gatherings of queer spiritual Asians and friends for fellowship and worship. *www.gayasianchristians.org.*

Griffin, Horace. *Their Own Receive Them Not: African American Lesbians and Gays in Black Churches.* Cleveland: Pilgrim Press, 2006.

King, J. L. *Coming Up from the Down Low: The Journey to Acceptance, Healing, and Honest Love.* New York: Three Rivers Press, 2006.

———. *On the Down Low: A Journey into the Lives of "Straight" Black Men Who Sleep with Men.* New York: Broadway Books, 2004.

Kirkwood, Neville A. *Pastoral Care to Muslims: Building Bridges.* New York: Haworth Press, 2002.

Lartey, Emmanuel. *In Living Color: An Intercultural Approach to Pastoral Care and Counseling.* London: Jessica Kingsley Publishers, 2003.

Montilla, R. Esteban, and Ferney Medina. *Pastoral Care and Counseling with Latinos/as.* Minneapolis: Fortress Press, 2006.

PANA Institute (Institute for Leadership Development and Study of Pacific and Asian North American Religion). *www.psr.edu/panahome.cfm.*

Smith, Archie, Jr., and Ursula Riedel-Pfaefflin. *Siblings by Choice: Race, Gender, and Violence.* St. Louis: Chalice Press, 2004.

"Two-Spirit People." A film of historical and contemporary Native American concepts of gender, sexuality, and orientation. *cart.frameline.org/ProductDetails.asp?ProductCode=T336.*

Way, Peggy. *Created by God: Pastoral Care for All God's People.* St. Louis: Chalice Press, 2005.

Williams, Walter L. *The Spirit and the Flesh: Sexual Diversity in the American Indian Culture.* Boston: Beacon Press, 1992.

Wimberly, Edward P. *Claiming God: Reclaiming Dignity — African American Pastoral Care.* Nashville: Abingdon Press, 2003.

"Ex-Gay" Ministry

Shidlo, Ariel, et al. *Sexual Conversion Therapy: Clinical and Ethical Perspectives.* New York: Haworth Medical Press, 2001.

Faith-Based LGBTQ-Affirming Resources

Affirmation: Gay and Lesbian Mormons. *www.affirmation.org.*

Affirmation: United Methodists for Gay, Lesbian, Bisexual and Transgender Concerns. *www.umaffirm.org.*

Al-Fatiha Foundation: an international organization which aims to support LGBTQ Muslims in reconciling their sexual orientation or gender identity with Islam. *www.al-fatiha.org.*

American Friends [Quakers] Service Committee. Programs Addressing Lesbians, Gay Men, Bisexuals and Transgender Persons. *www.afsc.org/pindx/lgbt.htm.*

Apostolic Catholic Church in America, an inclusive, sacramental, and liturgical Christian denomination welcoming all regardless of sexual orientation. *www.apostoliccatholicchurchinamerica.org.*

Association of Welcoming and Affirming Baptists. American Baptist Church. *www.wabaptists.org.*

AXIOS. Eastern and Orthodox Christian Gay Men and Women. *www.qrd.org/qrd/www/orgs/axios.*

Brethren/Mennonite Council for Lesbian and Gay Concerns. *www.webcom.com/bmc.*

Cathedral of Hope (Dallas, Texas). "World's largest gay and lesbian church." *www.cathedralofhope.com.*

Center for Lesbian and Gay Studies in Religion and Ministry. *www.clgs.org.*

Christian Lesbians. *www.christianlesbians.com.*

CLOUT. Christian Lesbians OUT. *www.andrew.cmu.edu/~riley/CLOUT.html.*

The Coalition. The United Church of Christ Coalition for Lesbian, Gay, Bisexual, and Transgender Concerns. *www.coalition.simplenet.com.*

Conference of Catholic Lesbians. *cclonline.org.*

Dignity Canada Dignité; Roman Catholic. *www.odyssee.net/~prince.dcd.html.*

Dignity USA. Lesbian, Gay, Bisexual and Transgender Catholics. *www.dignityusa.org.*

Emergence International, Christian Scientists Supporting Lesbians, Gay Men, and Bisexuals. *www.cslesbigay.org/emergence.*

The Evangelical Network (T-E-N). *www.theevangelicalnetwork.org.*

Evangelicals Concerned with Reconciliation (ECWR). *www.ecwr.org.*

Friends [Quakers] for Lesbian and Gay Concerns. *www.geocities.com/WestHollywood/2473/flgc.html.*

Gay and Lesbian Arabic Society. Networking for gays and lesbians of Arab descent or living in Arab countries. *www.glas.org.*

Gay Spirit Visions: to create a spiritual/healing community for gay men. *www.mindspring.com/~gayspirit.*

GLAD Alliance, Inc. The Gay, Lesbian and Affirming Disciples Alliance, Inc. Disciples of Christ. *pilot.msu.edu/user/laceyj.*

Honesty (Southern Baptist): Support, education, and advocacy for gay, lesbian, bisexual, and transgender Baptists. *www.geocities.com/WestHollywood/2032/honesty.html.*

Integrity. A National Association of Lesbian and Gay Episcopalians and Their Friends (U.S.). *www.integrityusa.org.*

Interweave. Unitarian Universalists for Lesbian, Gay, Bisexual and Transgender Concerns. *www.qrd.org/qrd/www.orgs/uua/uu-interweave.html.*

Jewish Mosaic: The National Center for Sexual and Gender Diversity. *www.jewishmosaic.org.*

Keshet Rabbis: Gay-Friendly Conservative/Masorti Rabbis and Cantors. *www.keshetrabbis.org.*

Lesbian, Gay, Bisexual, and Transgender Christian Scientists. *www.geocities/ WestHollywood/1892.*

The Lesbian, Gay, Bisexual and Transgender Religious Archives Network. A resource center and information clearinghouse for the history of LGBT religious movements. A project of the Chicago Theological Seminary. *lgbtran.org.*

Lutherans Concerned North America. *www.lcna.org.*

Mel White's Justice Net. Mel White is minister of justice for the Universal Fellowship of Metropolitan Community Churches; numerous full text reports, news articles, information. *www.melwhite.org.*

More Light Presbyterians. *www.mlp.org.*

National Association of Catholic Diocesan Lesbian and Gay Ministries. *www.nacdlgm.org.*

New Ways Ministry: "Ministering in new ways to Gay and Lesbian Catholics in the church." *mysite.verizon.net/~vze43yrc.*

Ontario Consultants on Religious Tolerance. Many full text sources related to religion and homosexuality and bisexuality. *www.religioustolerance.org/homosexu.htm.* This site attempts to present all sides of issues: pro, con, in between.

Open and Affirming Ministry. The Christian Church — Disciples of Christ. *www.gladalliance.org/oaa.html.*

Open and Affirming (ONA) Program — The United Church of Christ. *www.ucccoalition.org/programs/ona.html.*

Q-LIGHT. LGBT Quakers issues and communications. *groups.yahoo.com/group/Q-Light.*

Quest: An Organization of Lesbian and Gay Catholics in the UK. *www.users.dircon.co.uk/~quest.*

Rainbow Sash Movement: *www.rainbowsashmovement.com.*

Reconciling in Christ Program of the Lutheran Church. *www.lcna.org/ric.shtm.*

Reconciling Ministries Network of the United Methodist Church. *www.rmnetwork.org.*

Room for All of the Reformed Church in America. *www.roomforall.com.*

SDA Kinship International Inc. Gay and Lesbian Support Group. Seventh-day Adventists. *www.sdakinship.org.*

Stonecatchers. Presbyterian group seeking an inclusive church. *www.radix.net/ ~execware/stonecatchers.*

Unitarian Universalist Association (UUA). *www.uua.org/obgltc.*
    In Canada: *www.cuc.ca/queer.*

United Church of Christ Coalition for LGBT Concerns. *www.ucccoalition.org.*

Unity Fellowship Church Movement (U.S.). *www.unityfellowshipchurch.org.*

Universal Fellowship of Metropolitan Community Churches. *www.ufmcc.com.*

Universal Fellowship of Metropolitan Churches Canada/La Confrerie Universelle des Eglises Communautaires Metropolitaines. *www.ualberta.ca/~cbidwell/UFMCC/uf-home.htm.*

Welcoming Community Network (WCN) — Community of Christ. *www.galaweb.org/wcn.*

Welcoming Congregations. Provides lists by state of welcoming, gay-affirming congregations. *www.christianlesbians.com/congregations.*

World Congress of Gay, Lesbian, Bisexual, and Transgender Jews: Keshet Ga'avah. *glbtjews.org.*

Families, LGBTQ

Bernstein, Robert. *Families of Value: Personal Profiles of Pioneering Lesbian and Gay Parents.* New York: Marlowe & Co., 2005.

Drucker, Jane. *Lesbian and Gay Families Speak Out.* New York: Insight Books, 1998.

Weston, Kath. *Families We Choose: Lesbians, Gays, Kinship.* New York: Columbia University Press, 1991.

Gay Male Couples

Berzon, Betty. *Permanent Partners: Building Gay and Lesbian Relationships That Last.* New York: E. P. Dutton, 1988.

Clark, J. Michael. *Doing the Work of Love: Men and Commitment in Same-Sex Couples.* Harriman, TN: Men's Studies Press, 1999.

Driggs, John, and Stephen Finn. *Intimacy Between Men: How to Find and Keep Gay Love Relationships.* New York: Plume, 1991.

Isay, Richard A. *Commitment and Healing: Gay Men and the Need for Romantic Love.* Hoboken, NJ: John Wiley and Sons, 2006.

Mancilla, Michael, and Lisa Troshinsky. *Love in the Time of HIV: The Gay Man's Guide to Sex, Dating, and Relationships.* New York: Guilford Press, 2003.

Yip, Andrew. *Gay Male Christian Couples: Life Stories.* Westport, CT: Praeger, 1997.

Gay Men

Boisvert, Donald L. *Out on Holy Ground: Meditations on Gay Men's Spirituality.* Cleveland: Pilgrim Press, 2000.

———. *Sanctity and Male Desire: A Gay Reading of Saints.* Cleveland: Pilgrim Press, 2004.

Fellows, William. *Farm Boys: Lives of Gay Men from the Rural Midwest.* Madison: University of Wisconsin Press, 2001.

Nimmons, David. *The Soul beneath the Skin: The Unseen Hearts and Habits of Gay Men.* New York: St. Martin's Press, 2002.

Roscoe, Will. *Queer Spirits: A Gay Men's Myth Book.* Boston: Beacon Press, 1995.

Homophobia

Blumenfield, Warren J., ed. *Homophobia: How We All Pay the Price.* Boston: Beacon Press, 1992.

Pharr, Suzanne. *Homophobia: A Weapon of Sexism.* Little Rock, AR: Chardon Press, 1988.

Homosexuality

Jordan, Mark D. *The Silence of Sodom: Homosexuality in the Modern Catholicism.* Chicago: University of Chicago Press, 2000.

Oliveto, Karen, Kelly Turney, and Traci West. *Talking about Homosexuality: A Congregational Resource.* Cleveland: Pilgrim Press, 2005.

Sullivan, Andrew. *Virtually Normal: An Argument about Homosexuality.* New York: Vintage Books, 1995.

Lesbian Couples

Adelman, Marcy R., ed. *Midlife Lesbian Relationships: Friends, Lovers, Children, and Parents.* New York: Harrington Park Press, 2000.

Berzon, Betty. *Permanent Partners: Building Gay and Lesbian Relationships That Last.* New York: E. P. Dutton, 1988.

Clunis, D. Merilee, and G. Dorsey Green. *Lesbian Couples: A Guide to Creating Healthy Relationships.* Emeryville, CA: Seal Press, 2005.

Haley-Banez, Lynn. *Lesbians in Committed Relationships: Extraordinary Couples, Ordinary Lives.* New York: Harrington Park Press, 2002.

Laird, Joan, and Robert-Jay Green, eds. *Lesbians and Gays in Couples and Families: A Handbook for Therapists.* San Francisco: Jossey-Bass Publishers, 1996.

Marshall, Joretta L. *Counseling Lesbian Partners.* Louisville: Westminster John Knox Press, 1997.

Life Issues for LGBTQ people

Beck, Luane, director. *God and Gays: Bridging the Gap.* A film that explores sexuality and spirituality through the eyes of people wanting a relationship with the religion that rejects them. *www.godandgaysthemovie.com/about.html.*

Curry, Hayden, et al. *A Legal Guide for Lesbian and Gay Couples.* 13th ed. Berkeley, CA: Nolo, 2005.

Friskopp, Annette, and Sharon Silverstein. *Straight Jobs, Gay Lives.* New York: Simon & Schuster, 1996.

Garner, Abigail. *Families Like Mine: Children of Gay Parents Tell It Like It Is.* New York: HarperCollins, 2004.

Greene, Beverly, ed. *Ethnic and Cultural Diversity among Lesbians and Gay Men.* Thousand Oaks, CA: Sage Publications, 1997.

Heartstrong. "The Place for GLBTs from Religious Schools." *www.heartstrong.org.*

Kirk, Sheila, and Martine Rothblatt. *Medical, Legal and Workplace Issues for the Transsexual.* Watertown, MA: Together Lifeworks, 1995.

Kimmel, Douglas, et al., eds. *Midlife and Aging in Gay America: Proceedings of the Sage Conference 2000.* New York: Harrington Park Press, 2001.

Savin-Williams, Ritch. *The Lives of Lesbians, Gays, and Bisexuals: Children to Adults.* Wadsworth Publishing, 1995.

Sember, Brette. *Gay and Lesbian Rights: A Guide for GLBT Singles, Couples and Families.* 2nd ed. Naperville, IL: Sphinx Publishing, 2006.

Marriage, LGBTQ Ceremonies of Commitment

Ayers, Tess, and P. Brown. *The Essential Guide to Lesbian and Gay Weddings*. Los Angeles: Alyson Publications, 1999.

Deakin, Michael. *Gay Marriage, Real Life: Ten Stories of Love and Family*. Boston: Skinner House, 2005.

Ellison, Marvin. *Same-Sex Marriage? A Christian Ethical Analysis*. Cleveland: Pilgrim Press, 2004.

Jordan, Mark D. *Blessing Same-Sex Unions: The Perils of Queer Romance and the Confusions of Christian Marriage*. Chicago: University of Chicago Press, 2005.

Lewin, Ellen. *Recognizing Ourselves: Ceremonies of Lesbian and Gay Commitment*. New York: Columbia University Press, 1998.

United Church of Christ Coalition for LGBT Concerns. *Blessing Ceremonies: Resources for Same-Gender Services of Commitment*. Holden, MA: 1998.

Parenting, LGBTQ

Brill, Stephanie. *The Essential Guide to Lesbian Conception, Pregnancy and Birth*. Los Angeles: Alyson Books, 2006.

Clunis, D. Merilee, and G. Dorsey Green. *The Lesbian Parenting Book: A Guide to Creating Families and Raising Children*. 2nd ed. Seattle, WA: Seal Press, 1995.

Friends in Adoption. *www.friendsinadoption.org.*

Gay Parent magazine. *www.gayparentmag.com.*

Glazer, Deborah F., and Jack Drescher, eds. *Gay and Lesbian Parenting*. New York: Haworth Medical Press, 2001.

Johnson, Suzanne, and Elizabeth O'Connor. *For Lesbian Parents: Your Guide to Helping Your Family Grow Up Happy, Healthy, and Proud*. New York: Guilford Press, 2001.

Lev, Arlene. *The Complete Lesbian and Gay Parenting Guide*. New York: Berkley Books, 2004.

Martin, April. *The Lesbian and Gay Parenting Handbook: Creating and Raising Our Families*. New York: HarperPerennial, 1993.

Seyda, Barbara. *Women in Love: Portraits of Lesbian Mothers and Their Families*. New York: Bulfinch Press, 1998.

Strah, David, and Susanna Margolis. *Gay Dads: A Celebration of Fatherhood*. New York: Tarcher, 2003.

Symons, Johnny, director. *Daddy and Papa*. A film about gay fathers in America. *www.daddyandpapa.com.*

Pastoral Care and Ministry

AAPC (American Association of Pastoral Counselors): Its purpose is to promote the profession and the practice of pastoral counseling and to train future generations of the profession. *www.aapc.org.*

ACPE (Association for Clinical Pastoral Education): A multicultural, multifaith organization devoted to providing education and improving the quality of ministry and pastoral care. *www.acpe.edu.*

Alpert, Rebecca, Sue Levi Elwell, and Shirley Idelson, eds. *Lesbian Rabbis: The First Generation*. New Brunswick, NJ: Rutgers University Press, 2001.

CAPPE (Canadian Association for Pastoral Practice and Education): A national multifaith organization committed to the professional education, certification, and support of people involved in pastoral care. *www.cappe.org*.

Clinebell, Howard. *Basic Types of Pastoral Care and Counseling: Resources for the Ministry of Healing and Growth*. Nashville: Abingdon Press, 1984.

———. *Ecotherapy: Healing Ourselves, Healing the Earth*. Minneapolis: Fortress, 1996.

David, J. A. *Pastoral Care for the Mentally Ill*. Australia: Universal Publishers, 2001.

Dignity/USA. Letter on the Pastoral Care of LGBT People, 2007. *www.dignityusa.org*.

Friedman, Rabbi Dayle A., ed. *Jewish Pastoral Care: A Practical Handbook from Traditional and Contemporary Sources*. New York: Jewish Lights Publishing; 2nd ed., 2005.

Gerkin, Charles V. *An Introduction to Pastoral Care*. Nashville: Abingdon Press, 1997.

Graham, Larry Kent. *Care of Persons, Care of Worlds: A Psychosystems Approach to Pastoral Care and Counseling*. Nashville: Abingdon, 1992.

———. *Discovering Images of God: Narratives of Care among Lesbians and Gays*. Louisville: Westminster John Knox Press, 1997.

———. "Prophetic Pastoral Caretaking: A Psychosystemic Approach to Symptomatology." *Journal of Psychology and Christianity* 8, no. 1 (1989): 49–60.

Johnson, W. Brad, and William L. Johnson. *The Pastor's Guide to Psychological Disorders and Treatments*. Binghamton, NY: Haworth Press, 2000.

Kirkwood, Neville A. *Pastoral Care to Muslims: Building Bridges*. Binghamton, NY: Haworth Press, 2002.

Kübler-Ross, Elisabeth, and David Kessler. *On Grief and Grieving: Finding the Meaning of Grief through the Five Stages of Loss*. New York: Scribner, 2005.

Marshall, Joretta L. "Caring When It Is Tough to Care." *www.religion-online.org/showarticle.asp?title=300*.

Stone, Howard W. *Theological Context for Pastoral Caregiving: Word in Deed*. New York: Haworth Pastoral Press, 1996.

Switzer, David K. *Pastoral Care of Gays, Lesbians, and Their Families*. Creative Pastoral Care and Counseling Series. Minneapolis: Fortress Press, 1999.

Way, Peggy. *Created by God: Pastoral Care for All God's People*. Atlanta: Chalice Press, 2005.

Winston, Binford. *The Pastoral Care of Depression*. Binghamton, NY: Haworth Press, 1997.

Polyamory

Anapol, Deborah. *Polyamory: The New Love without Limits: Secrets of Sustainable Intimate Relationships*. Rev. ed. San Rafael, CA: IntiNet Resource Center, 1997.

Polyamorous NYC: An organization designed to nurture a prosperous polyamorous community in New York City. Web site contains much information: *www.poly-nyc.com*.

Unitarian Universalists for Polyamory Awareness. *www.uupa.org*.

Prayers and Liturgies of Welcome and Inclusion

Duncan, Geoffrey, ed. *Courage to Love: Liturgies for the Lesbian, Gay, Bisexual and Transgender Community.* Cleveland: Pilgrim Press, 2002.

Glaser, Chris. *Coming Out to God: Prayers for Lesbians and Gay Men, Their Families and Friends.* Louisville: Westminster John Knox Press, 1991.

Kittredge, Cherry, and Zalmon Sherwood. *Equal Rites: Lesbian and Gay Worship, Ceremonies, and Celebrations.* Louisville: Westminster John Knox Press, 1995.

Ritualwell.org: Ceremonies for Jewish Living: *www.ritualwell.org.*

Stuart, Elizabeth. *Daring to Speak Love's Name: A Gay and Lesbian Prayer Book.* London: Hamish Hamilton, 1992.

Turney, Kelly, ed. *Shaping Sanctuary: Proclaiming God's Grace in an Inclusive Church.* Chicago: Reconciling Congregation Program, 2000.

Psychology

Bradshaw, John. *Healing the Shame That Binds You.* Deerfield Beach, FL: HCI Publications, revised and updated, 2005.

Burke, Mary, et al. *Religious and Spiritual Issues in Counseling: Applications across Diverse Populations.* New York: Brunner-Routledge, 2005.

Campbell, Robert J. *Psychiatric Dictionary.* New York: Oxford University Press, 1989.

Collie, Robert M. *The Obsessive-Compulsive Disorder: Pastoral Care for the Road to Change.* Binghamton, NY: Haworth Pastoral Press, 2000.

Erikson, Erik. *Childhood and Society.* New York: W. W. Norton, reissue, 1993.

Fowler, James. *Stages of Faith: The Psychology of Human Development.* San Francisco: HarperSanFrancisco, 1995.

Greene, Sheila. *The Psychological Development of Girls and Women: Rethinking Change in Time.* New York: Routledge, 2003.

Hill, Clara. *Helping Skills: Facilitating Exploration, Insight, and Action.* Washington, DC: American Psychological Association, 2004.

Hopke, Robert H. *Jung, Jungians and Homosexuality.* Boston: Shambhala, 1989.

Lee, Wanda M. L. *An Introduction to Multicultural Counseling.* Philadelphia: Accelerated Development Group, 1999.

Levinson, Daniel. *The Seasons of a Man's Life.* New York: Ballantine Books, reissue, 1986.

McClintock, Karen A. *Sexual Shame: An Urgent Call to Healing.* Minneapolis: Augsburg Fortress, 2001.

Potter-Efron, Ron, and Patricia Potter-Efron. *Letting Go of Anger: The Eleven Most Common Anger Styles and What to Do about Them.* Berkeley, CA: New Harbinger, 2006.

———. *Letting Go of Shame: Understanding How Shame Affects Your Life.* San Francisco: Harper & Row, 1989.

Relationships, LGBTQ

Balka, Christie, and Andy Rose, eds. *Twice Blessed: On Being Lesbian, Gay, and Jewish.* Boston: Beacon Press, 1989.

Goss, Robert, and Amy Strongheart, eds. *Our Families, Our Values: Snapshots of Queer Kinship.* New York: Harrington Park Press, 1997.

Heyward, Carter. *Touching Our Strength: The Erotic as Power and the Love of God.* San Francisco:|Harper & Row, 1989.

Johnson, Robert. *A Study in the Contrast of Homoerotic and Homosexual Relationships* (audiocassette tape). Los Angeles: C. G. Jung Institute.

Shneer, David, and Caryn Aviv. *Queer Jews.* New York: Routledge, 2002.

Stiers, Gretchen. *From This Day Forward: Commitment, Marriage, and Family in Lesbian and Gay Relationships.* New York: St. Martin's Press, 1999.

Straight Spouse Network. Support for the straight spouse in a gay-straight marriage. *www.straightspouse.org.*

Stuart, Elizabeth. *Just Good Friends: Towards a Lesbian and Gay Theology of Relationships.* London: Mowbray, 1995.

Rural Life, LGBTQ

Murray, Tom, director. *Farm Family: In Search of Gay Life in Rural America,* a documentary film; *www.tjoemurray.com.*

Smith, James Donald, and Ronald J. Mancoske, eds. *Rural Gays and Lesbians: Building on the Strengths of Communities.* Binghamton, NY: Haworth Press, 1997.

Sexuality, LGBTQ

Bornstein, Kate. *My Gender Workbook: How to Become a Real Man, a Real Woman, the Real You, or Something Else Entirely.* New York, London: Routledge, 1998.

DeCecco, John P., and Michael G. Shivley. *Origins of Sexuality and Homosexuality.* New York: Harrington Park Press, 1985.

Henry J. Kaiser Family Foundation and MTV. *It's Your (Sex) Life: A Guide to Safe and Responsible Sex, www.kff.org/youthhivstds/upload/MTV_Think_IYSL_Booklet.pdf.*

Institute for Advanced Study of Human Sexuality. *The Complete Guide to Safer Sex.* 2nd rev. ed. Barricade Books, 1999.

Kinsey Scale of Human Sexuality. *www.kinseyinstitute.org/research/ak-hhscale.html.*

Klein Sexual Orientation Grid. *www.biresource.org/pamphlets/scales.html.*

Nelson, James B. *Embodiment: An Approach to Sexuality and Christian Theology.* New ed. Minneapolis: Augsburg Fortress Publishers, 1979.

Newman, Felice. *The Whole Lesbian Sex Book: A Passionate Guide for All of Us.* 2nd ed. San Francisco: Cleis Press, 2004.

Rahman, Quazi, and Glenn Wilson. *Born Gay: the Psychobiology of Sex Orientation.* London: Peter Owen Publishers, 2005.

Silverstein, Charles, and Felice Picano. *The New Joy of Gay Sex.* New York: HarperCollins Publishers, 1992.

Weaver, Andrew J., et al. *Counseling on Sexual Issues: A Handbook for Pastors and Other Helping Professionals.* Cleveland: Pilgrim Press, 2006.

Winks, Cathy. *The Good Vibrations Guide to Sex: The Most Complete Sex Manual Ever Written.* 3rd ed. Pittsburgh: Cleis Press, 2002.

Spirituality

Empereur, James L. *Spiritual Direction and the Gay Person*. New York: Continuum, 1998.

Fortunato, John E. *Embracing the Exile: Healing Journeys of Gay Christians*. New York: Seabury Press, 1983.

Glaser, Chris. *Reformation of the Heart: Seasonal Meditations by a Gay Christian*. Louisville: Westminster John Knox Press, 2001.

Helminiak, Daniel A. *Sex and the Sacred: Gay Identity and Spiritual Growth*. New York: Harrington Park Press, 2006.

Johnson, Toby. *Gay Perspective: Things Our Homosexuality Tells Us about the Nature of God and the Universe*. Los Angeles: Alyson Books, 2003.

————. *Gay Spirituality: The Role of Gay Identity in the Transformation of Human Consciousness*. Los Angeles: Alyson Books, 2000.

McNeill, John, S.J. *Both Feet Firmly Planted in Midair: My Spiritual Journey*. Louisville: Westminster John Knox Press, 1998.

Pepper, Michal Anne. *Reconciling Journey: A Devotional Workbook for Lesbian and Gay Christians*. Cleveland: Pilgrim Press, 2003.

Thompson, Mark. *Gay Soul: Finding the Heart of Gay Spirit and Nature*. San Francisco: HarperSanFrancisco, 1990.

Theology and Biblical Interpretation

Bellis, Alice Ogden, and Terry L. Hufford. *Science, Scripture, and Homosexuality*. Cleveland: Pilgrim Press, 2002.

Goss, Robert E., and Mona West, eds. *Take Back the Word: A Queer Reading of the Bible*. Cleveland: Pilgrim Press, 2005.

Helminiak, Daniel A. *What the Bible Really Says about Homosexuality*. San Francisco: Alamo Square Distributors, 2000.

Rogers, Jack. *Jesus, the Bible, and Homosexuality: Explode the Myths, Heal the Church*. Louisville: Westminster John Knox Press, 2006.

Scoggs, Robin. *The New Testament and Homosexuality: Contextual Background for Contemporary Debate*. Philadelphia: Fortress Press, 1983.

Stuart, Elizabeth. *Gay and Lesbian Theologies: Repetitions with Critical Difference*. London and Burlington, VT: Ashgate, 2003.

Stuart, Elizabeth, with John McMahon, Malcolm Edwards, Tim Morrison, and Andy Braunston. *Religion Is a Queer Thing: A Guide to the Christian Faith for Lesbian, Gay, Bisexual, and Transgendered Persons*. Cleveland: Pilgrim Press, 1998.

Tigert, Leanne McCall. *Coming Out While Staying In: Struggles and Celebrations of Lesbians, Gays, and Bisexuals in the Church*. Cleveland: United Church Press, 1996.

Transgender Resources: Identity, Legal Topics, Sexuality and Spirituality

Anders, C. "Welcoming Transgendered Jews." *Tikkun* magazine: www.tikkun.org/magazine/tik0509/article.2005-08-10.3345465137.

Boenke, Mary, ed. *TransForming Families: Real Stories about Transgender Loved Ones.* Imperial Beach, CA: Walter Trook Publishing, 1999.

Conover, Pat. *Transgender Good News.* Silver Springs, MD: New Wineskins Press, 2002.

Cook, Ann Thompson. *Made in God's Image: A Resource for Dialogue about the Church and Gender Differences.* Washington, DC: Dumbarton United Methodist Church (*www.dumbartonumc.org*) and Reconciling Ministries Network in Chicago (*www.rmnetwork.org*), 2003. See also *www.madeinimage.org.*

Emmaus Oasis. A Safe and Welcoming Place for Transsexuals and Significant People in Their Lives. Tucson, AZ. Contact: *SrLuisaOP@aol.com.*

Lev, Arlene. *Transgender Emergence: Therapeutic Guidelines for Working with Gender-Variant People and Their Families.* New York: The Haworth Clinical Practice Press, 2004.

Mollenkott, Virginia Ramey. *Omnigender: A Trans-Religious Approach.* Cleveland: Pilgrim Press, 2001.

Mollenkott, Virginia Ramey, and Vanessa Sheridan. *Transgender Journeys.* Cleveland: Pilgrim Press, 2003.

National Center for Transgender Equality. *www.nctequality.org.*

PFLAG. *Our Trans Children.* A Publication of the Transgender Network of PFLAG. *www.pflag.org/TNET.tnet.0.html.*

Sheridan, Vanessa. *Crossing Over: Liberating the Transgendered Christian.* Cleveland: Pilgrim Press, 2001.

Tanis, Justin. *Transgendered: Theology, Ministry, and Communities of Faith.* Cleveland: Pilgrim Press, 2003.

Tigert, Leanne McCall, and Maren C. Tirabassi. *Transgendering Faith: Identity, Sexuality, and Spirituality.* Cleveland: Pilgrim Press, 2004.

Transgender Law Center. *www.transgenderlawcenter.org.*

UCC Open and Affirming Program. *Transgender Pocket* ("Personal stories, articles, resources, etc. about transgender identities, experiences, and Christian life"). *www.ucccoalition.org/resources/ona.html.*

United Church of Christ and Filmworks, Inc. *Call Me Malcolm: One Man's Struggle with Faith, Love and Gender Identity.* 2004. *www.callmemalcolm.com.*

Violence

The Family Violence Prevention Fund. *www.endabuse.org./resources/facts.*

Fortune, Marie. *Sexual Violence: The Sin Revisited.* Cleveland: Pilgrim Press, 2005.

The Gay Men's Domestic Violence Project. *www.gmdvp.org/pages/myth.html.*

Miles, Al. *Domestic Violence: What Every Pastor Needs to Know.* Minneapolis: Augsburg Fortress Publishers, 2000.

———. *Violence in Families: What Every Christian Needs to Know.* Minneapolis: Augsburg Fortress Publishers, 2002.

Welcoming Congregation Resources

Alexander, Marilyn, and James Preston. *We Were Baptized Too: Claiming God's Grace for Lesbians and Gays.* Louisville: Westminster John Knox Press, 1996.

Anders, C. "Welcoming Transgendered Jews." *Tikkun* magazine: *www.tikkun.org/ magazine/tik0509/article.2005-08-10.3345465137.*

Flunder, Yvette. *Where the Edge Gathers: Building a Community of Radical Inclusion.* Cleveland: Pilgrim Press, 2005.

Glück, Robert, ed. *Homosexuality and Judaism: A Reconstructionist Workshop Series.* Wyncote, PA: Reconstructionist Press, 1993.

Hanway, D. G. *A Theology of Gay and Lesbian Inclusion: Love Letters to the Church.* New York: Haworth Pastoral Press, 2006.

Heskins, Jeffrey. *Face to Face: Gay and Lesbian Clergy on Holiness and Life Together.* Grand Rapids: Eerdmans, 2006.

Law, Eric. *Inclusion: Making Room for Grace.* St. Louis: Chalice Press, 2000.

Mattmann, Urs. *Coming In: Gays and Lesbians Reclaiming the Spiritual Journey.* Glasgow: Wild Goose Publications, 2006.

Oliveto, Karen, ed. *Enfold: A Reconciling Congregation Explores What It Means to Welcome All People.* San Francisco: Bethany United Methodist Church, 1997.

Oliveto, Karen P., et al. *Talking about Homosexuality: A Congregational Resource.* Cleveland: Pilgrim Press, 2005.

Schlager, Bernard. *With Open Arms: Gay Affirming Ministries in [San Francisco] Bay Area Faith Communities.* *www.clgs.org/5/open_arms.html.*

Shneer, David, and Caryn Aviv. *Queer Jews.* New York: Routledge, 2002.

Tigert, Leanne McCall. *Coming Out While Staying In: Struggles and Celebrations of Lesbians, Gays, and Bisexuals in the Church,* Cleveland: United Church Press, 1996.

UUA Office of Bisexual, Gay, Lesbian, and Transgender Concerns. *Living the Welcoming Congregation.* Boston: UUA, 2004.

————. *The Welcoming Congregation Handbook: Resources for Affirming Bisexual, Gay, Lesbian, and/or Transgender People.* Boston: UUA, 1999.

Waun, Maurine. *More Than Welcome: Learning to Embrace Gay, Lesbian, Bisexual and Transgendered Persons in the Church.* St. Louis: Chalice Press, 1999.

Index

abstinence from sex. *See* celibacy
ACPE (Association for Clinical Pastoral
    Education), 96
activism resources, 220
addictions. *See also* alcohol misuse; drug use;
    sexual addiction
  as caregiver's first priority, 99
  defined, 98
  resources, 99n12, 222–23
Advocates for Youth, 111
affectional (emotional) orientation, 5, 108, 218
African American value on validation of the
    individual, 73–74
AIDS, 92–94. *See also* HIV positive people
  church events remembering those with, 172
  pastoral care considerations, 45, 95
  prevention, 112n31
  resources, 220–21
AIDS Pastoral Care (Connolly), 92–93
alcohol misuse, 152–53
American Psychiatric Association, 133n3
American Psychological Association, 96
Anglican Church. *See* Episcopalian Church
Araujo, Gwen, 106
Asian Americans' religions and values, 74–75
Association for Clinical Pastoral Education
    (ACPE), 96

Belile, Jacki, 159
Berdache tradition, 75
BFLAG (Blind Friends of Lesbian, Gay, Bisexual
    and Transgender People), 104
biblical texts. *See also* theology and biblical
    interpretation resources
  on close friendships, 181–82
  on diverse forms of families, 212n33
  Exodus as coming out story, 158
  interpretations of, regarding LGBTQ people,
    3, 126–27
  stories of liberation, 186
  that affirm transgender persons, 211
Big Brothers and Big Sisters, 120–21
bisexuality, 110
  as a choice, 6, 125–27
  connotations and denotations of "bisexual,"
    6, 13
  resources, 221
bisexual people, 108
  coming out by, 138
  older, 122
  and sexual identity, 110

bisexual relationships
  abusive, 107–8, 109, 152
  first one(s) after coming out, 153–54
  negative stereotypes about, 155
Blind Friends of Lesbian, Gay, Bisexual and
    Transgender People (BFLAG), 104
British Association for Pastoral and Spiritual
    Care Counseling (APSCC), 81n43

Canadian Association for Pastoral Practice and
    Education (CAPPE), 94
caregivers. *See* pastoral caregivers
care receivers/seekers, 12. *See also* LGBTQ
    people
  caring intimacy with caregiver, 17–27
  clear boundaries with caregiver, 27–41
  confidentiality and outing issues in pastoral
    caregiving, 31–32, 111
  pastoral help with social system issues, 41–50
Catholic church
  celibacy case study, 202–4
  impact of position on homosexuality, 134
  language about homosexuality, 105
celibacy, 202–4
  resources, 221
Children of Lesbians and Gays Everywhere
    (COLAGE), 208
children of LGBTQ parents
  acceptance of, in churches and synagogues,
    208–9
  resources, 221
  through adoption or alternative insemination,
    205–6
churches and synagogues. *See also* congregations;
    faith-based LGBTQ pastoral care
  "All are welcome" message of, 3
  church-inflicted wounding of LGBTQ people,
    52, 56–57
  connection with violence against LGBTQ
    people, 105
  ethnic churches and homophobia, 73–76
  loss of closeted youth members, 134–35
  reconciliation with LGBTQ people, 63–66
  responses to coming out by members, 138
  sex education by, 102
  that consider queer people morally same as
    straight people, 133n3
  that create safe, positive, accepting welcome
    to LGBTQ members, 87, 111, 143
  that fear sexuality, 8–9
  that keep LGBTQ people from God, 46–47

236